EDUCATION UNDER SIEGE

EDUCATION UNDER SIEGE

A Sociological Study of Private Colleges

NIRMAL SINGH

CONCEPT PUBLISHING COMPANY
NEW DELHI

First Published 1983

Nirmal **Singh** (*b.* 1925-)

Published by
Naurang Rai
Concept Publishing Company
H-13, Bali Nagar
NEW DELHI-110015 (India)

Printed by
Mahajan Enterprises
at Hardev Printers Mayapuri,
NEW DELHI 110064

FOREWORD

THE PREAMBLE to the Constitution of India proclaims the solemn resolve of the People of India to constitute India into a Sovereign Socialist Secular Democratic Republic and to secure to all its citizens : Justice, Liberty, Equality and Fraternity. Further on in Part IV-A under the title Fundamental Duties, we have a succinct statement delineating the type of citizens who would be appropriate building blocks for the envisaged society. The citizens are to cherish and follow the noble ideals which inspired our national struggle for freedom, to promote harmony and the spirit of common brotherhood among all the people of India transcending religious, linguistic and regional or sectional diversities, to renounce practices derogatory to the dignity of women, to value and preserve the rich heritage of our composite culture, and to develop the scientific temper, humanism and the spirit of enquiry and reform. We have to strive towards excellence in all spheres of individual and collective activity so that the nation constantly rises to higher levels of endeavour and achievement. If we have to achieve these noble ideals enshrined in our Constitution, the pivotal role of education cannot be overemphasised. Education is the modern society's institutional device to produce and reproduce itself to move in the direction of the desired goals. It inheres within it organization and planning, reaching of deliberate decisions to formulate appropriate policies that join the present with the desired future and to devise mechanisms to overcome the negative elements. The institutions of higher learning — universities, colleges, research and professional institutes—have by definition a greater responsibility. Training and education of intellectual leadership—specialists, professional men and women as well as others with rounded personalities rooted in culture, arts and moral commitment—is their professed function. We can, at least in part, anticipate the conditions conducive to an unhampered fulfilment of these intellectual functions, with concomitant value commitment, knowledge spread, skill perfection and practical realization.

Introspection, self-reflection and systematic probing into the prevailing empirical conditions, both internal and external, relevant to the functioning of the institutions of higher (post-secondary or tertiary) education, is contributing not only in building a theoretical and practical fund of knowledge about knowledge but also to meaningfully provide necessary inputs for intelligent policy formulations. Thus they have a direct bearing on the practical realization of the ideals the country aspires to achieve.

The book presents the first full-fledged academic endeavour, coupled with the activist's zeal and sensitivity denied to the "neutral" observer and "pure" analyst alike, to unravel the conditions and consequences of private control of public education at the tertiary level. The problem has been tackled at two levels. At the macro-level the genesis and development of private control has been historically traced. It covers the entire period from the colonial times when modern education was introduced by the British rulers in the early nineteenth century, through the dawn of Independence, to the present times. The conceptual analysis has also followed a broad comparative and historical perspective. The empirical case material has been meticulously collected from available formal and informal documentary sources and through intensive field studies. This case material pertains to seven colleges of Kanpur university, selected on a purposive basis to bring out significant variables in diverse combinations. The details of the micro-level empirical evidence painstakingly dug out from the human actors involved and the records of the University, governing bodies, students' and teachers' organizations and obscure local journals make it difficult to escape the author's central conclusion. According to him "the private managements' are a redundant role and in practice they disoriented the teachers' role, the students' role and put them against each other as well as against their better selves, in fact, against education itself." The conclusions arrived at cannot be, automatically and with equal scientific justification, applicable to unexamined institutions and areas. They serve as illustrative material for the macro-level analyses advanced in the book on the conceptual-theoretical plane. As the micro-level empirical evidence goes well with the conceptual-theoretical scheme, it renders the latter quite plausible.

Since the advent of Independence, there has been a phenomenal all round growth of education in India. This growth, in quantity, quality and equality of opportunity, has not all been in accordance with the actual or felt needs of other areas of society like spheres of material production, spiritual-cultural activities, science-technology development or communication and administrative functions. This has resulted in many new imbalances and accentuations of some old ones while correcting others. The unplanned development has given rise to some internal imbalance within education, creating tensions between various levels of education, specializations and human components involved in educational processes. Much of the problems associated with education are the manifestations of these unintended consequences of allowing blind forces to determine the course of educational growth. It has been argued in the book that private control, having a major sway over higher education, has proved a structural barrier to the planned and balanced growth of education, since it has its own laws of autodynamics.

At the time of Independence, we had 17 universities and 626 colleges, while today the corresponding figures are 118 and 4460. This quantitative expansion has been marked in the case of privately managed affiliated colleges. The actual spread of private control is much more than the formal legal position. Dr Singh has amply demonstrated how control over college managements has been successfully used to occupy commanding positions in public institutions like the Universities, Boards of Secondary Education, State Legislatures and other political institutions. Today over 80 per cent of undergraduate enrolment and 50 per cent of postgraduate enrolment is in the colleges. Therefore, it would be little exaggeration if one were to assert that those who control college management control the entire educational resources and also related structures.

With the passage of time and the emergence of second/third generation of private managements private munificence has almost completely dried out and these managements take on more and more the characteristics of the ideal type of "pure management" described by the author on a Weberian plane. The colleges under the "pure managements" have a logical and historical tendency to develop "indulgency pattern"—'the teachers did not teach, the students did not study and the managers had no education to manage.' If quite a few colleges have been converted into degree-spinning factories and that too as a consequence of objective law-like tendencies and regularities associated with the institution of private control, the empirical and theoretical findings of the author deserve attention from many quarters.

The evidence collected from the seven colleges of Kanpur and described in some detail in the book impels the author to conclude that "private control of higher education subverts the professed national values of secularism, democracy, national integration, egalitarianism and scientific and modern outlook." This should cause many an eyebrow to be raised. If private control of colleges is eating into the very vitals of our value-structure, can we allow the policy of drift to continue any more?

The institution of private control of public education in India originated in the colonial period. This dubious distinction of its origin being situated in the deliberate decisions of the British did not prevent its later giving birth to alternative ideology and structures for the national platform of education. Thus private effort served both the colonial masters and the cause of national independence in the pre-Independence days. Now after the attainment of Independence this institution seems to have played out all its positive functions. In the context of continuing and some newly emerged inequalities, the two sets of educational institutions with two sets of classes to draw their students from and two sets of criteria for admissions, the existence of private control alongside with public (State) responsibility and funding seems to be making the task of ushering in an egalitarian society all the more arduous.

It is not necessary to agree with the author's methodological nuances, specificities of class analysis of the Indian State and society or his conceptual theoretical preference, to appreciate the importance of the issues involved in private control of higher education. The empirical analysis of the concrete contemporary situation carried out by the author to lay bare the conditions and consequences of the functioning of private control of higher education as a social institution stands out as a significant contribution to knowledge with the theoretical moorings or even independently.

23 February 1983 MOONIS RAZA

PREFACE

THE ARBITERS of India's destiny after Independence, as part of a grand design, forged a dual system of education with two sets of institutions at all levels, two sets of class clientele, two principles for admission criterion, and two bases for financing and two control mechanisms. The present study of private control of higher education, deals only with a fragment of this dual system of education.

I have studied, specifically, the control mechanism of seven colleges of Kanpur, which offer general courses in Arts, Science, Commerce, Law and Education, cater to a middle class clientele, are characterized by low to moderate educational standards and sell to students education carrying a very high public subsidy. This micro-study of actual conditions prevailing in a limited area has been attempted in a macro-perspective on education and society and their symbiotic relationship in India.

Groping for an appropriate conceptualization for the over-arching principle of organization leading to the pathological conditions permeating a number of these colleges, I stumbled upon the idea of specialized "pure" management. This ideal typical control mechanism increasingly expurgated itself of all commitment to internal educational norms and external societal ideals. It develops a specialist's expertise of manipulating men, money and material, making nonsense of the rules, regulations and legalities and obliterating any distinction between public trust and private appropriation. Its working hovered round an "indulgency pattern" gravitating towards a situation where the students do not have to study, the teachers do not have to teach and the managers do not have much of an education to manage. The emergence of "Bastard Colleges" that help open the guarded gates of the University for those whom the rules shut out on academic and extra-academic grounds is discovered as a logical development. These concepts have proved a helpful heuristic device to discover an underlying meaningful pattern in the chaotic conditions that were called colleges under private management.

The sociological perspective informing this study was, in many ways, removed from the dominant practice in the discipline. Sociological esoterica propounded in the name of professionalization had a conservative connotation for me. I believe the umbilical chord connecting sociological practice with society-in-action is vital for a living sociology's growth. It was felt that the prevailing definitions of sociological theory and methodology were stifling efforts to tackle substantive problems of public policy. The case for the perspective adopted for this study has been explicitly spelled out in a separate chapter. This has been done with a view to exposing my own "commitment, prejudices and blind-spots" to public gaze and to ward off possible criticism based on grounds which belong to questionable perspectives.

I have analysed the specific styles of effort for different colleges under private management. Divergence in origin, past performance, class and community composition of teachers and students and management make-up has been found to account for differential pace of overall growing convergence. Conditions helping or hindering the convergence were meshed up in a historical and contemporary context of the wider control mechanism of society and the internal norms and personalities constituting the managements.

The ideology of private control of higher education has been rationally reconstructed from the logical requirements of the control mechanism, the declared objectives and organizational principles of the managing bodies of the colleges and also the objective consequences of their actual actions. Direct and indirect conditioning of teachers and students' roles by managements' policies and practices have been analysed in detail to bring out the sociological consequences of the control mechanisms. The values fostered and foisted by the controllers of the colleges have also been discussed as indicative of the ideology and its consequences.

Not individuals but institutional arrangements were the target of sociological analysis. If in the course of reporting the findings of the study, taken up and conducted with the sole intention of analysing the private control of higher education, some individuals get named or identified in an unsavoury context, no personal characteristics should be read in the description. I offer advance apologies for any inadvertent irritation that illustrative empirical evidences of typified action may possibly cause to somebody.

I have been greatly benefited by free borrowing over a long time from diverse sources, living and dead. If some find mention in the text and others do not, memory at the time of writing has played the trick. In any case exhaustive listing is an impossible task. The selections for citation were biased in favour of building my arguments and not necessarily representative of the works of the authors cited. I express my gratitude for the ideas borrowed but the thesis, completed in 1978 and presented here, stands or falls on its own intrinsic logic and substantive support.

In this study I have been helped in varied ways by a large number of friends, colleagues, and institutions at various stages—planning, fieldwork, analysis and reporting. It is not due to my ingratitude to others but the desire not to dilute the effect that I mention one name and that is of Professor Yogendra Singh. He gave me advice and encouragement indirectly, directly, on seeking and without seeking in my "as is, where is" condition and in continuation of the perspective adopted for this study. I must also not fail to add grateful thanks to Professor Moonis Raza for his valuable foreword to this book.

Centre for the Study of Social Systems — NIRMAL SINGH
School of Social Sciences
Jawaharlal Nehru University
NEW DELHI

7 November 1978

CONTENTS

CHAPTER ONE

STATING THE PROBLEM

The colonial birthmark of modern education

MODERN education was introduced in India by its former British rulers in the early nineteenth century, as one of the many institutional mechanisms devised to serve their colonial interests. It was a device (i) to produce trustworthy servants for the Raj from among the Indians at a low cost, (ii) to form a new social base for their "modern" rule by recruiting from among the upper castes and classes by creating among them modern cultural needs and (iii) to propagate, as an adjunct to naked force, cultural values conducive to and supportive of the colonial rule. The institution of private control of public education likewise has the dubious distinction of owing its origin to the deliberate decisions of the colonial masters in pursuance of their basic educational policies, as part of the overall imperialist design.[1]

State and society after independence

With the transfer of power in 1947, the character of State power in India underwent a basic transformation. The new socio-economic structure was not sought to be built on the debris of the old colonial and feudal structures, Indian or foreign. It was built on the existing structures, with which the new rulers continue to have a dual relationship of protective partnership and gradual squeezing out, depending upon whether the conflict of the old structures is with the dominant ruling class or with its enemies.

The underdeveloped nature of the Indian capitalist class, with colonial historical constraints and the continuing neo-colonial curbs, its dual relationship with the precapitalist formations and ideologies like caste, communal prejudices and discriminatory practices has prevented the dominant class from risking a confrontation even in the interest of capitalist modernisation.

The situation gives rise to many social interests and provides them with typically Indian forms of "modernizing tradition", "traditionalising modernity", "resilience" of Indian tradition and structures and adaptability instead of replacement.

The path of development of India, since independence, being of arrested capitalism with feudal fetters and colonial curbs, we have an accentuated case of artificial appetites raised to ever increasing heights and an inherent incapacity of the social system to satiate them, even minimally. To keep the consequent discontent within manageable limits, mixed-up ideological manoeuvres and populist measures of "piecemeal socialism" are interspersed with solid institutional structures to guard the continued privileges of the upper classes.[2]

Educational system in India after independence

The new rulers took over the educational system as developed in the colonial period and began to build on this as the basic structure a quantitative expansion, a few qualitatively advaced super-structures and egalitarian-looking policy pronouncements with half-hearted implementation measures.

Naik, who was involved in various capacities in formulating and implementing the Indian Government's educational policies for decades, arrived at a similar assessment from his own characteristic standpoint. He sums up the situation in 10 points:

1. The system has been founded on the basic values of liberalism, individualism and competitiveness.... This helps the classes to strengthen their privileged position and makes education a weak instrument of social transformation.
2. The formal education system still functions on the basic concepts evolved at the opening of the nineteenth century....
3. The definitions of quality adopted in the system have a definite middle class bias and are not helpful for

the liberation of the masses or for social transformation.... In fact, our concepts of quality really support the status quo, strengthen the position of the well-to-do classes and build up a bridge between quality and privilege, especially because of the attempt to maintain a small number of quality institutions to which the privileged can secure admission while the bulk of the institutions, which provide access to the masses remain substandard.

4. The system almost totally ignores the non-formal sector. . . .
5. The system has obtained a virtual monopoly over the entire educational process: it alone can prepare individuals for well-established certificates, diplomas or degrees which have a value in the employment market. . . . .
6. The system is geared mainly to meet the needs of the class structure in power consisting of property, employment in the organized sector, and high education. . . . .
7. The policies adopted in the system even in secondary and higher education (which mainly benefit the well-to-do classes) are academically indefensible. . . . .
8. The system has grown to a fantastic size. . . .
9. The system has tended to be uniform and rigid and allows little initiative, freedom, creativity or experimentation within its boundaries. . . . . With every year that passes, the monster becomes larger, more entrenched, and more difficult to be moved or changed.
10. The performance of the system is poor and its efficiency low. Waste and ineffectiveness are writ large on every sector.[3]

Kamat, another perceptive social scientist engaged in the study of education, with a deep sense of his historical perspective, has noted the failure of the educational policies, pursued after the attainment of political independence, to measure up to the alternative national perspective developed in the colonial period itself. He notes that there is an amazingly close parallel between what is happening in education and what is happening in national economy. With an immense all-round expansion education has reached wider social strata, which were earlier untouched. It has reached all the middle sections of society and is extending its reach towards the lower sections also. Adult literacy efforts, practically non-existent, are visible. However, primary education has shown a slow inefficient growth pattern. Even fifty per cent in the age group 6-11 have not been drawn in and much less retained, the Constitutional obligation to provide free and universal education up to the age of 14 notwithstanding. Comparatively there is a much greater expansion in the secondary education but without useful terminal outlets. The growth of higher education has been found to be utterly indiscriminate and highly subsidized by the State. Standards have fallen or, at least, not improved in most cases. These standards are extremely asymmetrically distributed over different institutions in all sectors of education, depending upon the class clientele of the institutions.

For training and research in science and technology in the post-Independence period, national laboratories, research institutes, the I.I.Ts, regional engineering colleges and medical institutes were established. Their products could compete with the best in the world. Newer agricultural universities, medical colleges and advanced centres in the leading universities added to the elitist sector of our higher education. Many elite products from these institutions maintained at an immense cost to the public exchequer could find use and exchange value for their talent only in the rich Western countries.

For the bulk of the middle-class students, forming the bulge in the educational growth curve for higher education, the neglect of scientific, technical, modern managerial and business practices and proficiency in professional education continues unabated. "The uncontrolled and uncontrollable enrolment which is disproportionately large in terms of educability, manageability and employability" constitutes the principal cause of failure of the educational system at the higher level.[4]

Dual system of education mirrors class society

The Education Commission (1964-66) had noted with dismay the parallel existence of the minority of private fee-charging, better schools meeting the needs of the upper classes and the vast bulk of free publicly maintained but poor-standard schools utilised by the rest. The Commission lamented that access to these quality schools was determined solely by paying capacity. It issued appeals, in the name of democracy and socialism, long-term interests of the rich themselves and demand of national and social integration, to undo the increasing educational segregation, which was widening the existing gulf between the classes and the masses. The actual desegregation was to await a gradual improvement in the low-standard schools in twenty years to a point of where the rich would no more feel the need to send their children to separate elite schools.[5]

That the trend of increasing segregation in the schools has become all the more pronounced since the adoption of the Education Commission Report by the Government illustrates that exhortations are ineffective where vital class interests are involved. The full import of the phenomenon was not analysed by the Commission.

The dual system of education sustained by the policy decisions of the new rulers is an empirical reality, not only at the school stage as noted by the Education Commission but is very much in existence from the lowest to the highest level. It is functional to the existing socio-economic power structure.

From the ruling class point of view the educational system should ensure (a) perpetuation of the existing privileged position of the ruling class, (b) a minimum supply of scientists, technicians, managers of public and private[6] industrial and business establishments, competent professionals and civil servants, mainly recruited from the upper middle class, (c) a wider supply of personnel, recruited from the lower middle class and the new entrants to the class, to provide the lower-rung supervisory staff, with only a semblance of general education, which marks them off from those who work with their hands, holding a theoretical hope for the "really talented" to pass into the top elite by individual achievement, and (d) a general belief in the legitimacy of the regime as symbolising an open society, maintaining and extending an open-door educational set-up for the masses, keeping the dissatisfaction with the existing socio-economic arrangement channelized into an open race, where the handicaps are hidden.

The demand on the educational system enumerated in (a) and (b) above is met by :

(i) The elite schools open to all those who can pay or a chain of Kendriya Vidyalayas where admission is the exclusive preserve of Government servants whose loyalty is of crucial importance to the continuance of the regime.

(ii) High quality institutions of higher learning and research like I.I.Ts, institutes of management, national science laboratories, advanced centres in leading universities, engineering colleges, medical colleges, agriculture universities, national academies for defence or administration, etc., where admissions are open and by and large fair on the competitive principle of tested merit. (The class sieve having already weeded out the children of the poor, the rural, non-strategic and unorganised sectors at the school level, meritocracy principle at the higher level of elite institutions provides an effective mask for heavy Government expenditure on free and good quality higher education for private appropriation by those who have acquired the capacity to profit from it.)

(iii) A sprinkle of foreign-trained personnel from among those who failed to make a grade for the national institutions of higher learning and research in spite of the elite school ladder bought by their rich parents, but could pay their way through in Western educational institutions and from among those who graduated with credit from the elite national institutions and whose specialized further education abroad was financed by the state.

The demand on the educational system enumerated in (c) and (d) above is met by :

(i) publicly maintained but poorly equipped low-standard schools especially at the primary and elementary level, and

(ii) poorly equipped low standard higher secondary

schools and general education colleges established and maintained by private managements with two-thirds subsidy coming from Government grants and the remaining one-third from the fees.

The dual system of education, with two sets of institutions at all levels, two sets of class clientele, two principles as admission criterion, two bases of financing and two control mechanisms, more or less successfully meets the demand on the educational system by the existing power structure.

Private control and dispensation at the early school stage and private control at the higher education level take in two very different sets of students, from two opposite class origins. The total cost of education per capita being very low at the lower level and very high at the higher level, the system serves as a camouflage for State being an instrument in the hands of its keepers for private profit. The middle class can be alienated from the lower classes at cheap rate, with ideological affinity for the upper. The illusion can be kept up that the middle class in private colleges which largely gets this education is paying for its low quality white-collar-job-oriented education.

A scheme of association of five variables in educational institutions is presented in Table 1.1 to underscore the differential role of private control.

Private control of higher education as a sociological problem

Private enterprise at the school level especially pre-secondary is patterned on the pure market mechanism of quality goods/services offered to those who can pay. Resources for establishing and running these institutions were by and large the result of non-governmental (though not necessarily individual) efforts. These institutions are blatantly for the benefit of the upper classes. There is no mask, and it requires no sociological eyes to see the real face. To say so is not to belittle the work of those who told the obvious truth about these institutions as their continued existence contradicts the pronounced principles of State policies.

TABLE 1.1 : **Association of type of control, level of education class clientele, quality of education and students' share of cost**

	Level of Education	
	Lower	Higher
Private Control	(a) Upper class clientele (b) High educational standards (c) Very high students share in total cost of education	(a) Middle class clientele (b) Low educational standards (c) Low students share in total cost of education
Public Control	(a) Lower class clientele (b) Very low educational standards (c) Very low students share in total cost of education	(a) Upper class clientele (b) High educational standards (c) Very low students share in total cost of education

The mask, if any, in this case is common with private control at the higher level. The Constitution has guaranteed to the religious and linguistic minorities the right to establish and administer educational institutions of their choice. Moreover, the State is prohibited from discriminating in granting aid between institutions on the basis of their being under the management of a minority based on religion or language (Art. 30(1) and (2) of the Constitution of India). According to Supreme Court interpretations it is not necessary that all the members of a minority community should contribute funds for or be party to an institution's administration; a single philanthropic individual may do so. Both in mobilising resources and accepting as clients, members not belonging to the minority may be freely drawn in. Thus the Constitution and its interpretation have protected the continuation of one type of private institutions.[7]

A sociological analysis of private control of higher education can have a number of dimensions. Firstly, a conceptual analysis can show the possible relationship of other subsystems of society like polity, economy, family, religion, etc., with education as another sub-system, as mediated through private control over a part of higher education or total control in combination with all possible controls over other levels of education. Secondly, a historical study, of private control of higher education and its changing conditioning of and conditioning by other sub-systems, education proper and their reciprocal interactions, can be a fruitful dimension, with emphasis on the concrete ramifications rather than logical possibilities. Thirdly, one can take a broad macro view with national or regional aggregate data or one can look for the phenomenon in a micro setting which permits a more direct and detailed confrontation with the situation for a deeper probe, with the analytical, logical and macro-historical perspective taken as comparatively unproblematic for a specific study. The problem taken up for study here is detailed and concrete analysis of private control of higher education as it actually exists in a single city, with history of education at macro level, control pattern in changing context and conceptual analysis brought in as props to help the study stand up. There could also be other dimension worth studying.

Chitnis writes that the use of sociological concepts, methods and models to describe the patterns observed and to project the trends anticipated is probably the one single factor that distinguishes the sociological thinking on education from the non-sociological.[8] For this reason and more so for the realisation that there is and there can be no one single definition of "sociological" a detailed declaratory statement has been volunteered (Chapter II) with arguments that have appealed to me.

Issues the concrete evidence could decide

As the earlier conceptual and historical understanding has strongly suggested, the ideological position in defence of private control of higher education can be expected to be full of logical contradictions.

The case of private universities in the U.S.A. is cited in defence, where Lay Governing Boards have not really scuttled the academic reform and they have perhaps worked more closely with academics.[9] If the facts come out to be different in private colleges under study, the U.S. example would be declared as irrelevant. For a fair judgement we will look for the role of the managers in appointment and promotion of teachers, class-room teaching, library and laboratory work, examination reform and student policy, too. The issue is : Does the control system make commitment to knowledge a growing trend or does it negatively reward it ?

It is asserted that private control need to be sustained in order to retain their independent influence on the entire system even if by public money.[10] Autonomy of education is a coveted value, more so for higher education. This is corroded by norms of relationships developed in a polity, economy, religion and such other sub-systems, especially in class-divided society surreptitiously entering into the educational process. The aggression may come from political interference, economic subversions or religio-ideological distortions. Only evidencewill decide whether private control is a shield of academic independence and autonomy or allows apertures to alien elements or is itself the proverbial Arabian camel.

It is further argued that if private colleges and universities ceased to exist certain major goods to innovation and differentiation would disappear.[11] Specific rhythms and styles of colleges which make them into distinctive subcultures may be examined to answer related questions. Is the trend towards convergence or differentiation ? What is the role of private control in relation to this trend ? Does the management encourage or inhibit educational innovation ? Is the role of the management fortuitous or is it in its essence ?

Some have added educational excellence and service as additional points.[12] Does the claim stand in the face of scrutiny of actual practice ?

A common belief is that the private bodies have made a sizable contribution to the setting up of institutions of higher learning.[13] An interesting situation will develop if we find that municipal grants, State Government grants and even U.G.C. grants have been converted into private assets. Facts will answer if the financial contribution of private managers for the establishment and running of colleges is positive or negative. Is the trend towards greater munificence or profit-seeking ?

The colleges can be analysed as systems of interacting roles in continuity and change. Facts collected from the colleges will throw light on the suggestion that the private managers are a redundant role and in practice they disorient the teachers' role and students' role, and put them against each other as well as against their better self, in fact against education itself.

A counter thesis is that private control has reduced many a college into institutions where teachers do not teach, the students do not study and public resources of men, money and material are cornered by the managers. Students receive degrees and the teachers their salaries and the managers their power, prestige and pecuniary advantage as a by-product of managing the circus with the help of State purse. The strong thesis needs uncontestable facts to sustain it. Growth of "Indulgency Pattern" is a complex issue to be simplified by empirical findings.

Has the control of educational management acquired the characteristic of property, that it can be claimed in inheritance, alienated for profit, converted into political power and social prestige and vice versa? Is it because of this that it has developed indubitable resilience? Some of these questions will be answered in the pages that follow.

And finally, does private control prop up or subvert professed national values? Diversity of private managements united in practising the values of individualism, competitiveness, manipulation for personal or narrow group-interests may be fostering very homologous values among the teachers under their control and among the students put under their joint charge, on their way to full adult life.

A judgement on these issues, on the basis of empirical data collected from the concrete cases studied, would show as to how far the system of private control of higher education, sanctioned and supported by policy decisions of the dominant political leadership, fulfils the functional expectations. If these expectations are by and large fulfilled, the suggestions for its abolition would meet the same fate as the suggestion of the Education Commission for "common schools". If the suggestion is forced by popular pressure or a queer combination of teachers trade union interests articulated through strikes and street demonstrations and electoral compulsions, the form *alone* would be altered to its functional alternatives. A genuine alteration in the control mechanism of higher education may be part and parcel of efforts to seek a change in the broader socio-economic control mechanism.

REFERENCES

1. For details, see Chapter IV.
2. For a more elaborate discussion on the briefly sketched perspective on the Indian State and the path of development in India since Independence, see: (*i*) A.R. Desai, *State and Society in India: Essays in Dissent*. Bombay: Popular Prakashan, 1975 and (*ii*) Charles Bettleheim, *India Independent*. London, Haggikon and Kee, 1968.
3. J.P. Naik, *Equality, Quality and Quantity: The ilusive triangle in Indian education*. Bombay: Allied Publishers, 1977, pp. 106-109.
4. These ideas about the educational situation in post-Independence India are widely shared taken piecemeal but a coherent and systematic treatment is available in A.R. Kamat. See his *Education After Independence : A Social Analysis*. Bombay : Lala Lajpat Rai Institute, 1973-74. See also, A.R. Desai, "Social Change and Educational Policy" in Core *et al* (eds.) *Papers in Sociology of Education in India*. New Delhi : NCERT, 1967.
5. *Report of the Education Commission (1964-66) : Education and National Development*, New Delhi, Ministry of Education, Government of India, 1966, Chapter I, Para 36-38 and Chapter 10, Para 2-20. Also see, Recommendation No. 22 of "The 34th Meeting of Central Advisory Board of Education, and "National Policy of Eucation, Ministry of Education, Government of India (4)b" in Arbinda Biswas and Suren Agrawal (eds.) *Indian Educational Documents since Independence : Committees, Commissions, Conferences*. New Delhi : Academic Publishers, 1971, pp. 104 and 198.
6. It is interesting to note that in the U.S.A. the reference point for most partisans of private control, private industry directly invests in higher education and controls the production of its own requirements. It does not use control of the State for meeting its demand of scientists, technicians and researchers at the expense of the state exchequer, as is the case in India. For example, in 1969 I.B.M. engaged the services of a faculty of 31,417 offering 18,588,000 student contact hours of instruction, equivalent of nearly 40,000 full-time students. The trend toward major investments by Corporations in educational facilities and activities has by no means slowed down. (See Lewis M. Branscomb and Paul C. Gilmore, "Education in Private Industry: Modern Corporations need trained management personnel", *Daedalus*, Vol. II, Winter 1975).
7. See, G.S. Sharma, *Educational and Cultural Rights of the Minorities*. New Delhi : ICSSR, 1973.

8. Suma Chitnis, "Sociology of Education—A Trend Report" in *A Survey of Research in Sociology and Social Anthropology*, a Project sponsored by ICSSR. Bombay: Popular Prakashan, Vol. II, p. 169.
9. Y. Raghaviah and K.V. Srinivasan, "University Governance in India: A Case for Lay Governing Boards", *University Administration*, Vol. IV, No. 182, 1977, pp. 41-46.
10. Edward Gradd, "The American Credo. . .of Higher Education", Thesis No. 55, *Daedalus*, Vol. I, Fall 1974, p. 345.
11. The Assembly on University Goals and Governance", Theme 6, p. 325, *Daedalus*, Vol. II, Winter 1975.
12. Malcolm S. Adiseshaiah, "Why Private Colleges?", *New Frontiers in Education*, Vol. 2, No. 3, December 1972.
13. J.L. Azad, "The Financing of Higher Education in India" in Amrik Singh and Philip G. Altbach (eds.), *The Higher Learning in India*. Delhi: Vikas, 1974, p. 74.

CHAPTER TWO

SEARCH FOR METHODOLOGICAL WAY OUT IN SOCIOLOGY

THE SOCIOLOGICAL orthodoxy that ruled the roost, since the end of World War II, throughout the non-communist world, is in disarray.[1] Why and how the charisma, of Parsens-Merton "Social System" paradigm and "structural-functional" approach, has been washed out has been verily explained by different sociologists on the basis of autodynamics of the communal life of social sciences— introspection, self-consciousness and a return to philosophy— and a thorough-going shift in the socio-cultural setting— civil rights revolution and campus revolts of the sixties in the U.S.A., collapse of the collosus of the American armed might in Vietnam, consolidation of the communist regime in Cuba, exposure of the sinister C.I.A. activities, the downfall of the dollar and the dollar diplomacy, etc.—with shifting emphasis on different combinatorial choices about these subjective and objective factors.

Whereas the crumbling hegemony is on the way out, the pretenders are too many. The reconciliation of the irreconcilables in the phase of dethroning an incumbent is possible but not so in the phase of establishing and carrying out a positive rule. A bland statement that a pluralist model will replace the ruling paradigm, as has been made by Freidrichs, will not do, unless it is demonstrated that the plural positions do not suffer from mutual incompatibilities. This is one of the reasons prompting the author to delineate the sociological perspective that has informed this work.

When one works in what Thomas Kuhn has called the "Normal Science" phase, the fundamental images of reality that provide a science with a stable base are not in dispute, the domain of the discipline is well-defined and the problems to be researched dovetail into the previous practice. Moreover the tools and techniques of inquiry and procedural practices, sometimes called methodology, do not demand personal choice to be made by the researcher. The unifying logic of inquiry, analysis and justification follows a well-charted path. One can follow the available short-hand description to report on one's findings. In short everything is programmed. As I deliberately take a dissenting position and have followed an off-beat path, renouncing the *rite-dominated* sociology, it is necessary to declare the domain assumptions, the "logic-in-use" and its relationship with the "reconstructed logic"[2], and the procedural preferences with their rootedness in the assumptions. The deliberate departure from the mainline sociology, without opting out for a single-source alternative is another reason that calls forth a declaratory statement.

ESSENCE AND APPEARANCES

Marx, the founder of modern human-science approach, has remarked: "But all science would be superfluous if the outward appearances and the essence of things coincided."[3] Taking his point of departure from this distinction between appearances and essence[4], he rejected the naive inductionism and much of positivism and empiricism that deify "facts" and derive common comfort in the untenable belief that if enough "facts" are gathered an explanatory and predictive mechanism would spontaneously sprout up from this soil. Merton's distinction between the "manifest" and the "latent" functions, Popper's definition of sociology as the study of unintended consequences of intentional action and the like may create an impression that sociology, as a whole, looks for social reality beyond "the semblance, the cloak and the esoteric". But in most cases the acceptance itself is a semblance and the logic is not followed the whole way.[5]

A consequence of accepting the probe, for the essence behind the visible form, as the goal of social science is to take the fact as it appears at a particular moment in history as problematic and to look for its transcendence in its dialectical potentiality. To look for reality is not only to look for what "is" but also for what it "can be" which inheres within it what it "should be". Trent Schroyer has aptly said: "A critical theory, on the other hand, transcends its facts, rendering them meaningful, but at the same time placing them in the context of the tension between the given and the possible."[6] We will revert to this issue in the following section when sensitivity towards sociological issues and their sources are discussed.

Self-definition is only part reality

Recently sociologists have been flooded with books, critical of the "mindless empiricism" and positivistic methodology, couched in terminology quite similar to the dialectical approach of Marx. These efforts in the name of "symbolic-interactionism", "actors" definition of the situation, "ethno-methodology", "existentialism", "phenomenology" and the like have helped much in demystifying the prevailing Parsons-Merton paradigm but it must be seen that not all of these alternatives, advanced as "meaningful" approach to social phenomena, consistently look for the essence of these phenomena. Some of them break shells of objective appearances to lock themselves up in newer shells of subjective appearances.

Max Weber, the founder of *Verstehn* sociology, in his analysis of the capitalist system missed everything that did not constitute part of its self-celebration, for instance, exploitation, class conflict and its inherent irrationality.[7] He wrote after half a century of Marx's major works being published. Sociology is, no doubt, concerned with social acts or interactions and they involve meaningful phenomena and symbolic communication. But if we define the activities of human actors and institutions on the single parameter of self-definition and self-comprehension we misconstrue their real meaning. Human beings, their institutions and their activities cannot be comprehended within the four walls of their own belief and self-definitions. John Seeley holds simultaneously the logically contradictory propositions that (a) social facts tend to become what they are largely in virtue of beliefs about them and (b) problems exist whether or not they are recognised as problems.[8]

Thomas informs us: "A social institution can be fully understood only if we do not limit ourselves to abstract study of the formal organization, but analyse the way in which it appears in the personal experience of various members of the group and follow the influence which it has upon their lives."[9] This emphasis on the personal experience and the well-known concept of "actor's definition of the situation", while correcting the limitations of the behaviourists, has led to a craze for pyschologizing all social reality. It is maintained that criminals are criminals because some people "label" them as such and they accept the stigma. "What was called labelling theory grew out of the important assertion as against orthodox criminology that criminality or deviance was not an observable attribute of an act. There was a man who acted and another who labelled his act as deviant."[10] They would be conformists if they define themselves in those terms in their own culture. All distinctions vanish in such a position and sociology takes on more and more the characteristics of meaningless gibberish. To cite one example, Arthur Brittan writes: "Men perceive what they believe to be true in a situation, their common sense explanations are just as valid as the most elaborate theoretical scheme erected by the outside political analysis."[11] This makes all social sciences utterly redundant by asserting the belief of the perceiver as the *sole* basis of perception.

To present one more illustration of counterfeit sociology being pedelled in the name of "definition of the situation" and "everyday sociology", I quote Professor Zijderveld. He writes: "I define rationality as the search for means *believed* to be adequate for the realization of clearly envisaged goals. According to this definition, rain magic is as rational as scientifically designed irrigation systems since it is believed (in act of thought) to be an adequate means for the inundation of the fields—just as we moderns believe the jet plane to be an adequate means for reaching a certain destination fast and safely."[12] Though Andreski has titled his book, *Socil Science as Sorcery*, even he did not have this literal example of sorcery in view.[13]

It is possible to agree on the whole with Rex that "while the best of the phenomenologists" (e.g. Berger and Luckmann) continue to build the actor's definition of the situation into an approach to the study of social structures, others seem to be doing nothing more than describing the actors' perspective so that, instead of sociology, all we are offered is "the phenomenology of everyday life."[14] But even these authors, "the best of phenomenologists", while defining successful socialization as "the establishment of a high degree of symmetry between objective and subjective reality" advance the "fanciful" (their own labelling) theory of developing counter-reality and counterideology by just attaching new tags. They self-assuredly write : "If this process appears fanciful at first, it is beautifully illustrated by Gandhi's designation of *harijans*, that is, the children of God for the outcastes of Hinduism".[15] Only if labels could develop counter-reality objectively, social reform could have become a child's play. Thomas' statement that "if men define a situation as real, it is real in its consequences" is true but these consequences unfortunately do not include an automatic alteration of objective reality in the defined direction without the intervention of the activists' effort. The common saying, "If wishes were horses, beggars would ride them" has greater sociological truth-content than the "fanciful" theories of "everyday life" sociologists. These writers are not unaware that the definitions may also be manipulatively produced by the power holders and the definitions enforced by armed might are not less convincing on that count.[16] "False-consciousness" is an important conceptual tool available to sociology for an adequate explanation of "construction of reality" and its later transcendence.

Human behaviour : Counterfeit but authentic too

Goffman has contributed in no mean way to develop the perspective that human scene is nothing but pretence and putting up appearances. The dramatic metaphor that he has developed has correctly brought out that men often are aware of their inner and outer audiences and they do often attempt "impression-managements" for a favourable evaluation. But dangerous consequences flow from not recognizing that "often" is not "always" and even this "often" is also not a fixed quantity, as it varies from society to society, from segment to segment of the same society and from time to time for the same society or the same segment. It is the problematic nature of pretence as well as genuineness of human behaviour that makes the sociological game worth the candle. If for vulgar behaviourists all behaviour was genuine, for Goffman no behaviour is. The consequences for the practice of sociology are paradoxically identical. To quip, if all behaviour is pretensious so is sociologist's.

A unidimensional image of man leaves little to be discovered. Men act genuinely and they also fake appearances. They act consciously; they act unconsciously; and they also act false-consciously. Nature communicates but the communication has no addressee. She will not lie to anybody but the recipient can receive false communication content due to his own faulty reception outfit. In the case of human communication (so also other type of human behaviour), it can be deliberate distortion, calculated concealment or unwitting untruth on account of unawareness, even against one's own interest. Therefore a gullible guy is a sorry sociologist. But truthfulness, sincerity, genuineness and spontaneity are also attributes of human behaviour and interaction. As such, a person imbued with a devilish distrust in the existence of any qualities of veracity in human conduct can sire only suspect sociology.

"There can be no guarantee", as Rex puts it, "that our account of the other individual's behaviour and its meaning is accurate."[17] Neither absolute accuracy nor any unfailing guarantee can be the objective of sociology. Plausibility and not perfection should provide the criterion for evaluation of sociological enterprise.

A continuous critical re-evaluation of social sciences is necessary, if we aim even asymptotically to approach getting at the essence of social life. Gouldner's *The Coming Crises* was an attempt in the same direction. "If there is any point", he writes, "to *The Coming Crises*, if it can be reduced to a single theme it is precisely this : thinking that *their* theory is the result of an 'immaculate' theoretical conception, they fail to see that it is not only their political *enemies*' theory that is corrupted by their politics, but also their *friends*'and their own theory. They fail to see, even when they are sociologists, how *their* own theory is not only the product of a technical tradition of logic or of evidence but of their *whole social existence*."[18] The argument will continue.

SOCIOLOGIST AS A SELF-CONSCIOUS ACTOR IN SOCIETY[19]

The basis of the dissimilarity of approach, procedural techniques, the analysis, the conclusions arrived at and the criteria of validation and justification between the social sciences in general and sociology in particular on the one hand and the natural sciences, especially physics, on the other, is the fact that with the former there is epistemologically no separation of the knower and the subject-matter under study. This unalterable and broadly indisputable situation puts the sociologist in an advantageous as well as a precarious position. The situation is beautifully expressed in Andreski's description of psychologists' efforts as "man tries to lift himself by his bootstraps, using the mind to understand the mind".[20] The analogy is fully applicable in the case of sociology; as a branch of social knowledge, sociology is part of the "social construction of reality" which is also the object of its study. The perpetually approximate and ontologically tentative nature of our theoretical discoveries stems from this situation. As the phenomenologist philosopher Schutz has put it : "Whereas natural science involves having concepts about things, social science involves having concepts about things which have concepts."[21]

A triology of fundamental theses for sociology has been succinctly restated by Berger and Luckmann: "Society is a human product. Society is an objective reality. Man is a social product."[22] More than a century ago Marx said the same thing: "Thus the social character is the general character of the whole movement : just as society itself produces man as man so is society produced by him. Activity and enjoyment both in their content and in their mode of existence are social activity and social enjoyment."[23]

Berger and Luckmann further explain that society should be understood in terms of an ongoing dialectical process composed of the three moments of externalization, objectivation and internalization. They write : "The same is true of the individual member of society, who simultaneously externalizes his own being into the social world and internalizes it as an objective reality. In other words to be in society is to participate in its dialectic."[24] Now, nobody has been able to show that sociologists are beings descended on this earth from some other world and are, therefore, not covered by the phrase "individual member of society". Thus we come to the central thesis of this section : "The activities of sociologists are in many ways no different from those of the persons he studies."[25] It could reasonably be asserted that sociologists are fully covered by the individual-society dialectical relationship postulated above.

From this position, there ensues a methodological imperative as a corollary. The sociologist does what all other individuals in social interaction do. This interaction involves simultaneously sensing feeling and activist intervention or one follwing the other in all possible permutations. There is no clear "role separation" of the sociologist from all others, no "role switching" after the completion of field study and no "role distance" between participant observer and analyst. To maintain that "at these exalted levels only the sociologist understands social reality; he therefore divides the world into categories—experts and laymen—scientific knowledge on the one hand and folk wisdom on the other", is a false consciousness characteristic of the priestly mode of sociology.[26]

J.H. Huxley has said : "Science is nothing but trained and organized commonsense." What should distinguish a sociologist is a robust commonsense and its training and organization achieved through what Gouldner called "reflexive" activity. This is not to deride what commonly goes under the rubric of methodology, but this methodology should also be grounded in robust commonsense and reflexive activity on how and why some sociologists have produced and others failed to produce worthwhile sociological knowledge. The everyday actor in interaction with his fellows carries out this very process but not necessarily with equal self-consciousness.

The basic procedures for "the ordinary actors' everyday knowledge of society as a form of practical sociology, on the one hand, and the professional sociologists' knowledge of society as a form of common sense on the other" are the same and they feed each other knowledge or quackery as the case may be.[27] There is no reason to agree with Cicourel that "in actual practice, the actor's everyday theorizing is probably not much different from the observer-researcher" but "in the ideal, the actor and the observer-researcher employ different kinds of constructs and their procedural rules are distinct."[28] Both or either may outstep the rules or extend them but there is no *essential* difference between the actor's or sociologist's rules either in the ideal or in practice. In general, Cicourel's position as expounded elsewhere seems to be sympathetic to the one expounded here.[29] The difference between the practical sociology of the common actor and the sociology of the professional sociologist is one of level rather than of kind.

Lamenting the prevailing methodological approach Bierstedt recounts a humorous story. A little old lady inquired of the keeper of a zoo, if the animal in the cage in front was a male or a female hippopotamus. The keeper in all solemnness replied, "Lady, that is a question that could conceivably be of interest only to the other hippopotamus." Sociologists have to ask and try to answer questions which could conceivably be of interest to ordinary actors in society. The society sustains the sociologists' specialization. The mandate is likely to be withdrawn at any moment if the sociologists set themselves up above or against the rest of the society by addressing questions of interest only to professionals to the neglect of the rest of the society. His assigned role lies in doing in a more sophisticated way what all other members of society are always attempting—knowledge about social life. It is the abjuring of reflexive activity which led to sociologists becoming "mindless empiricists" and it is the recession from common folk concerns that resulted into what Redfield called "exercises in which something not very important is done very well".[30]

LANGUAGE FOR SOCIOLOGISTS

A sociologist's interest in language is at three levels : (i) it permeates the object of sociological investigation, i.e. society, so thoroughly that nothing remains to be investigated if language is left out; (ii) sociological investigation as a societal process involves language-based communication between sociologists and the rest of society under study; and (iii) the sociologist must report his findings to other sociologists and society at large and reporting obviously involves the language process in all its ramifications.

Language is a form of existence of thought and of its

expression. The sign-system, called language, is an instrument of cognition and communication. Thus no continuing consciousness exists outside of this system. It is the vehicle of transmission, crystallization and preservation of socially shared knowledge. Language is not identical with thought but only its carrier. In the process it becomes relatively independent with its own internal laws of action and development. As such, there is no one-to-one correspondence between word and concept or between sentence and judgement. Sapir has shown that not only is language, as a perfect symbolic system, capable of handling "all references and meanings that a given culture" has but new experiences necessarily "enlarge the resources of a language". Language through its independent existence, on the basis of its own internal logic, makes it possible for thought to go beyond more empirical knowledge and thus serves as a heuristic device. It is this heuristic function which is the hallmark of artificial language of mathematics. Sapir writes : "It is important to realize that language may not only refer to experience or even mold, interpret and discover experience but that it also *substitutes* for it. . . .[31]

The substitution of direct experience by the symbolic system creates a situation where falsification becomes possible. Moreover translation of one symbol system into another called "linguistic transfer" by Sapir, by further removing language from direct experience, not only enhances its capacity to successfully carry out its secondary function as a heuristic artifice but at the same time increases the artificiality and potential mendacity of the linguistic device.

A basic acquaintance with the dialectical relationship between direct experience, thought and language is a must for any serious student of society.[32] What has been discussed under "Essence and Appearances" applies with greater force when we focus on symbolic exchange. Most empirical sociology has faltered because of gullibility. " 'Coded' substantive responses are distorting, altering or truncating the meaning of the activities, objects or events for the actor", as Cicourel has warned.[33] A whole school of social anthropology called "structuralism" has gone astray by taking structural linguistics and semiology as a substitution for sociology and social anthropology.[34]

Both the Marxist and the existentialists in sociology posit man as an active agent and deny the one-sided Whorfian thesis that the language *determines* the world outlook of man. In the final analysis, it is life and reality that play the dominant role and not language per se. The experience of our life leads to refinement in thinking and in our language. People can respond to a given situation in new ways. "Language is capable of 'making present' a variety of objects that are spatially, temporarily and socially absent from 'here and now' ", as Berger and Luckmann note.[35] It is language which makes it possible and necessary for men to live in "second-hand worlds". We are aware of much more than we have personally experienced. The quality of our lives is determined by the meanings we have received from others.[36]

It is the meaning content of the language that the sociologists have to discover and also to determine the degree of correspondence between the actual experience and the symbolic expression. We can judge the real thought and feelings only by relating them to the actions of the individuals expressing them—to their social action.[37]

An element of language points out practical significance of a thing in its *denotation* which can be understood only by the context. The specification of the denotation is made clear as its *sense* by relating it to other words or an objective situation. Words as a rule have varied denotations and senses even within the same language depending upon to the context and the interpretation given by speakers and listeners. Here Garfinkel's concept of "indexicality" and "reflexivity" are helpful to establish the context and specificity as well as validation of meaning.[38]

Human languages do not as a rule use natural signs like smoke for fire; their signs are conventional signs, as such they are meaningless outside the specific system of signs of which they form part. Separated from the concrete situation and given an independent status by conventional usage and the diversity of its conventional usage makes the analysis of verbal communication both interesting and challenging. Gathering verbal responses is less than half of a sociologist's work. His real work lies in discovering its meaning and the degree of correspondence with other types of human responses.

Specialized Language

Should sociology have a specialized language of its own ? The desire to build up a specialized language of sociology springs from a number of undesirable, erroneous and illegitimate motives. The answer to the question depends on the typification a particular neologism answers to.

Firstly, new terms may be coined to label an old idea, with laboured justification to allow faithfuls to announce to the world the great "invention" of the originator. Surely this is no aid to the discipline of sociology; but minus the cult-of-personality involved a stray stylistic innovation may even sometimes serve to decrease the drabness of an otherwise dull description.

Secondly, a new language is attempted to build sociologists or some school within sociology as an elect group with their own exclusive "code" language and status symbols. This mantra-chanting group of sociological *brahmanism* does the double harm of (a) separating sociological practice from its life-giving source—the everyday social life—for raw data and validation criterion and (b) of producing hocuspocus of socially unserviceable sociology. This is the natural outcome of denying the thesis that sociologist is basically a self-conscious actor in society.

Thirdly, the sociologist may develop a special language to communicate in shorthand and in a precise way with other "self-conscious actors in society". If the object is achieved, the attempt is laudable but some sort of a test like the one proposed by Andreski[39] will have to be applied to ensure that the jargon has a justification within the third category and does not fall in the first two categories.

In any case, in everyday life, the common actors also coin and accept new symbols for newer experiences,[40] for precision or as measures of economy of expression. If the sociologist does that, he is only acting as the everyday actor does and his innovation sooner or later becomes part of general culture. Gouldner writes : "At decisive points the ordinary language and understanding fails and must be transcended. It is essentially the task of social theory, and the social sciences more generally, to create new and 'extraordinary' language, to help man learn to speak them; to mediate between the deficient understandings of ordinary language and the different and liberating perspectives of the extraordinary language of social theory. . . . To say social theorists are concept-creators means that they are not merely in the knowledge-creating business but, above all, in the language-reform and language-creating business. In other words they are from the beginning involved in creating a new culture."[41] For example, "socialization", "social stratification", "surplus value", "leisure class", "taboo", "totem" are some such contributions by social scientists to the common man's vocabulary.

Fourthly, there is the wholly illegitimate desire to get sociology and sociologists recognized as science and scientists by exhibiting the distinctive vocabulary as externalia of scientism. In outward appearances if "sociology" and physics look alike, it can pass as genuine scientific knowledge. Astrology, unlike astronomy, did not become science just because it also uses mathematical symbols and calculation apparatus.

Lastly, there is the possibility (in present practice it seems to be quite absent) that a specialized language may result in autonomous procedures and operations which can be performed with the symbols and results obtained which can be later on tested for empirical conformity with social reality. The analogy is of mathematical language and its relationship with experimental physics. The system of mathematical symbols is a complete language with elements, rules of combination and the rules of operation thereupon. No such demonstrable effort exists in relation to sociology. Mathematics, we are told, grew out of successive demonstrations, of the serviceability of its abstract symbolic operations in understanding and controlling nature.[42] In any case future development of a specialized abstract symbol system serviceable for sociology cannot be dismissed on logical grounds.

The above line of argument should lead us to agree with Peter Worseley as far as the present is concerned. He writes : "Many people feel that it is the business of scientists to develop a technical terminology and the scientist must move beyond mere 'commonsense' thought and 'everyday language' in order to obtain the refinement and discrimination of thought they need in their work. We would suggest that while the argument *might* hold good for other sciences it does not do so for sociology. . . . rather the concepts and theories which the members of society themselves develop must be built into the sociologist's model."[43]

If the language of sociology is far removed from the common everyday world, it violates the essential empirical world in which men interact.[44] It would be erroneous to believe with Schutz that sociologists' constructs being constructs of constructs or second degree concepts are the prerogative of professional sociologists.[45]

An impression might have been created that once the attempt at spurious, artificial and specialized language is given up, the problems associated with the language will dissolve themselves automatically. This is far from being true. Acceptance, by and large, of the common man's everyday language brings out into the open, in their very nakedness, the problems associated with the language of everyday discourse. The advantage is that the prestige of "science" associated with artificial plumage of esoteric vocabulary will not be available to the sorcery practised in the name of sociology, and it would unmask "sociological" apology for establishment for what it is. Take, for example, the folk concept of "power". Its exercise has been made to look legitimate (by Parsons and Lipset) by telling the powerless that definitionally this does not involve the use of brute force but merely the ability to mobilize resources for the system and by postulating that most of the things done by those at the summit of organization are socially necessary. The battle is won by a definitional stratagem and verbosity serves as camouflage. The concept of "ideology", which in common parlance may mean a net of ideas, has been successfully made to stand for deliberate distortion, falsehood and what not by those sociologists who were working for an "end of ideology" in the face of Marxian studies which were self-confessed ideology, of course with its commonsense meaning. Language is a weapon in the struggle for counter-construction of social reality. Sociologists should be shown up for what they are up to, their protestations of value-neutrality notwithstanding.[46] Bridgeman's idea of providing "operational definitions" should not give a licence to impose arbitrary definitions of everyday terms to serve as "spurious definitions" by furtively bringing into play common images to serve propagandist purposes.

SENSITIVITY TOWARDS SOCIOLOGICAL ISSUES

All domain assumptions are not equally conducive to the development of sensitivity towards sociological issues, a prerequisite though by no means sufficient condition for successful sociological work. Three basic assumptions about the relationship of sociologist and object of study, which the writer considers to be of help are listed below and the reasons for sharing them with a number of sociologists are also discussed.

(a) The existing situation is considered problematic.

(b) The sociologist is involved in helping bring about social change in the desired direction and resist changes in the undesirable directions.

(c) Sociologists must remain divided on the different sides of the battleline drawn in an internally divided society.

The problematic nature of existing situation

The materialist doctrine that men are products of circumstances and upbringing, which has been called "over-socialized conception of man", like the religious determinism called fatalism leaves man resigned to things as they are. An Indian saying rhetorically asks: "Why know the path to a village, if one has not to go there?" The deterministic assumptions deaden the will to know. On the contrary the thesis, "Just as society itself produces man as man, so is society produced by him" is an ever open-ended one. Both man and society continue to be in a state of flux. The relationships between individuals and groups and their circumstances as they exist at a particular point of time remain precarious; the fit is never complete and as such potentialities of creating an alternative future propel men to know the limitations imposed and the openings allowed by the present.

Sociological investigation creates a new "definition of the situation"; if the existing definition is not seen as problematic wherefrom could arise the impetus for a new definition? Unless the aim of sociology is operationally defined as producing university degrees in "sociology" and/or enhancing career prospects of "professional sociologists" there can be no sociology if existing situation is considered unproblematic.

The origins of modern sociology lay in the conceptualization of capitalist development as problematic in the dual sense of the term. It was seen as creating social problems and its own development was unevenly distributed among societies. Both Marx and Weber were the products of the problematic nature of capitalism. If Mills' "sociological imagination" encompassed global issues of war and peace, "power elite" and humanity's future, while his compatriots were busy with "middle range" studies of doctor-patient relations in a hospital, "one-year guarantee" by watch-repairers, or small groups of children, it was so because these respective aspects of social reality were seen as problematic by these sociologists. Similarly Desai studied "social background of Indian nationalism" and Srinivas' efforts to achieve illusory mobility (termed Sanskritization) within the caste hierarchy without challenging the ritual dominance of the Brahmin and the politico-economic dominance of the Kshatriya by the lower castes, because these were considered as problematic. History of knowledge in general and sociology in particular everywhere lends support to Andreski's statement:

> Whereas if you are living in a perfect society, which neither needs to be nor can be improved, you are unlikely to ponder about the fundamental questions of sociology.[47]

The type of sociology one does is a function of the conception of the problematic nature of social reality. It is society itself which is full of contradictions and hence problematic. As a consequence we may have contradictory sociologies.[48]

The value-neutrality stance of sociology traced from Weber to its coronation in post-World War II American sociology has been flogged verily as "myth" "cloak" "a disguise which permits the actual conservative activity", "reification", "pseudoneutrality . . . eminently profitable and at the highest level of skills it brings the benefit of being able to run with the hare while hunting with the hounds". As a result of this mounting onslaught a number of sociologists have formally accepted the impossibility of successfully sticking to the value-neutral stance, but have not been able to see its relatedness to the intellectuals' alienation in society or the desirability of devaluating this value of social science.

Anthropologists had long back realized that certain experience and knowledge were denied to those who were considered as outsiders. This led them to prescribe the technique of participant observation for data gathering. But the logic of the position was not fully understood, nor made explicit. The technique is narrowly conceived, emphasizing personal direct observation. The participation in action sensitizes an investigator to know what to look for. Most social scientists are of the view that involvement with the people under study impairs the capacity to observe and a role-distance between the scientist and the participant is recommended.[49] To me this position seems to be self-contradictory. A passionate involvement with the subject-matter, from the initial stage of recognition of the problematic area, through the stage of gathering sensitive data, down to the stage of analysis and reporting, is more helpful than playing it "cool". Disinterested research can generate information but of interest to no one.

Marx had brought out the inherent relationship of man, passion and knowledge when he wrote: "Man as objective sensuous being is therefore a suffering being—and because he feels that he suffers, a passionate being. Passion is the essential force of man energetically bent on its object."[50] John Horton has recently emphasized the same. He writes:

> "A truly human science like a truly human society must give full cognitive status to the whole man, which a reified reality fragments and hides; it must give cognitive status to consciously active men who strive to transcend their determination by things. He also says :
>
> "Science is politically intended activity and scientific knowledge a politically intended account of the world, not a theoretical reflection existing independently of human purpose and practice. The passive reflexive attitude is an

example of reification and reactionary politics."[51] Politics here stands for organised purposive action.

Gouldner has also recognized the advantages that accrue for scholars who engage in some form of political praxis and attempt to change some part of the social world in an emancipatory way, as they achieve a different and penetrating understanding of their social world; they can see certain things not seen by other scholars whose political praxis differs. It is not an automatic "response" to an action "stimulus" but results from reflection upon that experience.[52] All activists do not become scholars, only the reflecting ones may. It is not necessary for a scholar to participate in all actions directly but he should be one-piece with the movement to draw upon the sensitivities of the active participants. For a greater concentration on analysis disciplining one's emotional reactions is necessary, but this does not exclude emotional involvement, which prompts untiring curiosity. Marx is an outstanding illustration of the fact that profound insight into the working of society could be achieved by hating and admiring social reality.[53]

An offshoot of the activist sociology is that it is impossible to understand or explain social behaviour without imputing motives to the actors, as everyday actors, do to negotiate their own behaviour. What is required is not to shun imputing motives but to put checks on unreasonable imputations. A reasonable imputation of motives should be able to predict/anticipate action within a certain range. Congruence should be present in different forms of behaviour or the incongruence ought to be explained.[54] Methodological training and reflection may serve to act as prophylactic devices against erring on this score. The emphasis is on basic logic rather than on any specific technique.

No monolythic sociology under divided society

Declaring a particular situation, institutional arrangement or social process as problematic and accepting the activist mode of doing sociology necessarily leads not only to a heterogeneous view of sociology but of a scene replete with contradictory or even battling sociologies.

If there are antagonistic groups, classes, or interests

struggling for supremacy and establishing their own definitions of situations in the real world, the reflection howsoever distorted of this is bound to occur in social-science images of this reality. It is not an accident that some social scientists depict imperialist rule as functional[55] and others see human emancipation in wars of national liberation. Some sociologists study the impediments to productivity in a capitalist enterprise and contrive devices for better management of plant personnel, whereas others discover the dehumanization of the wage slave on the same plant and forge instruments for their emancipation. Some write about *Jajmani* system as a unifying principle of Hindu village life, others about the *Sudra* degradation and his struggle for the ending of caste bondage. Different sociologists may also employ different methodologies depending upon their sources and the vantage point from which they carry out their studies.

Therefore I accept the thesis, that a monolithic view of sociology under a divided society will only mean hegemony of the powerful, which will make the struggle for change in society as well as knowledge more torturous and tortuous. Moreover, apart from being a false picture, the consensual norm in sociology is counter-productive in another sense also. The norm leads to a self-censor on criticism of the methods and substance of the sociological work in the name of good professional image. The norm leads to a tolerance of charlatanism, parasitism and outright fraud practised in the name of sociology. Academic polemics on theoretical and substantive issues is more in consonance with the social reality that sociology purports to portray; and it portends well for scientific advance by weeding out the cancerous growth and preventing pretensions.[56]

STANDPOINT OF 'TOTALITY' AND DIALECTICAL APPROACH

The fall from pre-eminence of Parsons-Merton paradigm in the last decade has led many a sociologist to assert that there always has been a "conflict variously labelled as being between the mechanistic and organistic approaches, between atomism and holism, methodological individualism and collectivism and so on" and the present is only a new edition of the eternal conflict of the irreconcilabales. "The two sociologies" have, as they always had, two theories, two central concerns, two languages and two research specialisms.[57] The issue is incorrectly posed as an alternative between "sociological reconciliation" and "never-the-twain-shall-meet"—one more mutually exclusive dichotomy to serve as a prop for two mutually exclusive sociologies. The either/or approach in sociological analysis stems from reification of an analytical separation of aspects of social reality. Fortunately for sociology, no body has been able to do sociological research or report on it without drawing upon the concepts, analytical tools, theoretical insights and even language elements from the other sides, paying tribute to the unity of opposites that exists in the substantive reality under study. The neat property space representation of the dichotomous "major axes of sociological analysis" given by Roland Robertson[58] does not take into account the actual practice as well as the logical possibility of moving simultaneously along these axes in opposite directions and along various axes. A person cannot physically move in opposite directions and along different roads at the same time but the social reality and the thought processes do. The implicit physical analogy is too crude for understanding societal processes and their sociological reflections.

The theses, that (i) man and society are engaged in a continuous process of producing each other in ever newer forms of continuity and change at the same time and (ii) society is both a subjective and an objective reality, dissolve the mutually exclusive dichotomies (actor-system, value-meaning, conflict-consensus, micro-macro, order-control, society-culture, etc.) without wishing away the contradictions. But these contradictions are the very modes of social existence.[59] If the "oversocialized conception of man in modern society[60] is overdone, so is the assertion of the ethno-methodologists and phenomenologists that the social reality in which people live in their everyday activities is built not on the "objective" facts of a situation but on the "subjective" definitions of the situation.[61]

The overly subjective and voluntarist view, lacking in awareness of historical concreteness or objective existence of social structures leaves man without adequate knowledge to master the existing inhuman reality.[62] The dialectical approach helps in comprehending reality in all its complexity including contradictions and does not leave man defenceless against alien existence.

Not isolation but relatedness: Hallmark of sociology

Sociology, if it aims at an adequate comprehension of societal processes, has one more reason to take the standpoint of the "totality". No social object can be studied in isolation. As Mannheim has put it: "A thing is taken to be explained, comprehended, in so far as we have discovered its place in the currently accepted orders, series, levels."[63]

If, for example, education, the secondary socialization under the auspices of specialized formal agencies, is to be studied, any narrow conception of sociology based on the existing division of intellectual labour and boundary inviolability between social science disciplines will prove a crippling self-imposition. In its totality, even the context, leave apart the process proper of education, involves political, economic and psychological structures and processes. A narrow definition leaves out a large area of societal arrangements and activities from coming under the purview of any specific social science discipline. The present study of "private control of Higher Education" defies classification if disciplinary domains are narrowly defined. Even the internal differentiation of specialism like educational sociology, political sociology and organisational sociology could with equal justification or lack of it claim the problem under study.

If "neat" categories of discipline do not fit in, so much the worse for them. Birnbaum states :

> We do however confront the question as to whether an autonomous sociological analysis, which leaves to other disciplines and other perspectives the tasks of the analysis of the economy, of the state, and of culture is not in some danger of falling into either formalism or an artificial restrictiveness which is self-defeating.[64]

The question can be answered only by refusing to abide by the solitary confinement imposed by narrowly conceived definitions of social sciences.

The standpoint of the "totality" and the dialectical

approach by avoiding oversimplification of emphasizing a single aspect of social reality and rejecting narrowly defined boundaries of social science disciplines is helpful in building a more life-like picture of social reality and encompassing areas of study, which would otherwise remain "no man's land". If the method of isolation is the sine qua non of physical sciences, the interconnectedness of social phenomena and their inextricable interdependence, which is an aspect of the standpoint of the "totality", is the hallmark of sociological comprehension.

REFERENCES

1. This is exemplified and documented well in Robert W. Freidrichs, *A Sociology of Sociology*. New York : The Free Press, 1970, and Alwin W. Gouldner, *The Coming Crises of Western Sociology*. New York : Basic Books, 1970. The situation has only aggravated since then.
2. The terms "logic-in-use" and "reconstructed logic" have been used with the meaning given to them by the pragmatist philosopher of science, C.S. Peirce. "The former analysis explicates the rules guiding the practice of enquiry; the latter formulates criteria validity and semantic meaning in relation to the results of science. The positivist philosophy has worked within the reconstructed logic of science." (Trent Schroyer, "A Reconceptualization of Critical Theory", in J. David Colfax and Jack L. Roach (eds.) *Radical Sociology*. New York : Basic Books Inc., 1971, p. 138).
3. Karl Marx, *Capital*, Vol. III, p. 797. Also see, Trent Schroyer, "Toward a Critical Theory of Advanced Industrial Society" in Hans Peter Dreitzel (ed.) *Recent Sociology*, No. 2. London : MacMillan, 1970, pp. 210-234, especially pp. 227-228 for an exposition of Marx's position.
4. Three different but compatible meanings of essence—the German *Wesen*—have been assigned to the Marxist concept. The essentially sociological meaning is apparent when Marx writes : "The essence of man is no abstraction inherent in each separate individual. In its reality it is the ensemble (aggregate) of social relations." See, Karl Marx, *Economic and Philosophical Manuscripts of 1844* Moscow : Progress Publishers, 1974, pp. 12-13.
5. See, Maurice Roche, *Phenomenology, Language, and the Social Sciences*. London : Routledge and Kegan Paul, 1973, pp. 309-10.
6. Trent Schroyer, 1971, op. cit., p. 132.
7. See, David Beetham, *Max Weber and the Theory of Modern Politics*. London: George Allen and Unwin Ltd., 1974, p. 273. Beetham writes : "It also involves separating off capitalism from itself. The

consequence, if not the interaction of this method both in the *Protestant Ethic* and in *Economy and Society* was to produce a one-sided version of capitalism, and one which contributed to its ideological defence.

8. See, Richard Lichtman, "Social Reality and Consciousness" in Colfax and Roach, 1971, op cit., pp. 162-163.
9. M. Janowits (ed.), *W.I. Thomas on Social Organisation and Social Personality*. London : University of Chicago Press, 1967, p. 13.
10. John Rex, *Discovering Sociology—Studies in Sociological Theory and Method.* London: Routledge and Kegan Paul, 1973, p. 122.
11. Arthur Brittan, *Meanings and Situation.* London: Routledge and Kegan Paul, 1973, p. 125.
12. Anton C. Lijderveld, *The Abstract Society : A Cultural Analysis of Our Time.* Middlesex, Penguin, 1970, p. 142.
13. Stanislav Andreski, *Social Science as Sorcery.* London : Penguin, 1974.
14. John Rex, op. cit., 1973, p. 189.
15. Peter L. Berger and Thomas Luckmann, *The Social Construction of Reality.* London Allen Lane, The Penguin Press, 1967, p. 86.
16. Berger and Luckmann: op. cit., 1967, p. 137. Also see, Claus Mueller, "Notes on the Repressions of Communication Behaviour" in Hans Peter Dreitzel, 1970, op. cit., pp. 101-113.
17. John Rex, 1973, op. cit., p. 214.
18. Alwin W. Gouldner, *For Sociology, Renewal and Critique in Sociology Today.* London : Allen Lane, 1973, p. 148.
19. A convergent argument has been developed by Mark Harvey, "Sociological Theory : The Production of a Bourgeois Ideology" in Trevor Pateman (ed.), *Counter Courses—A Handbook of Course Criticism*, Middlesex, Penguin, 1972, pp. 82-111; building on Marx's Thesis on Feuerbach, delineating "the relations between theory, practice and the product of practice." Though I have to build my argument from a different angle, I find myself, in essentials, in agreement with Harvey's position.
20. Andreski Stanislav, 1974, op. cit., p. 25.
21. *Schutz Colleged Papers*, (eds.) Maurice Naleson, Arvid Broderson and Ilse Schutz. The Hague : Martinus Nijoff, 1944, quoted by Rex, 1973, op. cit.
22. Berger and Luckmann, 1967, op. cit., p. 79.
23. Marx, Karl, 1974, op. cit., pp. 91-92.
24. Berger and Luckmann, 1967, op. cit., p. 149.
25. N. Denizen, *The Research Act*, Butterworth, London, 1970, p. 299.
26. See, Arthur Brittan, 1973, op. cit., p. 15.
27. See, Maurice, Roche, 1973, op. cit., p. 311.
28. Aaron V. Cicourel, "Basic and Normative Rules in the Negotiation of Status and Role" in Dreitzel, 1970, op. cit., p. 38.
29. See, Aaron V. Cicourel, *Methods and Measurement in Sociology.* New York: Free Press, 1964 and also Maurice Roche, 1973, op. cit., p. 326.

30. Robert Bierstedt, "Sociology and Human Learning" in Claude C. Bowman (ed.), *Humanistic Sociology*. New York: Appleton-Century-Crofts, 1973, p. 39.
31. For a brief statement of Sapir's position see, Edward Sapir, "Language" (excerpts from his *Selected Writings in Language, Culture and Personality*, David Mandlebaum (ed.), University of California Press, 1949, pp. 6-20 in Kanneth Thompson and Jeremy Tunstall (eds.) *Sociological Perspectives*. London: Penguin Education, 1973, pp. 119-127.
32. For a brief discussion see, A. Kondratov, *Sounds and Signs*. Moscow, Mir Publications, 1969.
33. Cicourel, 1970, op. cit., p. 38.
34. See, Edmund Loach, *Levi Strauss*. London, Fontana Collins, 1970.
35. Berger and Luckmann, 1967, op. cit., p. 54.
36. See, C. Wright-Mills, "The Cultural Apparatus" in I.L. Horrowits (ed.) *Power Politics and People : The Collected Essays of C. Wright-Mills*. New York: Oxford Universi:y Press, 1967, pp. 405-422.
37. V.I. Lenin, *Collected Works*, Vol. 27, Moscow, p. 405.
38. Garfinkel and Sack, "On the Formal Structure of Practical Actors" in J. McKnney and B. Tiryakian (eds.) *Theoretical Sociology*. New York : Appleton-Century-Crofts, 1970.
39. Stanislav Andreski, *Elements of Comparative Sociology*, 1964.
40. T. Lomtev, "Internal Contradictions as a Source of Historical Language Structure Development" in *Engels and Linguistics*. Nauka Publishers, Moscow, 1972. In Lomtev's paper the basic internal contradiction is shown to be that "between the available resources of a given language and the growing needs of an exchange of thoughts". Refer to *Social Sciences*, Vol. 4, No. 3 (13), 1973, Moscow, p. 200.
41. Gouldner, 1974, op. cit., pp. 103-105.
42. L. Hogbon, *Mathematics for the Millions*. London : Ceorge Allen and Unwin, 1937.
43. Peter Worsely, *Introducing Sociology*, Middlesex, Penguin Books, 1970, p. 366. See also, Ely Chinoy, "Popular Sociology" in C.H. Page (ed.) *Sociology and Contemporary Education*. New York, Random House, 1963, pp. 115-133. Chinoy builds a trenchant argument against "vulgarization" of sociology by "Popular Sociology" but traces its sociological origin and appeal to the failings of sociology itself. He seems to lend support to the thesis that alienation of sociology from the common people as clientele leads to both the vulgarisations the "popular" minus rigour and formal rigour with too narrow a base.
44. Arthur Brittan, 1973, op. cit., p. 122.
45. Alfred Schutz, "Concept and Theory Formation in the Social Sciences", in Thompson and Tunstall, 1973, op. cit., p. 95.
46. See, Andreski, 1974, op. cit., Ch. 6 and 12 and Gouldner, 1974, op. cit., p. 74.
47. Andreski, 1974, op. cit., p. 220.

48. See, David Frisby, "The Frankfurt School : Critical Theory and Positivism" in John Rex (ed.) *Approaches to Sociology—An Introduction to Major Trends in British Sociology*. London : Routledge & Kegan Paul 1974.
49. See, M.N. Srinivas, "Village Studies, Participant Observation and Social Science Research in India", *Economic and Political Weekly* Vol. X, Nos. 33-35, (Special), 1975.
50. Karl Marx, 1974, op. cit., p. 138.
51. John Horton, "The Fetishism of Sociology" in Colfax and Roach, 1971, op. cit., pp. 177, 194.
52. Gouldner, 1974, op. cit., p. 115.
53. Andreski, 1974, op. cit., p. 105.
54. John Rex, 1973, op. cit., p. 197.
55. See, R. Mukherjee, The Sociologist and the Social Reality", *Sociological Bulletin*, Vol. 23, No. 2, September 1974, pp. 179-180. Mukherjee cites Lucy Mair (1934), Wilson and Wilson (1945) and Malinowski (1945) as apologists for the imperialist rule in Uganda.
56. Andreski, 1974, op. cit., p. 15. Peter Worsley argues a case for successive and synchronically rival versions even of Marxism. See, Peter Worsley, "The Reification of Marxism: Rejoinder to Lazar", *Sociology*, Vol. 9, No. 3, September 1975, pp. 496-502.
57. See, Alan Dawe, "The Two Sociologies", *British Journal of Sociology*, Vol. 21, 1970, pp. 207-18.
58. John Rex (ed.), 1974, op. cit., pp. 107-124.
59. See, Marx, 1974, op. cit., pp. 92-93 and also Berger and Luckmann, 1966, op.cit., Parts II and III.
60. D.S. Wrong, *American Sociological Review*, Vol. 26, pp. 184-93,
61. See, Draitsel, 1970, op.cit., p. xii.
62. For a brief and succinct statement of the strength and the weaknesses of the phenomenological and ethnomethodological approaches in sociology, see, Richard Lichtman, "Social Reality and Consciousness" in Colfax and Roach, 1971, op. cit., pp. 160-165.
63. Irving M. Zeitlin, *Ideology and the Development of Sociological Theory*. New Delhi : Prentice-Hall, 1969, p. 267.
64. Norman Birnbawm, "The Crises in Marxist Sociology" in Colfax and Roach, 1971, op.cit., pp. 119-120,

CHAPTER THREE

SPECIFICITY OF EDUCATIONAL PROCESS AND CONCRETE METHODOLOGICAL CHOICES

"EDUCATION", writes Durkheim, "is the influence exercised by adult generations on those. . .not yet ready for social life. Its object is to arouse and to develop in the child a certain number of physical, intellectual and moral states which are demanded of them by both the political society as a whole and the special milieu for which he is specially destined."[1] Here, Durkheim in his characteristic overemphasis on the total submission of the individual to the demands of the "political society" and the specially destined milieu for each individual, has brought out the basic sociological definition of education as the "influence exercised by adult generation on those not yet ready for social life". The education process involves two principal parties, those who impart education and those who receive it.

Inherent hierarchy in educational process

That education, like all other societal processes, is an interactional process involving give and take should not warrant the conclusion that the educational process per se has no peculiar characteristics of its own as distinct from other societal processes. The first peculiarity of the educational process stems from the fact of the hierarchy inherent in the organisation of the principal parties involved. One aspect of this hierarchy is made explicit in the Durkheimian definition. It is essentially the adult society which controls the content, the techniques and actual procedures of transmitting the crystallized experience of the past generations, helping the new generation in getting an awareness of the place of each one of them individually and collectively in society's arrangements or imparting the skills to carve out a new place and in the flowering of hitherto dormant human capacities and capabilities. This emphasis on the *relatively active and powerful* role of the adult society in the educational process does not mean that the young ones, who are essentially at the receiving end, play an absolutely passive part or do not exert any influence on the process or the end-product.

Education is a never-ending continuous process. Even educators have to be continuing students, if they are to carry out their task successfully. Here too the specificity underlined above persists. Firstly, the educators get their continuing education from books, which are the repositories of the wisdom of the past adult generations and, secondly, they are enabled to engage themselves in the process of self-education by the education proper which precedes it, whose complementary and continuing process this self-education happens to be. In fact the actual proportion of guided education and self-education in the overall process of education is also controlled to a great extent by policy decisions made by the adult society, without giving equal voice or vote to the new generation. Of course, the recipient of education exercises his or her own selectivity in accepting or rejecting in part the education offered or attempted to be imposed by the adult society. As such the educational end-product can never befully determined.

The other aspect of the inherent hierarchy involved in the educational process has been a little obscured from public vision by various devices developed, of late, under the guise of "student participation" in decision-making regarding educational processes. These devices have been developed, by and large, as hurried measures of half-sincere adjustment to students rebellions on the campuses in the sixties. But as Andreski has pointed out, "no amount of disingenuous fraternization can alter the fact that education consists of passing knowledge from those who know to those who do not."[2] The blurring of the realistic picture of inequality of responsibility and knowledge between the educator and the recipient of education, apart from serving the demogogic purpose of concealing the power equation and consequently accountability, takes on a pseudo-radical garb to cover intellectual timidity. The educators must accept that they know more about the subject they are teaching than any of their students. Ehrlich has bluntly put the point: "I am saying that you have no business being a teacher unless you really know a great deal more than those who come to study with you."[3]

As a consequence of the unalterable inequality of age, knowledge, power and responsibility and the recurring process of obliteration of the same with the successful completion of formal education, in each case, social relationships and the processes involved in education must bear a stamp, which is in many respects independent of the specific character of the social apparatus designed by the adult society, for the transmission of knowledge and bringing out the potentialities of the individuals born in society will vary from society to society; but the basic difference between the adult transmitters and creators of knowledge and their relative hold on it and the young recipients who are relatively ignorant with lesser power and responsibility remains a universal characteristic.

The norm underlying educational process

Gouldner in his paper, "The Norm of Reciprocity : A Preliminary Statement"[4], has discussed the efforts made by a number of sociologists and anthropologists to comprehend "the totality of man" and "the vital principle of society" in the norm of reciprocity—the scheme of giving and returning the equivalence. Neither reciprocity, demanding that people should help (only) those who have helped them and not injure those who have helped them, nor its complementary part called complementarity by Parsons, wherein the duty of one to give implies the right of the other to get from the first and vice versa can explain *all* social life adequately. Gouldner has demonstrated the theoretical inadequacy of the reciprocity principle, conceived narrowly or with more liberal connotation, to explain various normative orientations. He cites the case of help and care given to the children, old people and mentally or physically handicapped to show that different kinds of orientation are required to develop the appropriate moral code. The applicability of the so-called principle of reciprocity as the overarching principle of moral code was rejected by Marx and

Engels long back. That each has a right to the product of his labour or that no one shall reap where he has not sown would exclude the duty of feeding children and deprive each generation of the right to live since each generation starts life with what it inherits from the preceding generation was noted by Engels.[5] This duty of feeding the children subsumes the duty of transmitting accumulated knowledge and equipping them with skills for specific jobs or bringing out their capabilities to meet the future, in short the duty of imparting education. No system of education of the young can exist if it is based on the principle of equivalence of exchange or what is called reciprocity norm.

Gouldner, while showing the inapplicability of the principle of reciprocity-cum-complementarity to explain moral codes, advances (i) beneficence, (ii) moral absolution and (iii) exploitation as alternative and additional normative principles explaining the organization of societal processes. It is my contention that Gouldner's additional normative principles are as inapplicable in understanding educational processes as the reciprocity-cum-complementarity principle he discarded. To the extent that these normative principles inform the actual behaviour of the educators (the controllers of education, educational administrators and teachers) and the recipients of education, the process of education will get distorted. It is the central thesis of my study that the invasion of the alien normative orientations into the educational territory has caused chaotic conditions and it is possible to mend the defence lines if we first mark out the soft spots.

The principle of beneficence has been alternatively called by the name of "indulgency pattern" and "leniency pattern" by Gouldner. This so called "indulgency pattern" was discovered by him in the course of his early factory studies. The pattern is defined as giving more than the takers' rights. Obviously it is applicable in an area where the "rights" are decided by the prior rights of the factory owners by virtue of ownership and the free wage contracts entered into by the workers under compulsive conditions of power asymmetry. It is only under these conditions that the managers may earn the goodwill of the workers by showing "leniency", "indulgency" or giving more than the worker's "rights". It is strange that the reflexive sociologist could not see that the indulgency pattern is a veiled version of the exploitation pattern. The "leniency" shown is like the unwritten and informal part of the contract, e.g. the tips paid to the bearers outside the bill paid to the hotel managers. These fringe benefit payments are a form of wages, though generally not formalised. In the case of education there are no contractual rights of the new generation beyond which they can be bestowed with "leniency" and "beneficence". In this case the "indulgency" pattern is only an agreeable name for an unagreeable reality—wherein managers mismanage education, converting public resources into private benefits, teachers do not teach and students do not study—allowing the tag of education to stick to institutional arrangements, where every thing but education is given or taken.[6]

The moral imperative or absolutism goes beyond "beneficence" of doing a good turn or giving others such help as they need. This norm is translated into the imperative. The code must be obeyed. This principle substitutes the deified secular society for the supernatural sanctioning of social codes. By doing so it puts beyond the purview of social investigation and reflection that which is essentially a social product and therefore has a logical tendency to degenerate into ritualism, suppression of dissent and an apology for status quo. Applied in the field of education, it will lead to an inculcation of an unquestioning attitude, "learning" by rote and dispirited dissemination of outmoded and lifeless knowledge. Development having been denied, the knowledge enterprise will degenerate into non-human automechanism repeating itself endlessly a picture of ossified society.

The principle of exploitation is operative under the conditions of asymmetrical distribution of power. The rich and the powerful can and generally do take without giving back in adequate measure. The power disparity permits the powerful to coerce to the weak into acting against their own interest and even against their own will. For an exploitative relationship to prevail, an asymmetrical distribution of power and a will of the strong to exploit the weak must simultaneously be present. The presence of only one of these is not sufficient for behaviour to be governed by this principle. What has been said about the inapplicability of the reciprocity principle in feeding the children, and each generation starting life on the inheritance from the preceding generation, is all the more true for the *exploitation* principle. Human beings have inherited from their animal ancestry a sense of oneness and continuity of their lives with their progeny's. If the *exploitation* principle were to determine behaviour of the adults towards their young ones, human race would have reached "the end" long back. The biopsychic make-up of man excludes any widespread building of parent-child relationship on the principle of conscious exploitation and education is only an aspect of this relationship.

As a consequence of differentiation and specialization developed by various institutions of modern society, the possibility of exploitative relationship entering into the educational field is not ruled out, especially because the transformation of the parent-offspring relationship into the wider adult-child relationship may distort the original relationship as the child one deals with is not one's own. But no parent would willingly or knowingly allow his or her child to be inducted into an exploitative relationship. Hence to the extent that the exploitation principle has entered the field of education, it is an alien principle distorting the process of education and the line of division is actually drawn, not between the educators and the recipients but between the powerful and their progeny on the one side and the weak with their offspring on the other.

Education is extended socialization

Then what is the principle of normative orientation that ideally could determine the relationship in the educational field? Education, not conceived as a narrow formalized process carried on by specialized institutions alone, is indistinguishable from what sociologists, psychologists and anthropologists have called socialization. It is "the comprehensive and consistent induction of an individual into the objective world of society or a sector of it." In the early education, primarily imparted by the mother, father and other members of the family of the child, and then by playmates in the form of primary socialization, society plays its most important confidence trick on the individual by making the accident of his birth all that important. Now the only motivation that informs the parents or other members of the family, who serve as the first conscious educators for the child, is to see a continuation and fulfilment of their ownselves in the socialized child.

It is the parents, who within the conditions imposed by their own circumstances, select other agencies of socialization and deliberate education for their own children, in the following stage of secondary socialization, which is marked by a comparative growth of rational capacity of the child, the primary socialization being marked by highly charged emotionality. At the secondary stage, when role-specific knowledge is acquired, specific vocabularies and skills are learnt, and capabilities to imaginatively face novel situations are developed, *more* rational and formalized procedures are adopted as appropriate, because the base has already been formed in primary socialization. Relatively speaking more alternatives present themselves at the secondary stage of socialization. The development of modern education is only an extension of secondary socialization taking place under the auspices of specialized agencies.[7]

It stands to reason to hypothesize that a moral orientation at all stages of education should be the one that informs the parents in the initial stage, that is, the educator finds himself fulfilled in the education that is imparted to the recipient. It isnot a sufficient condition of carrying out the task of education, but it is a necessary one. If this motivation is absent, to the extent that it is absent or is substituted by incompatible motivations, the educational process will be impaired.

Significance of autonomy of educational institutions

The autonomy of educational enterprises, accepted as a value in modern societies, acquires a living meaning, when we are able to see that it is an institutional device to keep out other principles of societal organization from distorting the educational process, even when they are considered appropriate in other spheres of social life. The value of autonomy of education is greater in a society which is, by and large, run on the principles of exchange—reciprocity, exploitation, complementarity, beneficence or moral imperatives and any possible mix thereof. We have yet to learn of a society in which the educational process, as distinct from the substance of the arts and science taught, is organized consciously on any of these principles. It may be considered perfectly honourable to use force and fraud to subdue your adversary in business or politics but no parent would approve of behaviour built on these principles between their sons and daughters and their educators. Otherwise education as a process comes to a grinding halt, though side advantages may still accrue for a short while to some individuals.

Self-fulfilment—The only permissible orientation

Keeping in view the foregoing it is concluded that (i) in the field of education, only the *self-fulfilment* principle can ideally serve the normative orientation for the educator's behaviour, (ii) to the extent that other principles of societal organization enter the field, the process of education is distorted, (iii) in all ongoing societies and at all stages of development autonomy of education is relatively ensured, to protect education against being atrophied by infiltration by alien principles of societal organization and (iv) a sociological study of educational pathology is to look into the empirical reality for deviation from the principle of *self-fulfilment* and for the extent to which institutional arrangements leave opening for infilteration by alien principles of organization. The theorem for education pathology is : The greater the deviation from the principle of self-fufilment, normatively guiding the behaviour of the education and the lesser the autonomy of the educational process the greater is the distortion of the process.

Significance of the Study of Private Control of Higher Education

Private control extends to formally public institutions

In relation to educational enterprises the word "private" is used in India as counterposed to "public" or "State". We have educational institutions established, maintained and run by private interests individually or jointly and others by public agencies like the State, local bodies and other autonomous bodies established by the State, just as we have the private or public sector in industry. We have purely public institutions as ideal types; in practice the inputs in large measures in private institutions are public and the appropriation of the output even in formally public institutions is private. Thus for the purposes of operational manageability of the study the concept of "private control" may be used in a narrow technical and legal sense of the non-governmental agency establishing, maintaining and administering an educational institution. As an analytical concept it encompasses the wider connotation of actual raison d'etre of running an institution and the mode of appropriation of the benefits or the motivating force for the actions of the various elements constituting the educational enterprise. Government institutions may not be free from private control. One can reasonably assume that there is greater private control in "private" institutions than in "public institutions".

By whom and in whose interests control is exercised in an educational institution decisively determines the immediate context in which the educational process takes place and, as such, provides the "hidden curriculum" both for the teachers and the students. The nature of control also provides the aperture for various normative patterns to penetrate the educational process and thereby contribute to determining the quality of the next generation. The issues in education have been traditionally identified by educationists as issues in education like in learning, in teaching and in curriculum[8] or as issues in evaluation. Others under the growing cultural influence of sociology have focussed on the interplay of community and education, by studying the socio-economic and family background of the teachers and students, the constitutional provisions for education, the financial support available and of late the fit between the educational product and the jobs available in society and the "indiscipline" of students. The question of control has on the whole been kept in the domain of "non-decision" for public policy by declaring it academically a "non-issue"[9]. "A Selected Bibliography of Sociological Foundations of Higher Education in India"[10] mentions only one article and no book on the problem of private control and the extensive "Bibliography on Indian Higher Education",[11] includes no book on the issue and refers to three articles on this topic and two more on Christian education which indirectly pertains to the problem.

It is not my contention that the broader interaction of society and education are of lesser importance or the internal issues of the content and the mechanisms of class-room education can get dissolved in the immediate-context of control on education. The importance of the study of control lies in the understanding that the impact of societal norms on educational processes get mediated through the control mechanism, the internal issues of education are insoluble in a countermanding context and the area has been largely neglected by the students of society and education.

While the academics have shown a general insensitivity to the issue involved the teachers' organizations and the broad student bodies have always considered the control issue as vital in the educational process. It figured centrally in the abortive efforts at legislative reform of education by the first Namboodiripad Ministry (1957-59) in Kerala, in statewide strike actions by teachers of Bihar (1973) and Haryana (1972)[12] and a host of other demonstrations. The issue acted as the starter for the Chiman Bhai Patel Ministry's ouster outbursts on the Gujarat Campuses in 1974. The National Conference of "Educators for Secularism, Socialism and Democracy" unanimously urged the authorities concerned to "abolish the private management system in education, as this system has largely created exploitation and distortion of the national goals and has indeed obstructed (the) growth of progressive, socialist and secular educational structure".[13] The Madhya Pradesh Government announced, in October 1975, a panel to probe into the allegations of mismanagement against private managements. The Tamilnadu Government has issued an Ordinance for the take-over of mismanaged private colleges.[14] The Bihar Government has also taken steps in the same direction. In short, private control of education is a live public issue and as such deserves detailed sociological analysis.

The choice of seven Kanpur colleges : An explanation

I have tried to argue that private control of education is a live public issue, which deserves a detailed sociological analysis. A general historical review of the growth of modern education (discussed in Chapter 4) has revealed that (a) private effort in establishing and managing educational institutions was hybrid in its origin, (b) its character changed with the changing political context and the corresponding manifest and latent functions of modern education, and (c) the organization of Indian education has been and continues to be top-heavy or rather light-in-foundation, coming of Independence notwithstanding. It has also been observed that the ruling class—earlier the British colonialists and now the Indian capitalists—had an uneasy alliance with the private controllers of education.

These are general observations based on a macro study of Indian education in its historical setting. A number of issues that arose out of the general proposition that private control of higher education is part of the education policy of the ruling class have already been framed (Chapter 1). The general proposition and the logically related deductions with expected practical contradictions in working out the policy need corroboration, corrections and refutations by studying the phenomenon in concrete instantiation and multiple manifestations. The actual intricate inter-relationships of the various variables involved would acquire living meaning only if studied in detail in a field situation. It was with these considerations that seven colleges of Kanpur for a detailed dissection were selected.

Choice of the sample

In making the choice of the field I have been guided by a number of additional assumptions, which I considered reasonably tenable. Firstly, it was assumed that a focus on the state of affairs in higher education would bring into bold relief the strength and the weakness of the phenomenon in a more vivid way, because of the top-heavy organization of education in the country. Secondly, it was assumed that an operational decision to concentrate on the control mechanism and its consequences in formally-speaking private managements in affiliated colleges of formally-speaking public (State) University allowed a closer study of private control in duelling relationship with public purpose. Considerations of manageable limits for a single-handed study did not permit inclusion of private-'private', private-'public', 'public'-private and 'public'-public educational institutions for a comprehensive and comparative study. Thirdly, it was assumed that the known diversity of private control of college education in Kanpur would more than offset the disadvantage due to narrowing down of the field for purely practical considerations to one city.

The Kanpur colleges were known to have a variety of private managements, old and new, religious, denominational and secular, high on the discipline-scale and those displaying chronic indiscipline, political and non-political, single-lineage or individual dominated or with a broader democratic community base, controlling one institution or a chain, managing colleges for boys, girls or both, with post-graduate and research students or only under-graduates, located in posh areas or near-slums, with a great disparity in subjects, faculties, number of teachers and students, etc. A prior acquaintance with the field not only helped in deciding in favour of the city of Kanpur as the geographical area of study, but was also the basis of further cutting down the number to seven out of a total of sixteen privately managed colleges located in the city. A glance at the Table 3.1 of Private Colleges of Kanpur will indicate that those variables have been kept in mind in selecting the sample of the seven colleges on a purposive basis. (These seven include four colleges managed singly and three of a chain management; spread over a time span from 1892 to 1965 regarding their year of origin). They included two girls' colleges and five others with a varying mix of boys and girls. One is a first-degree college with teaching only one faculty and six others are post-graduate colleges with many faculties with or without research students. The selected list includes minority institutions in the name of Christians, Muslims and Sikhs, as well as Hindu sects—Arya Samaj and Sanatan Dharam. We have a Rashtriya Swayam Sevak Sangh dominated, person-based-politics dominated and without-any-politics dominated managements in our sample. Looking at the size we find institutions with thirteen teachers as well as with over three hundred approved teachers and a corresponding number of students ranging from a bare 250 to one which had touched 6,500. The heterogeneity on all those variables was included and yet this number is seven (which was manageable). The list was discussed with the leaders of the Kanpur University Teachers Association, who were agreed about its

TABLE 3.1 : **Private Colleges of Kanpur with known characteristics**

S. No.	Name of the College	Year of Founding	Faculties	Post-graduate/ First Degree	Managements
1.	*Christ Church	1892	Arts, Sc., Comm.	P.G.	Christian
2.	*Dayanand Anglo-vedic	1919	Arts, Sc., Comm.	P.G.	Dayanand Shiksha Sansthan (DSS)
3.	*V.S. Sanatan Dharma	1921	Arts, Sc., Comm., Law	P.G.	Sanatan Dharma
4.	D.A.V. Law	1958	Law	F.D.	DSS
5.	*Dayanand Girls	1959	Arts, Sc., Ed.	P.G.	DSS (Girls)
6.	Pandit Pirthi Nath	1959	Arts, Sc., Comm.	P.G.	DSS
7.	*Dayanand Brijendra Swarup	1959	Arts, Sc., Ed.	P.G.	DSS
8.	S.N. Sen Balika Vidyalaya	1956	Arts	F.D.	Independent (Girls)
9.	*Halim Muslim	1959	Arts, comm., Ed.	P.G.	Muslim
10.	Brahmanand	1961	Arts, Sc., Law	F.D.	Brahmin
11.	Juhari Devi Girls	1961	Arts	P.G.	Marwari
12.	Jwala Devi Girls Vidya Mandir	1962	Arts	P.G.	DSS Allies (Girls)
13.	*Guru Nanak Girls	1965	Arts	F.D.	Sikh (Girls)
14.	Dayanand Women's Training	1958	Ed.	P.G.	DSS (Girls)
15.	Mahila Vidyalaya	1969	Arts	F.D.	DSS (Girls)
16.	International Centre	1973	Ed.	F.D.	Independent

*Selected for intensive study.

Abbreviations:

Sc.: Science;
Comm.: Commerce;
Ed.: Education;
P.G.: Post-graduate;
F.D.: First Degree;
D.S.S.: Dayanand Shiksha Sansthan.

representative character. An analysis of these colleges will hopefully reflect (but it may not) the diverse reality of private managements much beyond the narrow confines of the seven colleges studied.

Sensitivity and personal reality

Another important consideration in selecting the specific field was that much of the reality of educational processes at Kanpur had become "personal reality" to me. I got my education at three different colleges of the city, established and maintained by three important managements operating in the city. Later, I served as a teacher in two colleges in the city. In a way the study is a continuation of the knowledge gained through these roles on a more self-conscious, systematic and sociologically informed basis. The sensitivity attained about the significant aspects of the problem in everyday life in the earlier career is carried forward and is tempered with sociological disciplining of the later period. A gap of a decade between the earlier teaching activity and the present research endeavour has hopefully helped in controlling a purely subjective understanding. The justification for this methodological choice is a logical derivative from "sociologist as a self-conscious actor in society"—thesis discussed in Chapter 2.

Field work

The actual data collected for the study mainly came from the intensive field work for more than one full academic session 1974-75. The sensitivity towards the type of data to be collected and the possible sources go back into the personal experience gathered as a student and a teacher earlier and numerous readings.[15]

The bulk of the information is based on prolonged personal interviews with teachers, students, their leaders and functionaries of the Managing Committees. Officers of the University and the Directorate of Higher Education for the State were also interviewed. Neither the number of interviews nor their duration nor the number of sessions with each interviewee was pre-fixed. In case it was felt at the early stage of an interview that the interviewee did not possess the desired information or decisively refused to cooperate the interview was cut short. In other cases either the process of establishing rapport was a prolonged one or material could be secured only piecemeal and a number of sessions had to be gone through. Similarly, if interviewing three or four persons led to same facts being reported over and over again, other interviewees with a similar make-up were not tackled. If newer or diverse information was forthcoming, the number of interviewees had to be increased. A process of cross-checking did not follow any routinized structure. Satisfaction of the researcher, that all available alternatives within the limitations of time and money have been gone through to arrive at a finding, was given a greater credence than formal structuring of questions, interview validation and accepting nothing that cannot be fully proved in a court of law. *Plausibility* rather than foolproof *certainty* has been the basis of accepting or rejecting a statement or a piece of information.

Even withholding of information has been analysed for probable motivation.[16]

For documentary evidence and supplementary sources the published Magazines and Prospectuses of the colleges, minutes of the Executive Committee and the Academic Council of Kanpur University since its inception, files of the *National Herald*, an English daily of Lucknow, for 1973-75, *Jagran*, a Hindi daily of Kanpur, for 1974-75 and *Ailga*, a Hindi weekly of Kanpur, for 1971-75 were scanned. Some memoranda of the Kanpur University Teachers' Association, teachers' representations to different authorities, handbills issued by students at the time of union elections or strikes were also used. Published memoranda of the constitutions of the managing committee and unpublished budget layouts were looked into. All these documents proved helpful as checks on the memory of many interviewees by fixing certain chronological order of events or as a recall mechanism as an additional source of information which is not within the experience of available living respondents or as a check on the veracity of information gathered through interviews. These documents have been extensively used in presenting the findings.

The general methodological assumptions have already been discussed earlier in Chapter 2. But no programmatic statement can provide adequate justification. Hence I proceed to the substantive part of my study in the hope that the results will provide justification for the methodological stance adopted for this study.

In Chapter 1, I have already outlined the theoretical context and the issues were framed. The data were collected around these issues. The structure of management has been analysed in the case of each of the seven colleges studied. Their distinctive subcultures with roots in historical make-up, constitutional arrangements, and present practices were researched in. So also I gathered information on the tendencies to obliterate past differences to gravitate toward a common "pure" type. "Genetic imprint" and common diverse environs conditioning contemporary practices were looked for. The teachers' role as conditioned by college managements has been analysed in two separate chapters, first, the direct conditioning by teacher-policies and next indirect conditioning by student-policies and control of the University. The students' role as conditioned by the management policies has been discussed. The roles have been analysed as dependent variables and the extent to which they are defined and enacted independent of or even opposed to the constraints put by managements, which themselves are neither assumed to be uniform nor actually found as such, studied. The values, openly propagated or fostered as such through "hidden curriculum" that the control system is, were noted and analysed for all the three elements—managements, teachers and students.

REFERENCES

1. Emile Durkheim, *Education and Society*. Glencoe, Illinois : The Free Press, 1956, p. 71.
2. Stanislov Andreski, *Social Science as Sorcery*. London : Penguin, 1974, p. 236.
3. Hans J. Ehrlich, "Notes from a Radical Social Scientist : February 1970" in J. David Colfax and Jack L. Roach (eds.) *Radical Sociology*. New York : Basic Books, 1971, p. 207.
4. Alwin W. Gouldner, *For Sociology, Renewal and Critique in Sociology Today*. London: Allen Lane, 1973, pp. 224-259.
5. Fredrick Engels, "Outlines of Critique of Political Economy" in Karl Marx, *Economic and Philosophical Manuscripts of 1844*. Moscow: Progress Publishers, 1974, p. 163.

6. See, A.R. Kamat, *Education After Independence—A Social Analysis*. Bombay: Lala Lajpat Rai Institute, 1973-74, p. 11.
7. In my understanding of education as a socialisation process as such I have drawn freely on the treatment in Peter L. Berger and Thomas Luckmann, *The Social Construction of Reality*. London: Allen Lane, The Penguin Press, 1967, pp. 147-182.
8. See, for example, Mary Alice White/Jan Duker, *Education—A Conceptual and Empirical Approach*. New York: Holt Rinchart & Winston Inc., 1973, Section 3.
9. For the concepts, see, Peter Bachrach and Morton S. Boratz, "Two Faces of Power", *American Political Science Review*, 56, December 1962, and "Decisions and Non-decisions: An analytical framework", *American Political Science Review*, 57, Sept. 1963. Also see, Frederick Frey, "Comments: On issues and non-issues in the study of power", *American Political Science Review*, 65, December 1971.
10. S.P. Ruhela (ed.), *Contributions to Sociology of Education in India, Vol. I*. New Delhi: Jain Brothers, 1969, pp. 121-151.
11. Amrik Singh and Philip G. Altbach (eds.), *The Higher Learning in India*. Delhi: Vikas, 1974, pp. 420-446.
12. An interesting personal account is available in B.R. Garg, *Educational Crisis in India*. Ambala : Associated Publishers, 1977. The author is a former Principal of a private college in Haryana, sacked by the private management.
13. "Statement of the Conference of Educators for Secularism, Socialism and Democracy, New Delhi, 19-21 Sept. 1975" in *Secular Democracy*, September 11, 1975.
14. See, UNI report in the *Rajasthan Patrika*, a Jaipur daily, 23 November, 1975.
15. For example, William Foot Whyte, *Street Corner Society: The Social Structure of an Italian Slum*. University of Chicago Press, 1943: Howard S. Backer, *Sociological Work—Methods and Substance*. London : Penguin, 1971.
16. For example, even a copy of the "Rules & Regulations of the D.A.V. College Trust and Management Society, U.P. Kanpur", which were in force earlier or of the "Rules and Regulations of the Dayanand Shiksha Sansthan, U.P. Kanpur" which were in force, could not be procured from the College office, Sansthan office or Kuladhipati in spite of repeated promises. These were public documents which were procured only through circuitous routes. So also the budget supposed to be circulated among members of the various Management Boards of the institution affiliated to the Sansthan, though cyclostyled in hundreds, is kept a closely guarded secret in the Kuladhipati's office. The chance of corroborating or refuting certain allegations of financial irregularities was denied at Government office at Allahabad. The inference is obvious that there were many skeletons in these cupboards. Note the contrast with Guru Nanak and Halim Colleges discussed (Chapter 5).

CHAPTER FOUR

EDUCATIONAL POLICY AND PRIVATE ENTERPRISES IN EDUCATION

A. ORIGIN AND GROWTH OF MODERN EDUCATION IN INDIA

The Government policy

"THE FOUNDATION of modern education in India was established by the British. Its historical landmarks are Macaulay's policy of 1835 to promote European learning through English, Sir Charles Wood's Despatch of 1854 which for the first time recognized the need for mass education with private and missionary help and gave up the policy of selective education known as the 'filteration theory' and finally the first Indian Education Commission of 1882 which recommended the initiative of private agencies in the expansion of education."[1]

The situation in the eighteenth century is briefly stated by Kuppuswami. He writes: "Thus the main aim in starting of the schools for children as well as the institutions of higher learning in the eighteenth century were to propagate Christianity, to have competent scholars in the Muslim and Hindu Law, and to train the British civilians in Indian languages, Indian law and Indian history."[2] As this period does not bear directly on the development of modern education in India and has not left much legacy to be taken care of in understanding the present condition, a detailed discussion can possibly be of interest only to students of history.

The process of modernization started in India under the British rule and that too discernibly in the nineteenth century. It would be an idle exercise to speculate as to what course of development India would have taken had the British rule not been there. The undeniable reality is that whatever aspect or area of modern institutional set-up we may try to look into, the impact of the British political domination stands out, not only in the historical context but also as live legacies that persist like indelible birth-marks, marring and making the present. Students of Indian society and history differ on the rejuvenescence or stupefascience produced by the British impact on the economic, political, social and ideological development, but they are unanimous that all departments of modern India carry characteristic marks of contact and conflict with the West, as a consequence of British rule. Education is no exception.

The notorious Macaulay Minute of 1835 proclaimed in no ambiguous terms the objectives of the British, in providing to the natives some acquaintance with English literature and Western science. Prior to this Clause 43 of the East India Act 1813 served as the basis of the British educational policy in India, namely, to encourage the learned natives, the Ulemas and Pandits, review and promote their literature and advance a knowledge of science among the inhabitants of the British territories. As against the previous policy of encouraging the learned natives and reviving indigenous literature Macaulay declared: "A single shelf of a good European literature was worth the whole native literature of India and Arabia." The objective of Public Instruction in India was spelled out in the statement: "We want a class of persons Indian in blood and colour but English in tastes, in opinions, in morals and intellect." The endorsement of the Macaulay Minute by William Bentick on 7 March 1835 put the government seal on the policy of promoting "European literature and science among the natives of India" and declaring "that all the funds appropriated for the purpose of education would be best employed on English education alone", a policy based on a total disregard for the indigenous learning.[3]

The policy was concretized and operationalized by the Wood's Despatch of 1854 by accepting the task of creating a scheme of education from primary school to the university. Actual execution of a policy always involves compromises with adverse circumstances, in the interest of achieving the main objectives. Moreover, a number of unanticipated and undesired consequences follow, whatever course the policy formulator may decide upon. Therefore, a policy cannot be judged on the basis of the objective consequences alone; neither can we judge a policy merely on the basis of stated objectives either, as they invariably are couched in public-interest terminology. The policy of Wood's despatch was "not only to produce a higher degree of intellectual fitness but to raise the moral character of those who partake of its advantages and so to supply you (the British Government) with servants to whose probity you may with increased confidence commit offices of trust. . ." This policy was to protect the material interests of imperialism by ensuring "a large and more certain supply of many articles necessary for our (British) manufactures and extensively consumed by all classes of our population, as well as an almost inexhaustible demand for the produce of British labour."

The despatch crystallized a number of hitherto amorphous aspects of educational policy. It is marked by comprehensiveness and detailed tackling of related issues. The fundamental contradictions of the British educational policy, inherent in the effort to build a modern system of education in India and yet keep the interests of colonial domination unchallenged, is more than apparent. The elements of modernization contained in the despatch policy could be enumerated as: (i) the decision of imparting information and knowledge available through the medium of English, even to "far larger classes who are ignorant of, or imperfectly acquainted with, English", by employing vernacular language, (ii) the decision in favour of active measures of government and increased expenditure to convey useful and practical knowledge to the great mass of people "who are utterly incapable of obtaining any education worthy of the name of their own individual efforts", (iii) the declaration that "the Government ought to give to the native female education in India its frank and cordial support", (iv) the declaration that the education imparted in the Government institutions should be exclusively secular and the Government should prevent even the suspicion that the intention was to use its influence for the purpose of proselytism, (v) decision to make arrangements for training of teachers and to ensure them sufficient salary and inducements such as were held out in other branches of public service, (vi) decision to establish universities in India and (vii) acknowledgement that education of the people was the duty of the State, though maintaining that "the most effective method of providing for the wants of India in this respect (providing adequate means) will be to combine with the agency of the Government the aid which may be derived from the exertions and the liberality of the educated and wealthy natives of India and of other benevolent persons."[4]

Of these seven pillars of educational policy, the first three refer to the extension of the catchment area of education, by providing differential approach and specialized attention to the education of the socially cramped and historically handicapped segments of society. The apparent intention of the rulers in haltingly proposing secular education and declaring a policy of the Government to be of religious neutrality was to allay popular suspicion of the Government's intention of spreading Christianity. A large number of educational institutions were manned by Christian missionaries who had the support of the Government. Macaulay's total condemnation of Sanskrit and Arabic mediums as "false history, false astronomy, false medicine", we find them in company of false religion" had to some extent already injured the religious susceptibilities of orthodox Indians. The Government thought it impolite to alienate the local opinion any further.[5] Whatever the immediate motivation, the policy of secular education provided a vital component of modernization in a society where diverse religions had entrenched themselves through history and tradition, providing the adherents with a clamouring for the byegone's perspectives. The fifth and sixth elements pinpointed the need to build appropriate institutions to carry out the educational tasks. The introduction of the grants-in-aid system, to draw upon support from local sources, had the dubious purpose and consequence of initiation of a process and yet keeping it under control in the interest of colonial rule.

The paradox for the rulers was that the demand for cheaper and loyal servants from amongst the local people, the need to create a cultural base for the British rule and the desire to ensure a continuous growth of raw material for export and expanding market for British manufacture strengthened the policy of educational modernization and expansion, and this brought in its trail the "undesirable" consequence, the conscious desire to break free from the fetters of foreign rule.

British produced their own negation

The political relevance of modern education, historically speaking, lay, firstly, in its overtly political origin in the policy decisions of the foreign rulers and, secondly, in the political outcome of this education in the form of the growth of the modern middle classes, which provided the leadership as well as the social base for Independence struggle.[6]

The period that followed the Despatch of 1854 is a long span of a century or so, marked by a recurrent effort at containing the contradictions inherent in the British policy of spreading modern education—a quantitative increase in the educational institutions at various levels from the primary to the university, of diverse types from the general education through vocational to professional education, and a grappling with the issue of encouraging local initiative while tightening the alien Government's control over the process and products of education. For example, the Indian Education Commission (1882-1883), apart from emphasizing the elementary education of the masses, encouraging indigenous institutions also and to adapt them to modern requirements, recommended at least one model high school to be established in each district by the Government, while recognizing the ultimate goal of running of higher education by the people of the country themselves. The Commission's report evoked the cryptic evaluation by Basu: "The net result achieved by the Commission was not commensurate with the volume of the report. It practically reiterated the principles which had already been accepted years ago in Wood's Despatch. It only elaborated some of the points and added some emphasis here and there."[7]

The Indian University Commission (1902) recommended reorganization of the administration with defined jurisdiction and improvement in course content and library facilities. It also recommended direct teaching by the University apart from strict supervision of conditions of affiliated colleges.

The Resolution of the Government of India on the

Educational Policy (1913) deals in some detail with school housing, teachers' working conditions and qualifications, inspection mechanism, separation of the role of the universities and high schools and their organizational structure. Some shift in favour of local bodies in the primary education and away from accepting fresh responsibilities of the Government in secondary education or curbs on expansion in university education could also be discerned. Thus apart from the suggestion of establishment of teaching universities as distinct from the examining-affiliating role they had carried till then, it was only a question of dealing with the process and the products of education getting out of the Government's control—the central problem that Curzon had to grapple with.

The Calcutta University Commission set up by the Government in 1917 under the chairmanship of Dr M. E. Sadler made a systematic and comprehensive study of secondary and higher education in India. It recommended separation of intermediate classes from the university and joining them for administrative management with high schools under autonomous boards with representatives of Government, high schools and intermediate colleges and the universities. For the management of the university, the principle of internal autonomy giving more powers to the teachers, formation of selection committees with experts for appointing teachers, constitution of academic councils, faculties and boards of studies to decide upon academic issues and a full-time vice-chancellor seems to have been recognized as a functional necessity for organizing education at the university level. The Commission also recommended specialized efforts for educating women and Muslims to overcome their historical backwardness in the field. These, as well as the recommendation of high school plus two-year intermediate education followed by three years of the first university degree and the institution of honours courses, as distinct from pass courses, look as relevant today as when they were made some six decades back. Or, maybe the educational situation today remains the same as in 1917 ! As regards the basic approach there appears no departure from the Macaulay-Wood policy delineated in the middle of the last century.

Outside the official orbit

The only important development, before the advent of independence, affecting the development of modern education, outside the orbit of the governmental efforts and decisions, was the expression of Indian resentment at the total subjugation of Indian languages, culture and traditions by the English language and the Western culture. A number of efforts, inspired by diverse motivations and orientations, were made to counterpose and evolve an alternative system of modern education. The main current surfaced in the form of the National Education Movement of Bengal, which resulted in the establishment of National College at Calcutta in 1907, which eventually grew into the present Jadavpur University[8] and a large number of National High Schools started by the Society in Bengal and many more in East Bengal (now Bangladesh). The movement was an outgrowth of the nationalist upsurge at the time of partition of Bengal, which prompted many students to boycott the official schools and colleges and others were removed by the authorities. The case of Samarth Vidyalaya near Poona, which was suppressed by the Government under the Criminal Law Amendment Act, is illustrative of the extreme hostility of the Government the movement had to face.

The second phase of the movement coincided with Gandhiji's call to the students to boycott the official educational institutions in 1920, which evoked widespread response. Pattabhi Sitaramayya, the official historian of the Indian National Congress, refers to the emergence of "National University of Aligarh, the Gujarat Vidyapith, the Bihar Vidyapith, the Kashi Vidyapith, the Bengal National University, the Tilak Maharashtra Vidyapith and a large number of National Schools of all grades, with thousands of students on the rolls" within four months. This time, even though the declared objective of attaining independence within one year did not succeed, some among the alternative educational institutions that came up continued to challenge the official educational monopoly throughout the British rule.

Indian control, teaching of love of motherland, opposition to servile imitation of the West and also to the domination of the English medium, and emphasis on vocational education formed the corner-stone of the alternative ideology of education. It was not a rejection of the modern scientific content of the Western knowledge but a synthesis of the best by combining self-respect with openness to accept new and useful ideas from all sources.[9]

The establishment of Gurukul at Kangri by the Arya Samaj and Dar-ul-Uloom at Deoband and at Lucknow by Muslim religious leaders, though developed as alternative educational set-ups to the British system do not qualify for inclusion here as they are not based on an acceptance of modern scientific attitude as such.

Growth characteristics

As has already been noted the total development of education under the British Raj followed the basic policy objectives laid down in the Macaulay Minute and Wood's Despatch. Both in origin and subsequent growth the educational system catered to the demands of employment in Government administrative service and professions, especially legal practice, with the exception of the weak sporadic and side emergence of a nationalist alternative. Lord Hardinge's proclamation in 1844 that preference should be given to English educated persons in recruitment for Government jobs clearly stated the central motivation for the educational endeavour, both of the organizers and the recipients. As the Government was almost the sole employer, people apparently asked for the type of education the Government asked for in the qualifications preferred in recruitment. It is erroneous to confuse the apparent demand for some type of education as the real cause of development of education in that direction.[10]

The development of education in India since the early nineteenth century in all periods shows (i) emphasis on the English language and medium, (ii) concentration of effort on the growth of the so-called higher and secondary education as against mass literacy, elementary education and original contribution to extension of knowledge and (iii) expansion of general arts and science education as against vocational and professional training. All these characteristics especially the "top heavy"[11] growth were directly linked to the policy of demanding "baboos" to be produced by education.[12]

The educational institutions being largely reduced to

certificate-spinning machines can also be traced to the same root cause. The Hartog Committee Report had observed in 1929 : "But the theory that a university exists mainly, if not solely, to pass students through examinations still finds too large-acceptance in India; and we wish that . . .the universities regarded the training of broad-minded, tolerant and self-reliant citizens as one of their primary functions."[13] The picture of the educational growth in the three decades of independence does not show any major break with the above-stated characteristics.[14]

Aparna Basu, analysing the 1898-1920 period, says, "The total number of pupils under instruction in 1896-97 was over four million, by 1920 the number had more than doubled. In 1898 there were five universities, by 1922 there were 12. Between 1896 and 1922 the number of Arts colleges increased from 115 to 152 and pupils in them from 13,933 to 45,224. The number of English secondary schools increased from 2,760 to 4,904 and the number of pupils in them from 3,39,704 to 8,23,416."[15] This overgrowth of pupils at the secondary and college levels took place in the period when the stated official policy was to restrict and control higher education. "In 1917-18 the population of Bengal and U.K. was equal around 45 millions and so also the population of students working for a University degree around 26 thousands."[16]

The growth anomally is made all the more glaring when we note that the Hartog Committee had found that the male literacy rate had progressed from 13 in 1892 to just 14.4 by 1922. The Report had noted that "while much attention had been paid in the past to a consideration of the higher forms of education, the problems of primary education have been comparatively neglected." Nurullah and Naik pointed out that Wood's Despatch, Government's review of education, 1866-70, Education Commission, 1882, Government's Resolution of 1904 had also made similar observations.[17] If in spite of these observations the problem still remains to be squarely and fully faced, the cause must be sought deeper down in the basic motivation informing the educational system.

Kamat, analysing "the educational situation" in the post-Independence period, writes that during the eighteen years (1950-1968) the enrolment increased three-fold in the primary, fourfold in the middle, fivefold in the higher secondary classes and almost sixfold in the higher education.[18] Thus, the dice continues to be loaded in favour of those for whom it was originally meant.

The intended function of education in the past had been to prepare the individuals to take up the middle-rung baboo jobs, that is, recruitment to the middle class and providing means of individual advancement within the class. If it resulted in any (i) training of minds who would bring together the material and human resources, (ii) intellectual analysis and imaginative insight, (iii) intellectual adventure, (iv) an integrated way of life, (v) commitment to the national values of freedom, justice and liberty, equality and fraternity, (vi) love for higher values of life, (vii) breaking ground for new values, (viii) training for leadership or (ix) comprehending the cultural unity of India with its past greatness and contemporary values through critical study and a sense of oneness of the world (aims of education formulated by the Radhakrishnan Commission 1948-49),[19] it was only an unintended by-product. Rudolphs writes: "The functions of universities under British rule were intellectual, cultural and political; to connect Indian education to European knowledge; to transmit the cultural values specific to Britain and Europe ; and to make available to the Raj a class of clerks, bureaucrats and political collaborators."[20] It is the last manifest function which subsumed all others and remained dominant like a "genetic imprint".

B. PRIVATE ENTERPRISE IN EDUCATION : THE CHANGING CONTEXT

Difficulties of empirical analytical separation of private from public

Nurullah and Naik equate private enterprise in education with the non-official efforts.[21] To begin with the distinction between the official and the non-official or, to be more exact, between the government and non-government effort is a useful classificatory device. It is obvious that the distinction between the private and the public though more meaningful than the government and non-government may not be easily discernible in an empirical institutional analysis. The distinction between public and private enterprise is blurred because (i) agreement over what functions and interests are to be termed public generally does not exist, (ii) what are generally recognized as private individuals or organizations may usurp public functions, (iii) the public authorities may delegate their own powers and functions to private individuals or organizations, (iv) public institutions may serve private interests and (v) private individuals and organizations may serve public interests.[22]

Nurullah and Naik give a fourfold classification of non-official attempt in education : (a) the educational institutions conducted by the missionaries, (b) the educational institutions conducted by officials of the Company in their individual capacity or by non-official Englishmen resident in India, (c) the educational institutions of the modern type conducted by Indians themselves, and (d) the indigenous educational institutions.[23] Another frame for studying private enterprise could be to grade the institutions on a continuum based on the relationship with the Government. First, we have institutions which were neither aided nor recognized by the Government, which could be further subdivided into those imparting indigenous education and those imparting modern education. Secondly, we have institutions recognized by the Government for sending up candidates for common public examinations, teaching the same courses as the Government-run institutions but receiving no financial aid from the Government. Thirdly, we have institutions which were recognized and received financial grants from the Government. Now any one of these could be established and managed by secular Indian interests, caste or other sectional Indian interests, or Christian missionaries with varied foreign backing. If "private" is understood as the opposite pole of public (i.e. Government) the latter frame has much to recommend itself.

British squeeze out indigenous institutions

Indigenous institutions had to face a difficult time for survival when the British rulers made a definite choice of introducing modern education through the English medium, changing the court medium to English and of giving preference to English-educated persons in Government employment. As the indigenous industry was destroyed and the Government became the monopoly employer, the indigenous educational products had no way to make a decent living. The educational institutions which had been supported by *muafis* ceased to function as the East India Company deliberately followed a policy of resumption and confiscation of these *muafi* lands.[24] A majority of village-level indigenous schools were allowed to die out and a minority was absorbed into the aided and recognized schools. Others catered mostly to religious teaching and indigenous system of medicine; they have already been referred to by giving the examples of Gurukul at Kangri and Dar-ul-Ulooms at Deoband and Lucknow. Their contribution to secular education is that a stream of ancient knowledge was kept flowing under adverse circumstances till it could be fruitfully merged at least partially into the mainstream of modern education after Independence.

Private efforts in public cause

Amongst the unaided and unrecognized educational institutions, we should also count the National Education Movement institutions established during the Swadeshi Movement after 1905 and again in 1920, the call by Gandhiji for boycott of the British educational system. These institutions brought into open the lopsided approach of the British educational policy in India, published the need and demonstrated the practical possibility of an alternative modern but national approach towards education. Most of them could not survive the unequal competition with the officially recognized and backed system of education, but such ones as were able to survive presented an example of private efforts for public cause, both on the part of organizers and the teachers.

Private effort as adjunct to British Government

The educational institutions conducted by officials of the Company in their individual capacity or by non-official Englishmen referred to by Nurullah and Naik have only a historical importance as they came into a short-lived existence when the Government had no clear-cut policy on education and after the initial gestation period were almost always absorbed as Government undertakings.[25]

Missionary effort—Changing context

Now we take up the recognized/aided Christian educational institutions established and run by Christian Missions or by Indian private managements. The *missions* were the first to attempt a cultural conquest of India on behalf of the West. But their efforts were naturally built round proselytizing. They started with the poor, the low caste elementary education and through the medium of modern Indian languages. They were also the first to embark upon women's education. Thus the very origin of missionary effort had a democratic aspect in a caste-ridden tradition-bound society. But their proselytizing zeal, foreign men and money-source and close links with the rulers aroused hostility among Indians, especially the upper castes. Up to the time the British Government decidedly embarked upon English education in India, the missionaries were mainly involved in elementary schools, teaching through Indian languages. In the 1833-53 period they shifted their efforts to the secondary schools and colleges, teaching through English. The desire to go in for English language and Government jobs in the upper castes and well-to-do Indians weakened the barriers between them and the missionaries managing these English-medium institutions and, for the first time, the missionaries had an access beyond the poor, the orphans and the low caste—the recruitment base for "Vice Christians".

Missionaries ordinarily worked under the shadow of political authority of the foreign rulers, who were generally in sympathy with the missionary cause.[26] The cautious attitude of the British rulers towards the missionary effort was totally due to the political consideration of avoiding unnecessary alienation of the local people.[27] The relative neutrality was first started with the assumption of political power in 1765 but was relaxed in 1813 and again asserted after the 1857 war of independence, when the Government was transferred to the British Crown. The differential rate of growth of missionary enterprise in education was directly related with the quantum of cordiality between them and the officials; comparatively lean periods were 1765-1813 and 1858-1882. Thereafter, the missionaries having lost the monopoly of educational control to the Government and the Indian private effort and even the leading position in the private sector, decided, by 1902, to restrict their activities to a few educational institutions in as higher a state of efficiency as possible, but the concentration of their efforts in tribal and backward communities continued.

We may conclude that the missionary enterprise in education was largely complementary to the official effort. Their specific contribution lay in bringing the printing press as a tool of education, the development of modern Indian languages as the medium of instruction, catering to the education of the socially handicapped sections of society and presenting some fine examples of devoted and efficient teaching as voluntary effort. Their indirect contribution to the modernizing process has been the growth of secular approach in public education as reaction to their over-zealous proselytizing, though mainly motivated by the Government's considerations of political exigency. In the course of time the missionary institutions grew also as minority institutions guarding the "special" interests of Indian Christians and Anglo-Indians with concomitant complications, which would be discussed later.[28]

Indian private effort—Hybrid character

Indian private enterprise in modern education has a continued history of dependence upon playing an auxiliary role and recurrent opposition to the government policy in education. The founding of Elphinstone College in Bombay and Hindu College in Calcutta, which later on became Presidency College[29] amply demonstrate that the Indian private enterprise in its origin was hybrid. British officers' sponsorship was an essential condition for opening private Indian purses.[30] The real growth did not take place till the Despatch of 1854 declared that Government aid should be combined with the liberality of the educated and wealthy natives of India to provide for the educational needs of India and the system of grants-in-aid was introduced. This is not to deride the efforts of Raja Ram Mohun Roy, Jagannath Shanarset, Jotiba Govindrao Phule and others like them, who, moved by a genuine desire to synthesize Eastern and Western cultures, to reform the social condition of their fellow countrymen and to regenerate the social life of the country, contributed to the organization of Indian efforts to spread modern secular education.[31] By and large the private Indian enterprise was the result of the Government policy of gathering non-government financial resources, avoiding direct accountability for failures in the educational field and yet aiming at governmental control over the process and the products of education. That the policy of back-seat driving did not show consistently satisfactory results is a different issue.

In 1854 private enterprise practically meant missionary enterprise but by 1882 the situation was reversed in favour of Indians except in college education where the missionaries maintained their lead. There were five colleges managed by Indians as against 18 by others. But in the case of secondary and primary schools the Indian-managed schools outnumbered others by 1,341 to 757 and 54,662 to 1,842 respectively. Indian enterprise accounted for 10 out of 28 professional colleges and schools.[32]

Quantitative growth of private enterprise and finance

Some idea of the growth of private enterprise can be had if we look at the distribution of educational finance. An analysis of three-quarters of a century, 1881-1956, shows a steady rise in the income from fee up to 1941-42, after which year there is a vertical rise probably due to the increased rate and later due to a rise in enrolment. The income due to other sources which include donations, subscriptions and endowments follow the course under the fee curve, with the gap widening. The fee receipts rose from Rs. 43.66 lakhs in 1881 to Rs. 37.9 crores in 1956; whereas that from other sources from Rs. 37.5 lakhs to Rs. 18.2 crores.[33]

The Table 4.1 further shows the growth of private enterprise in India.

The figures for private managements include the Christian managements. But some estimate of reality can be made if we make note of the fact that even in 1901-1902, the Christian institutions did not constitute as much as one-fourth of the private management institutions in Madras, where their share was the maximum in India. Later figures for the whole of India tell us that Christian institutions and the pupils studying in them fall below 10 per cent and their share goes on gradually decreasing. If the rate of increase in the number of institutions and the pupils studying under them in the private sector has not kept pace with that in the public sector, it

TABLE 4.1 : **Growth of public and private management education, 1901-1955**

Year	Under Private Management		Under Public Management	
	No. of institutions	No. of pupils	No. of institutions	No. of pupils
1901—1902	82372	2646852	22250	1239641
1921—1922	117025	4398318	56274	3343907
1937—1938	135758	7134523	83037	6299895
1946—1947	94277	7608969	109596	10141294
1955—1956	125563	11632140	241078	22291453

Source : A.N. Misra, *Education Finance in India*, 1962.

is so because the private sector shied away from professional education except law and lately education, technical and vocational education and primary education of the backward sections or adult education. Spread of education in these areas increased the public sector. The private enterprise in education concentrated on general arts and science colleges and higher secondary schools imparting general education wherein with a moderate investment they could control disproportionately bigger human resources.

Private entrepreneurship undergoes metamorphosis

The proportionate contribution to the maintenance of education by endowments, donations, subscriptions, etc., shows, a clear-cut and continuous decrease since 1881-82 and almost dried up after the advent of popular ministries in 1937. With this development and the greater and greater attraction provided by the Independence movement for those who held public service higher than self, after the appearance of Gandhiji on the scene, the character of private entrepreneur in education underwent a metamorphosis. With a few notable exceptions like J.R.D. Tata's or J.C. Bose's contributing to the establishing of scientific research institutes or more recently Hari Singh Gaur's donation for the establishment of Sagar University, entrepreneurship now meant manipulation capacity to secure Government grants and recognition in popular subjects by appropriate boards, university or Government bodies. Monopolising or snatching control of management of existing institutions also engaged the talents of many. The description of private colleges managed by Indians given by Curzon as "devoted more to profit than to learning; the teachers were underpaid, the buildings unsanitary and unsuitable, and the teaching superficial. Some depended for their existence wholly on fees and admitted students without limit or enquiry . . .[34] began to fit more and more the growing reality. The advent of electoral politics gave further fillip to the possibility of converting control of educational resources into non-educational services and goods.[35] That the disease of converting assets meant for educational institutions into private property was not entirely unknown in earlier times was noted in the Minute of Lord Moitra 1815.[36] Rudolphs recognizes the changed "entrepreneurial and administrative talent of a sort that may not be compatible with intellectual and academic values".[37] The changed circumstances have also seen the rise of second generation managers of private educational institutions with educational management as the major occupation. With them educational management has been developed into a specialism separated from the content and the process of education.

Uneasy alliance of foreign rulers and private Indian managements

The backseat driving, that the foreign rulers intended to practise by helping the Indians found and manage educational institutions, as a result of the policies enunciated in the 1854 Despatch and the Indian Education Commission (1882-83), soon got into rough weather. Where the Indians were in command, they showed, according to Lord Curzon, a mischievous independence of government." The Act of 1857 entrusted the entire management and supervision of the affairs, concerns and property of the universities to the senates, which had a growing number of Indians as its members. Curzon feared that the Senates were developing into "a potent political instrument, wielded by ill-educated vakils" and the universities would develop into "nurseries of discontented characters and stunted brains". According to Curzon, Goroodas Banerjee, the Indian member of Raleigh Commission, was holding brief for "the poor and unworthier class of students whom we want politely to suppress". In 1913 Calcutta University, among others, proposed three names as lecturers, who were considered by the British politically unsuitable and the Government wanted to prevent the exertion of an unsettling influence on students, as "the political situation did not allow trifling with sedition." Even Sir Asutosh was not given a new term as Vice-Chancellor. Curzon was also disappointed to know that the Government could not effectively control the choice of text-books. Stricter rules for recognition of schools and affiliation of colleges and revised constitutions of universities ensured a greater governmental control on education. The whole development displayed, on the one hand, that Indian partners in the British educational enterprise had a tendency to go against their original sponsors and to get out of hand politically and on the other their inherent weak position, as they could always be browbeaten into submission.[38] The uneasy partnership continued with the Indian managers of aided and recognised educational institutions becoming more and more alienated from the freedom struggle. The question of standards which was raised by Curzon was never seriously taken up. If the private managers played to the political tune of the Government, the question of educational norms was relegated to the background, funds protection and even Government titles were liberally bestowed. But due to the circuitous nature of control the alliance remained uneasy and precarious as there existed an inherent tendency of the Indian managers to assume independence.

Trends in the changing character of private entrepreneurship

From the above discussion we may conclude that private Indian enterprise had a start, like their half brothers the missionary institutions, under the political patronage of the British rulers. Intitially an important motivation was the service and well-being of the people, which demanded and secured sacrifice of money, time and effort. With the passage of time and the changed political context the service motto gradually began to be replaced by a realization that control over educational resources can be an institution of profit and power. Private entrepreneurship in education can grow into a pure managerial skill of procuring political patronage, government grants, university affiliation or Board recognition with the minimum of conditions of recognition/affiliations being fulfilled and it can become completely free from encumbrances of educational norms. Private educational enterprise will concentrate on colleges of general education and secondary schools where with lesser resource investment greater resources can be brought under control for conversion into profit and power. These managements will resist public control by all means possible but to remain in business will grudgingly yield to a determined bid for control by public authority.

REFERENCES

1. Yogendra Singh, *Modernization of Indian Tradition*. Delhi: Thomson Press, 1973, p. 102.
2. B. Kuppuswami, *Social Change in India*. Delhi: Vikas, p. 230.
3. For *Section 43 of the East India Act 1813*, *Macaulay Minute* and the unsuccessful rearguard action fought by Princep, see, *Selections from Educational Records*, Delhi, National Archives of India, 1965, pp. 22 and 107-130. Hereafter cited as *Educational Records*.
4. See, B.D. Bhatt and J.C. Aggarwal (eds.), *Educational Documents in India* (1831-1965). New Delhi: Agra Book Depot, 1969.
5. Syed Nurullah and J.P. Naik, *A History of Education in India*, (During British Period). Bombay: MacMillan, 1951, p. 24.
6. See, R.C. Majumdar et al., *An Avdanced History of India*, pp. 888-98; Aparna Basu, *The Growth of Education and Political Development in India, 1898-1920*. Delhi : Oxford University Press, 1974, Chapter 8; A.R. Desai, *Social Background of Indian Nationalism*. Bombay : Popular, 1948; S. S. Dikshit, *Nationalism and Indian Education*. Delhi: Sterling Publishers, 1966, Chapters I and IX; Jawaharlal Nehru, *The Discovery of India*. Calcutta: Signet Press, 1956, pp. 336-341.
7. A.N. Basu, *Education in Modern India*. Calcutta: Orient Book Co., 1947, p. 56.
8. See, Haridas Mukherjee and Uma Mukherjee, *The Origins of the National Education Movement*, (1905-1910). Calcutta: Jadavpur University, 1957.
9. See, Kuppuswami, 1972, op. cit, p. 232; A.R. Kamat, *The Educational Situation and Other Essays on Education*. Delhi : People's Publishing House, 1973, pp. 215-232; Sampurnanand, *Memoirs and Reflections*. New York : 1964, p. 23; Aparna Basu, 1974, op. cit., pp. 46-47; Nurullah and Naik, 1951, op. cit., pp. 558-572.

10. As examples of erroneous understanding, see Kuppuswami, 1974, op. cit., p. 22, arguing for growth of English education on these lines, of Aparna Basu (1974, op. cit., pp. 101, 102) stating that the process of educational expansion was self-generating and would continue with or without Government aid.
11. Correct expression should be "light in its foundation", see Nurullah and Naik, 1951, op. cit., pp. 758-59.
12. Ibid., p. 860; Atmanand Misra, *Educational Finance in India*. Bombay: Asia, 1962, p. 18.
13. Bhatt and Aggarwal, 1969, op. cit., p. 38.
14. Suresh Chandra Shukla, "Notes on the Educational Situation", *Mainstream*, February 6, 1971.
15. Aparna Basu, 1974, op. cit., p. 105.
16. Ibid., pp. 101, 107.
17. Nurullah and Naik, 1951, op. cit., p. 669.
18. Kamat, 1973, op. cit., pp. 301, 336-37.
19. As adopted by Bhatt and Aggarwal, 1969, op. cit., pp. 98-115.
20. Susanne Hoeber Rudolph and Llyod I. Rudolph, *Education and Politics in India: Studies in Organization, Society and Policy*. Delhi: Oxford University Press, p. 1.
21. Nurullah and Naik, 1951, op. cit., p. 164.
22. For the discussion of the public policy-making role played by private interests, see, Mark V. Nadel, "The Hidden Dimensions of Public Policy: Private Government and the Policy-Making Process", *The Journal of Politics* , Florida, Vol. 37, No. 1, February 1975.
23. Nurullah and Naik, 1951, op. cit., p. 164.
24. J. L. Nehru, 1956, op. cit., pp. 1336-37.
25. Nurullah and Naik, 1951, op. cit., pp. 184-189.
26. Educational Records, op. cit., p. 3.
27. Ibid., pp. 4-6.
28. See, Nurullah and Naik, 1951, op. cit., pp. 59-69, 169-172, 239-245 and 252.
29. Educational Records, op. cit., pp. 78, 163, 197-98.
30. Rudolphs, 1972, op. cit., pp. 14-15, Nurullah and Naik, 1951, op. cit., pp. 88-89.
31. Ibid., pp. 192-202.
32. Ibid., p. 260.
33. Atmanand Misra, *Educational Finance in India*. Bombay: Asia, 1962, pp. 307-08.
34. Aparna Basu, 1974, op. cit., p. 17.
35. Rudolphs, 1972, op. cit., p. 101.
36. Educational Records, op. cit., p. 26.
37. Rudolphs, 1972, op. cit., p. 32.
38. Aparna Basu, 1974, op. cit., pp. 13-49.

CHAPTER FIVE

ORGANIZATION OF HIGHER EDUCATION IN KANPUR AND STRUCTURE OF PRIVATE MANAGEMENT

HIGHER education in Kanpur is mainly organized under Kanpur University, established in January 1966, under the Kanpur and Meerut Universities Act 1965. The University with its jurisdiction in the area included in the districts of Allahabad, Fatehpur, Kanpur, Etawah, Farrukhabad, Jhansi, Jalaun, Hamirpur, Banda, Lucknow, Unnao, Rae Bareli, Sitapur, Hardoi, Lakhimpur-Kheri and Barabanki,[1] started with the colleges of this area, affiliated to the Agra University, on the day of its inception, transferred to it as affiliated colleges. Though the University has the powers to provide for instruction in such branches of learning as the University may think fit and to make provision for research and for the advancement and dissemination of knowledge",[2] it continues to be a purely affiliating-examining university. Kanpur has an Indian Institute of Technology, established under an Act of Parliament. Kanpur University is a State University.

At present there are, in Kanpur, four professional technical colleges all maintained by the State Government, eight purely women's colleges including two First Degree colleges and nine boys', or co-educational colleges including two First Degree Colleges.

Of the sixteen private colleges functioning in the city of Kanpur, three are run in the name of minorities—Christians, Muslims and Sikhs—six are directly affiliated to Dayanand Arya Samaj, one is a Sanatan Dharam college, and one is a Brahmin sub-caste college. Of the remaining five Colleges, two are linked indirectly to the Dayanand group through the controlling interests and the other three though exhibiting some caste and linguistic group biases do not clearly belong to any specific segment of the community.

For the purposes of this study, only seven colleges have been selected out of these sixteen colleges.[3] The Government colleges and the Municipal College have been excluded with a view to keeping the study within manageable limits, moreover professional colleges have their own ethos, which makes them uncomparable with other institutions. The Indian Institute of Technology has been excluded for the same reasons.

Christ Church College

It is difficult to fix the exact year of the foundation of Christ Church College, which produced most of the teachers and managers of other colleges established in the city in later years. However, the Revd. R. G. Slater, a former Principal of the college, had accepted 1892 as its foundation year.

The mission that established this college, or rather developed it out of the school that had existed since 1837, was called Society for the Propagation of the Gospel (SPG). The Westcott Brothers had come to Kanpur in 1889 from England to organize the affairs of the SPG.

The college was getting an annual government grant of Rs. 1,200 against Rs. 6,000 and Rs. 9,000 for Meerut and Bareli Colleges in 1901-2, which did not have M.A. classes. The following year the College had its grant, from the Government, doubled and it also received Rs. 1,600 and Rs. 600 as donations from two local Hindus and another Rs. 1,000 from the Municipal Board. This information was dug up and is included to emphasize that though a good part of the effort and the money did come from the founding agency, in this case the S.P.G., it was supplemented by a Government contribution as a continuing phenomenon as well as sporadic contributions by other non-Christian sources. The college also received a grant of a spacious playground from the Government in 1901.

The distinctive sub-culture

The founders of the college not only personally participated in the teaching work, lived in the hostel with the students but were active in the games on the playground and on the stage for cultural programmes. This active sharing of life and leadership with the students of the college grew into a distinctive tradition of the college. This also found reflection in the heroic help rendered by the college during the days of the Plague Riot in April 1901. Again, when in 1931-32, the city was paralysed by communal riots, "The Principal and four of the staff, following the tradition of the Westcott brothers, did all they could to relieve the suffering and assuage the fears and suspicions." This is in contrast not only with the communal approach of the management of a sister college in the city, but more so with the deliberate encouragement of the communal division of the college students indulged in by the same Indian Principal in 1940-41 session (whereas two members of the S.P.G. Brotherhood resigned from the college to dissociate themselves from the Principal's actions).[4]

In this college dissent and tolerance of opposition was one of the important values imparted by the British Christian Missionaries both in the matter of religion and politics. The type of the management and control, historically represented by Christ Church College, Kanpur, is in a way revealed by the working of C. Ackroyd, a member of S.P.G. Brotherhood, who joined the college "in 1932 after achieving no little notoriety at St. Paul's College, Calcutta". He organized a College Parliament, a "survey of Some Industrial Housing in Cawnpore" and another survey, "Passenger Transport in Cawnpore". He took the students to work with the labouring classes and made available to them radical and even Marxist literature in the thirties. Under his editorship the College Magazine published "The International" as a consequence of which "the angry and frightened" Director of Public Instruction intervened and Professor Ackroyd was persuaded to resign from the college but he continued his work with the peasantry and his intellectual contacts with the young radicals. He rejoined the College in July 1937 when the political climate had changed in favour of the Congress to resign again in 1940 to checkmate the approach of communal division resorted to by Principal Chatterji. In the "Quit India" movement of August 1942, Revd. Thorne, the then Principal, is credited with disallowing the police to enter the campus to suppress the defiant students. This attitude is markedly different from that of the Revd. R. G. Slater, the next Principal, describing the same movement years later as "Quit India and leave us to Chaos". In any case it was a question of one's evaluation and not playing to the tune called by the British rulers. In his *The Story of the College*, Slater refers to only two politicians as former students of the college—Ajoy Ghosh, who led the Communist Party of India, and Balkrishna Sharma, a Congress M.P. In contrast, the other two pre-Independence colleges of the city proudly refer to Deen Dayal Upadhyaya and Atal Behari Vajpayee, the two successive presidents of the Bharatiya Jan Sangh, as their former students in their respective *Golden Jubilee Souvenir* issues of the College Magazine.

On the question of religion also the tradition built up by the controllers of the college in the pre-Independence days was definitely not of proselytism. The reference, to three generations of college inferior staff from a Hindu family and the removal from service of a Christian head clerk in 1943-44 in a case of faked attendance records, the presence of only seven Christian students and five Christian teachers in 1943-44 and the Principal's lament that the religion classes which had been optional since 1936 had almost ceased to exist do not indicate any special interest taken in the spread of Christianity. "The college was founded on this conviction, and with the hope that it would provide", wrote the Rev. Slater, "leaders for the Indian Church and for the administration, profession and education of India; men of integrity inspired by a vision of God's will being done in every activity of society." The actual instance of the former students of the college coming up as leaders for the Indian Church could not be discovered, though it is easy to agree with the Rev. Slater that "no one may say that the Westcotts set out to provide only 'baboos' for Government offices.[5] R. N. Dey, I.C.S., a former student of the college (1914-18), observed that the faith of the Christians, who guided the college, was itself very liberal and recognized that other religions also had a valuable contribution to make for the enrichment of the human spirit."[6] Balkrishna Sharma describes his conversation with his teacher

Edwin Warring Ornerod and quotes him as saying: "Yes, even the scriptures you must read with a critical mind. Conviction comes when Reason is reasonably satisfied."[7] These are only picked up illustrations but there seemed to be a general agreement among the former students of the college that it filled its students more with a questioning faith than an orthodoxy.

Other features that stand out in the pre-Independence history of the college management are the absence of a mercenary motive, emphasis on the playground and limited numbers. How far these and other characteristics survived the "Indianization" of the college management will be discussed in the chapters that follow.

Structure of the management

The structure of the controlling body called Governing Body went through a number of changes since its inception in 1892. The Revd. G. H. Westcott, the founder of the college, along with his brother Foss Westcott, was the representative of the S.P.G. Mission. He was the Head of the S.P.G. Brotherhood that he had founded in Kanpur, as well as the Principal. Thus the management was a unified authority. Canon Fisher took over as head of the Brotherhood in 1910 as well as Chairman of the Governing Body and there follows a period when the Principal, head of teachers in the college, is not the formal head of the Governors of the College. Canon Fisher continued to work from behind the scene and the three principals of the college that worked with him till 1935 were given all the power and support to run the college. From 1923 to 1942 the Head of the Brotherhood was the Vice-Chairman of the Governing Body of which formerly he was the Chairman. From 1942, the representative of the S.P.G. Mission replaced the Brotherhood Head in the Governing Body. In 1946 on the eve of Independence, the college ceased to be the property of the S.P.G. Mission and was transferred to the Lucknow Diocesan Trust Association.

In 1956 the Christ Church College Society was registered under the Societies Registration Act-XXI of 1860 with the Registrar, Joint Stock Companies, Uttar Pradesh[8]. It is this Body headed by the Bishop of the Diocese (Lucknow) which runs the college. It is to be noted that the changes in the constitution of the Governing Body did not affect much the working of the college because the principle of vesting all power and responsibility in the office of the Principal was always upheld. The changes in the legal status of the body owning and maintaining the college as a property in 1946 and again in 1956 were pre-emptive actions to meet the possible changes that the Government might enforce in running schools and colleges in the interest of secular policy. The property built with Mission support, local non-Christian support and above all with the Government's donation and grant-in-aid for the college and school is sought to be protected as religious trust property. The Rules and Regulations, as they stand, have written-in clauses (Clauses 4, 58 and 49) to ensure a perpetual and absolute control of the college by the Bishop of the Diocese. But clause 47 binds the Principal and the Governing Body to carry out "any special powers or duties which the Education Department or the University to which Christ Church College, Kanpur, is affiliated, shall allot", in the way and manner thereby directed. This is the only opening left. The Principal of the college continues to be the secretary of the Governing Body, but this is not binding by the rules and regulations and therefore an arrangement that can be dispensed with. In the objects of the Society occurs clause 2 (e): "To maintain sufficient staff to preserve and strengthen the Christian character and purpose of the Institution." If a narrowly constructed meaning is imposed on this clause, which would not be altogether difficult keeping in view the wording, the clause can be exploited for rabid communal discrimination in the appointment and promotion of the staff to the detriment of educational norms.

Dayanand Anglo-Vedic College and the Shiksha Sansthan

Under this rubric we discuss D.A.V. College proper, Dayanand Girls College and Dayanand Brijendra Swarup College as the latter two were literally conceived and given shape by the former and are controlled and managed by the parent body which was established to administer the Dayanand Anglo-Vedic College.

D.A.V. College, Kanpur, was founded in 1919, by the D.A.V.

College Trust and Management Society, U.P., as part of the D.A.V. movement, started by Lala Hansraj, a follower of Swami Dayanand, in Lahore.[9] In April 1867 Dayanand, the founder of the Arya Samaj, attended the great *Kumbh* fair at Hardwar. There he is said to have hoisted flag a bearing the inscription "Pakhand Khandani Pataka" (Hypocrisy-Demolition Standard). Can one apply this very standard to evaluate the work of the organization which claims to work in his name?

The D.A.V. College Trust and Management Society, founded in 1892, shifted its headquarters to Kanpur in 1919 as some influential members resided here and Babu Bansidhar bequeathed Rs. 25,000 and about 50 acres of land for building the college at Kanpur. Some more funds were raised and the college was established after the pattern of the D.A.V. College, Lahore with Lala Dewan Chand, a former Professor of the Lahore College as Principal. Initially the founding society had decided, on the Lahore pattern, not to go in for a Government grant but the policy was soon given up and substantial Government grants were secured. Rai Bahadur Anand Swarup was the President of the Society from 1919 till his death in 1931. On his death his younger brother R.B. Brijendra Swarup, an equally flourishing lawyer, took over as President to hand over to his son Devendra Swarup in 1952 due to old age. By this time the D.A.V. Trust had already become a sufficiently powerful organization whose control carried prestige as well as material advantages, and Sri Devendra Swarup was edged out from the Presidentship by his younger brother Sri Virendra Swarup in 1957 who continues to preside over the affairs since then. The Trust, in 1969, when the college celebrated its Golden Jubilee, was controlling 19 institutions, 10 at Kanpur, 5 at Dehradun, 2 at Unnao and 1 at Lucknow.[10] Thus from its very beginning, unlike the Christ Church College, the D.A.V managers took no direct part in teaching, games or hostel living. The management was an activity apart from and standing above the educational process as such, mainly concentrating on procuring and managing resources. The missionary origin and the assertive personality of the first Principal, coupled with the contest of flourishing law practice being the main occupation of the first two Presidents, for whom educational management was a side job, had made him quite central to the control and running of the college. The college maintained a steady growth under his stewardship. With 70 students and 10 teachers in 1919, the college had already blown into the only college in Agra University with four faculties—Arts, Science, Commerce and Law—having 772 students and 36 teachers in 1940 when Lala Dewan Chand retired as Principal.

Rise of specialised 'pure' management

Sixteen years of principalship of K. P. Bhatnagar meant a record quantitative growth and all that goes with it. In 1956 there were 5,336 students and 215 teachers surpassing the older institutions like the Agra College, the St. John's College, Agra, the Bareilly College and the Meerut College to claim the dubious title of being "the biggest college of the biggest University of the biggest State of India". By this time the importance of controlling educational resources, for using them to corner still more, of converting them into political inputs, deriving economic benefits by manipulating the complex funds, providing full-time and part-time jobs, for managing the elections to the University Senate from the Registered Graduates Constituency, the Principals Constituency and similar constituencies in the Board of High School and Intermediate Education, had become too apparent. The control of a complex of colleges and schools would mean control of the University and the Board. The control over these institutions meant prescribing books, appointing examiners and many other points of patronage and privilege. The presence of Graduates Constituencies and Teachers Constituencies for election to the U.P. Legislative Council meant a politicization of educational management. Control of these Legislative Council seats was fed back as control of universities (especially Agra University, which was an affiliating-examining university), as control of the U.P. Board having sway over all the High Schools and Intermediate Colleges and control of various educational institutions and vice versa. The situation was ripe for a second generation of educational managers to specialise in "pure" educational management.

The "purity" involved (i) taking it up as a primary occupation, (ii) freeing it from the circumvention due to aims set by the original founders like sacrifice, self-help (except with an altered meaning), economy (except for using the capitalist market ethos of maximising profit for the owner-controller) or adherence to out-of-date Arya Samaj dogmatism, and (iii) freeing it of encumbrances due to internal norms of the educational process like autonomy of the principal and the teachers, providing congenial conditions of work for teachers and students, for curricular and co-curricular activities.

The specialization consists of mastering the legal as well as extra-legal mechanism of securing Governmental grants through various agencies, of obtaining or obstructing affiliation in profitable subjects and faculties, with or without conditions imposed by the formal rules, and skilful use of one authority against another or to coalesce various groupings for concerted action including students' or teachers' demonstration or their break-up.

Factors contributing to the rise of 'pure' management

A quick succession of changes in the Principal's chair—5 in 9 years—further helped in corroding the authority of the Principal and internal autonomy of the college and the emergence of "pure" management. The placement of a former Principal of the college as Vice-Chancellor of Agra University for a good part of this period helped the manipulative capacity of "pure" management to expand by fission[11], by grafting[12] and also by takeover from other managements of the uneconomic units.[13] The management could soon be compared to an education resources bank dealing in managerial knowhow, technical personnel, principals and teachers—part-time or full-time, on term appointment or permanent tenure. How far the model of a centrally controlled giant industrial corporation with all parts reduced to inhuman cogs except the controlling "boss" fits in can be answered only after the analysis of its working that follows in other chapters.

One of the three former Principals of the college interviewed informed me that donations to the Society or the college were unknown since the last days of Lala Dewan Chand. "With the expansion of the college the Boys Fund was surplus to the extent that the earlier deficit was cleared and a huge reserve fund built. Otherwise donations were nil. Every college shows the actual number studying in the university returns and in the internal accounts but a lesser number is shown to the Government to secure deficit grants. The Government makes a sample checking only and the auditors can always be tackled. Thus more and more money was accumulated." The informant regretted that it was under him that the practice of charging a capitation fee of Rs. 300 per candidate was started for admission in a particular class but proper donation receipts were issued and the money was properly utilized for purchase of equipment. Later as the practice enlarged its area of operation and multiple points of collection were contrived to avoid detection by the Government, collection-commissions began to be charged with ever increasing rates and percentages. Soon the distinction between personal profits and donations to the society vanished. Other colleges were opened on the basis of the assets of the D.A.V. College Society. No transfer of money takes place but the immovable properties of the Society provide the basis for "showing" necessary funds for the new colleges. Much of this "on paper" manipulation is possible according to the interviewee because the inspecting and affiliating authorities are "softened." The picture was corroborated by the other two Principals. It may be mentioned that two of them are still heading Managing Committees of the colleges affiliated with the group. The motivation in withholding even public documents as closely guarded secrets is obvious.[14] (These informants would not part with information regarding the Managing Committees they were currently heading except acknowledging that they did not hold real power and were mere "rubber stamps" of the one at whose pleasure they hold these offices.

Kuladhipati is the Sansthan but . . .

"The Rules and Regulations of the D.A.V. College Trust and Management Society, U.P." which came into force after 1 September 1940, apparently indicate a democratic character of the Managing Committee of the Society. It tries to keep a delicate balance between the Arya Samaj units sending representatives to constitute the membership of the society and others who are members by virtue of being members of the Managing Commitee. But it gives to the then President overriding power, so much so that he can perpetuate himself in office with or without others' support (clause 2, 8(a), 15, 30, 33, 45, clause 50 read with 49 and 53, 56, 63, 82, 85 and 93 (b), (c), (d) and (e)). Clause 93 (e) stating the functions and duties of the President mentions : To superintend all Establishments belonging to the society and all departments under its control . . . by taking upon himself the duties of the absentee. Clause 104 states that the Boards of Management for each institution will be appointed by the Managing Committee of the Society and these Boards will exercise powers of management subject to the general control and exercise of emergency powers of the President by him through "Secretary" for College and Manager for Inter College or High School . . . . Such Secretary or the Manager as the case may be shall give effect to the orders of the President or the Board of Management concerned.

"Rules and Regulations of the Sansthan" currently in force, by Clause 5, give to the Kuladhipati the right to suspend any member and the term of the office-bearers was increased to five years from the earlier three years. The Powers, Duties and Functions of the Kuladhipati give him the right to preside over any meeting of any Board of Management of Colleges affiliated to the Sansthan and to take part in the meetings of any other authority or body under it. Similarly, he can call a meeting of any Board of Management or bodies working under them. He maintains general control over the colleges, is responsible for discipline and can take action immediately in urgent matters and report forthwith for approval to the Board concerned. He has the power to sign cheques and draw amounts, to deposit, invest and keep on behalf of the Sansthan immovable property in accordance with the rules, etc. He can nominate seven heads of the institutions affiliated to the Sansthan to the Karya Karni Parishad (Executive Committee). Thus the new rules and regulations make the Kuladhipati even more powerful than the former President that he replaced for all practical purposes. Through various provisions Kuladhipati is the Sansthan using as rubber stamp its various bodies and boards of management of the institutions affiliated to the Sansthan. His writ runs unquestioned. One learnt that a former principal who rose to become the Vice-Chancellor of Agra University discontinued attending the meetings of the Management because of its being reduced to one man's show and because original aims had been relegated to the background. Almost everybody connected with the Society and the University agreed about the complete identity of the D.S.S. with the present Kuladhipati.

But as we shall have occasion to see, wherever he had to exercise power through other offices the possibility of subversion, usurpation and even challenge cannot be ruled out. We have already seen how the collection of "capitation" fee gave an opportunity to the lower links to arbitrarily define their own share and rights. Both Dayanand Girls College and Dayanand Brijendra Swarup College in their own way display these tensions more than the D.A.V. College itself. More of this in the following chapters.

Vikramajit Singh Sanathan Dharma College

The college was founded in 1921 by Shree Brahmavart Sanatan Dharam Mahamandal, Kanpur, specializing in commerce education.[15] But now it is a post-graduate college with Arts, Science, Commerce, Law and Education faculties. If the aim of the Arya Samaj was to protect Hinduism from Islam and Christianity, especially the former, and to reform the perverted Hinduism of the Puranic age by a call back to the Vedas, Sanathan Dharma considered even the Arya Samaj as a corruptive influence.[16] The Sanatan Dharam in the words of Nehru "combined religious obscurantism of an extreme type with fervent or at any rate loudly expressed loyalty to British rule."[17]

The college founded by the Sanatan Dharam Mahamandal, presided over by Rai Bahadur Vikramajit Singh, had the support of the British industrialists.[18] Sir Spencer Harcourt Butler, Lt. Governor of U.P., Zamindars and Raises[19] Marwari businessmen[20] and a host of Rajas and Maharaja's.[21] Thus we had the college aim "at combining reverence with knowledge and modern scientific thought with ancient Aryan culture". The class composition and political exigency taking the upper hand in the management could be detected in the promise made in the Address to the Lt.-Governor that the College Committee could lay their scheme before Raja Sahab of Mahmudabad, a Muslim feudal lord, and in the inclusion of Khan Bahadur Makbul Hussain, Registrar of Joint Stock Companies, U.P., in the Advisory Council for the College (1921-22). It would be wrong to conclude from this that the Sanatanist character of the management had no communal or denominational sectarian consequences for the staff or the students, which we would be discussing later.

Instability in Principal's chair

The emphasis on a Commerce faculty and availability of a large hostel had made this college an attraction for students from all over U.P., Madhya Bharat, Rajputana (Rajasthan) and even other provinces in the pre-Independence days. As newer colleges were opened in other parts of the regions, students from far-off places stopped travelling long distances for studies. A glance over the list of the Principals of the college reveals a Telugu and a Bengali figure among the nine who occupied the chair since the birth of the college. For the first seventeen years, this chair could see no stability. Except for the first incumbent who never got a permanent tenure, the remaining had to leave the college principalship within one to four years for unstatable reasons.[22] One Principal was removed on the advice of the Executive Council of Agra University even against the wishes of Vikramajit Singh, the Management boss.[23]

The indelible mark of "Rai Bahadur Saheb"

As already mentioned the Management of the college, from its inception, was not only Sanatanist (a movement emphasising adherence to an orthodox Hindu, scripturally prescribed way of life, including rituals with pronounced abhorrence of not only Islam, Christianity but also the Arya Samaj) but had support from the British rulers, British capitalists of Kanpur, Marwari capitalists and businessmen and Zamindars. It was Sanatan Dharma College but after the death of Rai Bahadur Vikramajit Singh, the first Secretary of the Management who continued to control the destiny of the college till his death in 1942, the name of the college became Vikramajit Singh Sanatan Dharma College, which it always had been in practice. The personality of the "Rai Bahadur Saheb" has left an indelible mark on the character of the college. True to the British bestowed title of "Rai Bahadur" he was never with the National Congress movement. He was associated with the Hindu Mahasabha throughout his life and was its all-India President for some time. A number of teachers got appointment in the college, not on the strength of their academic qualifications but their nearness to him. For example, B.N. Chopra, who was close to Rai Bahadur, was only an Intermediate and the paid secretary of the U. P. Chamber of Commerce, was appointed to the college and later made the Principal, and Satya Narain Pande, who later became head of the Sanskrit Department was a reciter of the Ramayana at Rai Bahadur Saheb's residence and secretary of the Hindu Mahasabha before his appointment in the college. Principal Sheshadri had to sever his connection with the college, causing students' demonstrative resentment against the management's policy. Vikramajit Singh wanted to retain Principal Bhattacharya, who had caused a breakdown of the cohesion of the staff but had to leave due to the University's intervention. All this evidence placed together from the writings in the *Golden Jubilee Magazine* of the college is summarized in the statement of Ayodhya Nath Sharma, the head of the Hindi Department from 1926-1958 in the following words: "His life was extremely busy. So he depended for matters related with the College on those he had more confidence in or who had easy access to him . . . . Consequently many able and eminent teachers had to sever their connection with the college."[24] In contrast with the position of Christ Church College management or D.A.V. College in the Dewan Chand period, the Principal of V.S.S.D. College had always a lesser say, allowed by the Management, in running the college.

Family grip on management

Not only Vikramajit Singh but his family too had been important in controlling the college. It was not the donation of Rs. 10,000 by him or Rs. 1,000 by Dwarka Pd. Singh but his organising capacity that helped in establishing a tightening grip of the family on the Management. First it was the secretaryship, then an additional membership of the Committee, then an assistant secretaryship also and finally secretaryship, joint secretaryship and two members on the Board of Management that constituted the family share.

Unlike the D.A.V., the secretary's post has been the most powerful post in the S.D. College Management. It has passed from father to son and there are clear indications that the joint secretary (the grandson) will inherit the mantle, when the need arises. But compared to the D.A.V., the Management still has some other power positions and persons sharing in a minor way control of the college. Moreover the personal interest of Narendrajit Singh, the present secretary, in the educational process as such going on in the college and his interest in the Rashtriya Swayam Sevak Sangh teachers and students in particular has prevented the Management from being reduced to the "pure" type.

Sanatanist ideology to R.S.S.

The R.S.S. ideology that dominates now, in a way, is a continuation of the Sanatanist ideology. Narendrajit Singh devotes his energies and time on the College as a major occupation but derives no economic benefits from his position, as the most important person in the Management. His being Sar Sangh Chalak for U.P. and his comfortable economic assets and the desire to recruit Swayam Sevaks (volunteers) for the R.S.S. mitigates the tendency towards "pure" type of management but gives rise to other types of distortions. The personality cult of "Barrister Saheb" as he is "popularly" called in the college is buttressed by combining the power position, piety of personal life and politico-ideological partisanship with an appeal in the name of "ideals". His two sons are being groomed in the Committee taking up the control of the college after him on the same lines.

Like the Christ Church and the D.A.V. the college management and the ownership and control of the properties are vested in two different bodies. It is the Brahma Vrata Sanatan Dharam Mandal, the wider body, that controls property and the Board of Management runs the college. The Management is subordinate to the former but has direct control over the live resources. The most important position in the Mandal is that of the President and in the Board of the Secretary according to the Constitution given in "The Memorandum of Association" of the Mahamandal and "Rules and Regulations" of the college. It is no strange phenomenon that the "Rai Bahadur Saheb", later "Barrister Saheb", held these offices simultaneously and continuously.

Important points impinging upon the working and control of the college in the Memorandum are : (1) The aims and objects of the Society include (a) preaching of "Sanatan Dharma based on the Shruti (Vedas), Smritis, the Ithihasas and the Puranas", (b) "to preserve the caste system among the Hindus as enjoined by the Shastras", (c) to improve the religious and social training of all the Hindus and to diffuse the principles of Sanatan Dharma by means of schools, colleges, etc., and (d) to improve the unhappy conditions of the Hindu sacred places of pilgrimage and to protect the cow. How far these aims contravene the Indian Constitution is a moot question; (2) If any meeting is postponed for want of quorum, the next meeting can be held without any regard to quorum, the office-bearers are eligible for re-election endlessly and can be removed from the roll of its members for any reason by three-fourths of its members; (3) The Managing Committee of the Society alone has full power and control over all the funds and the properties of the Mandal; (4) Every affiliate shall be entitled to frame its own rules and regulations but they shall not conflict with the principles and rules of the Mandal; (5) Every patron shall be entitled to vote in any meeting of the Managing Committee without his election being made, to inspect the head office or the affiliates and to call the meeting of the Managing Committee through the Secretary. A Sanatanist who makes a donation of Rs. 5,000 or more to the Mandal becomes a patron.

Clause 2 of the "Rules and Regulations" relating to the college states that the Board of Management shall be elected by the Mahamandal at its Annual General Meeting or any adjourned meeting thereof and shall hold office for life. Clause 3 stipulates that the Principal of the College will be ex-officio member of the Board but will have no vote. Clause 8 gives the right to the Board to appoint its office-bearers for any term that it may please. Clause 12 makes quorum unessential in adjourned meetings. Clause 14 compels the Board to submit an annual statement of account duly audited to the Mahamandal. As already stated Clauses 18 and 19 give to the secretary most important powers. Clauses 28, 29 and 30 make religious training compulsory for all Hindu students and the resident scholars of the college (not only Hindus) are required to practise rituals and daily observances enjoined by Sanatan Dharma and observe festivals as far as possible and the Principal is enjoined upon to ensure compliance. Naturally this rules out a non-Sanatanist as principal and threatens even non-Sanatanist resident students. The ideology of the management is brought out in bold relief by an interesting incident, described by D. S. Nag, a former Prime Minister of the College Students Union. The College Union decided to cut down the expenses (which used to amount to two-thirds of the total budget of the Union) on Janmashtami and invite a Harijan to initiate Puja and distribute "prasad". Rai Bahadur Vikramajit Singh, orthodox teachers and Sanatan Dharam Kumar Sabha boycotted the celebrations.[25]

Halim Muslim College

In the city of Kanpur, the Muslims formed about one-third of the industrial labour. They have no share in the ownership of major industries. The only comparatively rich section comes from tannery owners, hide merchants and those who run general merchandise shops (Bisatis). On the whole the Muslims have been economically and educationally a backward section of the Kanpur population. The small number of families, who belonged to the middle and upper classes, used to send their sons to Aligarh Muslim University or those who could not send them to Aligarh took advantage of Christ Church College, where the Muslims constituted almost half of the student population up to 1947. When Christ Church College also embarked upon a policy of reluctant expansion, the ratio of the Muslims fell as the demand for education did not grow among them equally with the Hindus, probably due to the differential class composition. The migration of the middle class leadership of the Muslim League to Pakistan was a contributing factor. The point that is being made is that the demand for higher education amongst the Muslims as well as the organizing capacity was comparatively low, mainly due to class composition of the Muslim population.

From middle school to a post-graduate college

Hafiz Mohd. Haleem, the founder of Halim Muslim College (which in his times was only a school) was a hide merchant, who along with some others established the Muslim Association. The Association, amongst other service organizations, started a Middle School in 1911, which was raised to a High School in 1916. This high school, the only Muslim-managed High School in Kanpur, could be elevated to an Intermediate college only after two decades, through the efforts of S. N. Bashir, son of Mohd. Haleem, and some Muslim members of the Bar and hide merchants. It became a Degree College in 1959 mainly due to "the efforts of some philanthropic hide merchants of Kanpur and Janab Al-Haj Baboo Mohd. Abdul Barkat, its president (1961-62), in fulfilment of the desire of his late father Janab Al-Haj Baboo Mohd. Hamza who was its president till 1956. . . ."[26] The formation of the Degree College was further helped by the personal efforts of the Principal of the Intermediate College who became the first Principal of the Degree College and the policy of the then Vice-Chancellor of Agra University to affiliate more and more colleges to the University, especially if the Management was helpful in maintaining his group's grip on the University.

Control vests in hide merchants

An important characteristic of this college's management is that the controllers and the donors were overlapping from the very beginning. It is not only a Muslim management but even formally a hide merchants organization. Article (3) (a) of the "Memorandum of Halim Degree College, Kanpur" states: "The Executive Committee of the Muslim Association, the Parent Body will elect eight members including the office-bearers from among the Hide Merchants and Tannery Owners who are the members of the Muslim Association." The next clause empowers the Executive Committee of the Muslim Association to nominate five members from amongst the donors and industrialists, apart from the Principal and the teachers' representative, to constitute the 15-member Managing Committee. There is no bar to the same persons being elected again after the expiry of their three-year term. The Managing Committee is entitled to remove its office-bearers with two-thirds of the actual members concurring therein. The Managing Committee has the power to invest funds of the Muslim Association placed at its disposal or the income from the college property.[27]

The absence of people engaged in the legal profession and the actual dominance of the hide merchants in the Management from the very beginning has prevented the growth of "pure" educational entrepreneurship in this case. Another contributing factor has been the peculiar characteristics of the community providing students to the college which resulted in lack of pressure for admissions. Three members of the Managing Committee and all the teachers interviewed said that the college got second-rate students even from amongst the Muslims, as good or upper-class students continue to prefer Christ Church College. The college offered Arts and Commerce facilities for the first degree and Urdu and Sociology for M.A. and B. Ed. as a professional degree for teachers. Urdu offers no job opportunities and Sociology has to face competition from Christ Church, the oldest college with better facilities of staff and library, apart from other colleges.

Scramble for power

The scramble for control of Halim College till 1973 was not serious, as it always needed financial support from the parent body, the Muslim Association. The college taking the clue from the D.A.V. group and Christ Church management constructed some shops on the Campus and the college suddenly became a viable economic proposition, even without the Muslim Association's aid. Some conflict over the control have of late developed. Bashir, a leading industrialist and the son of the founder Mohd. Haleem, and his sons have been out of the Management as they, unlike Haleem, are not in the hide business. In 1973-74 the college had gone under a Government nominated Administrator, due to a dispute between the Management and the dismissed Principal, who had been spending most of his time in the U.S.A. The

Management was informally advised by the University and also the State dignitaries to accept Bashir as President, but it did not agree to any change in its composition. The dispute with the former Principal had led to the students going on strike in protest against the Management. The controllers of the Managing Committee suspected Bashir supporters' hand behind the trouble. They volunteered to hand over the management to the Government Administrator for the period of inquiry into the charges and counter-charges and let the Vice-Chancellor nominate an acting Principal.[28] In the last elections, two aspirants offered themselves for presidentship but sensing lack of support one of them withdrew. But this indicates a possibility of future conflict, now that the initial stage of investing money has been crossed.

Absence of pure-type management explained

Another factor that contributed to the lack of growth and non-emergence of a "pure" type of management was that the first Principal, who had been promoted from the Intermediate college, was not fully qualified and had to get exemption from the University. Hence he did not have the ambition of presiding over a post-graduate college. His retirement age being near, his interest was more in the extension of his term than in the expansion of the college and consequent growth of the power of the controllers. The next Principal, as luck would have it, was from the very start with one foot in the U.S.A. Thus absence of managerial initiative in educational entrepreneurship could have given a free hand to the principal to develop the college, but this end too faultered.

An interesting fact to be noted is that in the six Aims and Objects of the college written into the Memorandum, there is nothing to show that it is a Muslim college. One Hindu hide merchant has been continuously elected to the Managing Committee. Hindus outnumber Muslim students, the ratio being 3 : 2. Forty per cent of the staff is Hindu. The college has not sought protection under the minority clause of the Indian Constitution, unlike the Christ Church College which has secured this status and the D.A.V. management which used this threat to wrench a compromise with the University to regularize irregular appointments in D.A.V., D.G., D.B.S.

and D.A.V. Law College. B. Gopala Reddy, Governor of Uttar Pradesh, in his Convocation Address in 1971, said about the College: "It has been founded by the Muslims. The endowment is paid by Muslims but now the doors are open for the Hindu boys also to get their education. The best boy of the college who has just received a prize from the Vice-Chancellor is a Hindu. . . ." Every year the students and the staff elect either the President or the Secretary from amongst the Hindu members in their respective organizations. In some years both the offices go to the Hindus. In short the Muslim character is present only in the name of the college, the parent body managing the college and the principal (both the permanent principals were Muslims but a Hindu has also acted as the principal) and the office staff.

Guru Nanak Girls Degree College

The College has grown out of a primary school started in 1949 to cater to the needs of the refugee girls from West Punjab, which became Junior High School in 1953 and Higher Secondary School the following year. It became an Intermediate College in 1960 and finally a Degree College in 1965. All this growth has been under the continued patronage of Baba Mohan Singh, a Sikh holy man, who is the founder President of the Guru Nanak Vidyak Society, the parent body running the Girls' Degree College, Girls' Inter College, Boys' Inter College, Girls Primary School, Nursery School and a Boys' Primary School. There is a Managing Committee but the overall control and patronage of Baba Mohan Singh, the life President of the Vidyak Society, is accepted without any question.

Apart from the forbearing personality of Baba Mohan Singh, who has no English education but commands respect among a large number of Sikhs and can help collection of funds, the Management Committee is elected on a democratic basis by the Vidyak Society, which itself is run on a democratic basis subject to the acceptance of Baba Mohan Singh as the final arbiter. Note (iii) (i) of "Memorandum of Association and Rules and Regulations of Guru Nanak Vidyak Society, Kanpur" states that "Shri 108 Baba Mohan Singhji shall be the President of the Society for his lifetime." After his death even this office will be filled democratically by patrons, donors, representatives of general members and representatives of the Gurdwara Kirtan Garh (established and run by Baba Mohan Singh). The patrons, donors and general members are those who pay Rs. 1,100, Rs. 500 and Rs. 101 and a monthly fee of Rs. 21, Rs. 11 and Rs. 5, respectively. Thus it is controlled by those who give donations or can collect large sums, as in the controlling Executive Committee these categories are allotted, 4, 4 and 10 seats respectively out of a total of 21. The reports of the Vidyak Society, with accounts of the college and so also of other institutions run by it, are available for every year. From the published reports it seems the Management as compared to the Dayanand Shiksha Sansthan and the V.S.S.D. has not much to conceal.

The college and the controlling Vidyak Society has openly a Sikh character, in many ways more pronounced than the religious denomination of the other colleges of the city. The Memorandum of Association of the Guru Nanak Vidyak Society declares through clause (b) (iii), the aim : "To preach Guru Nanak's Gospel of Peace and Universal Brotherhood." Clause 2(ii) (c) and (d) demand proficiency in Punjabi (Gurmukhi) and a declaration of being a true follower of Guru Nanak as a condition for membership of the Society. The Secretary of the Society in his annual report for 1968-69 draws the attention of the managers of the institutions run by the Society: "Prayers is an important part of our schools. Principals, staff and the students will please compulsorily participate in the prayer. Moreover, the Society recommends that the principal or teachers should lecture every day for 10-15 minutes on Gurbani (Sikh Guru writings) and Sikh history so as to reform the lives of students" (translated from Punjabi, N.S.). The college prospectus declares in the General Rule (2) : "The prayer will be held during interval time and all the students have to attend it. Most of the information will be given at the time of prayer." As against this it must be mentioned that the Principal is a non-Sikh and a very small percentage of the teachers are Sikh, indicating thereby that no communal considerations have prevailed in the appointment of the staff.

The Managing Committee takes special interest to promote

the study of Punjabi.[29] Apart from the money collected by Baba Mohan Singh and the Vidyak Society from the Sikhs, the college has received substantial grants from the U.G.C., State Government and land donation from Kanpur Municipal Corporation.[30] This money is going to create landed property for the Society, a repetition of the process through which the Christ Church College property was built and later vested with the larger body controlled by the Bishop from Lucknow.

Signs of fissures

In spite of open allegiance of every body to Baba Mohan Singh, the Society is divided into a number of factions. Initially the division was between a group of refugees who had migrated from Sargodha in West Punjab led by a small capitalist family and another faction of migrants from Gujarat along with a Saluja family. The latter were dominant especially in relation to the management of the Girls Inter and Degree Colleges. Now this group has further been divided and the Gujarat faction seems to be dominant.

The members of the Managing Committee interviewed were of the view that the internal dissension and a scramble for control may increase. The Management has to contribute money only in the initial stages when buildings are to be constructed. Now it is a viable running unit and those who control it do not have to sacrifice anything, but they get public acclaim (*Yash*). The office-bearers are able to build up contacts with Government officials and political leaders which they convert into personal advantage. The business dealings on behalf of the college can be done with parties in whom one may have personal or other interest. For example, a manager changed the bank of the college, even without authorization, to boost his own interests. As has already been mentioned, the struggle for control of the college through control of the Vidyak Society is not very open but as an elected President is to take control of the Society and consequently of the huge properties and other resources after the death of Baba Mohan Singh, any sign of his impending demise is bound to accentuate the struggle. The factional struggle is bound to have consequences for the role performance of the students and the teachers. We will have occasion to confront the issue in the following chapters.

A general tendency towards "pure" type of management

Thus we have seen that the "private colleges" in Kanpur differ in their historical growth, have followed different adjustment processes to the wider political context and display dissimilarities in rules and regulations guiding their managements. Apart from the historical context in which an institution takes birth, the ideology of the parent-body founding the institution, the personality of the key person(s) constituting the management committees and the principal and, to a lesser extent, other members of the staff and the class of student-clientele contribute to make the colleges and their managements what they are. These differences notwithstanding, there is a tendency to gravitate towards the "pure" type of management, where manipulative skills to secure Government, University and political support as resources count and the interchangeability of educational resources, political resources and economic resources is increasingly recognized. This stage is reached when the institutions become viable after the initial teething trouble is overcome. The techniques developed in one management serves others by borrowing the experience or sometimes personnel also. The movement of teachers and students from one college to another and the common university context also helps in rounding off the angularities. We can see the persistence of differences of historical make-up as well as their obliteration under the impact of common present-day context.

REFERENCES

1. After the field work was completed a new University with jurisdiction in Jhansi, Jalaun, Hamirpur and Banda has been carved out of Kanpur University and the Kanpur Agriculture College has been raised to the status of Agriculture University.
2. The Kanpur and Meerut Universities Act 1965, Chapter II, Clause 5(i).
3. See Table 3.1 (Ch. 3) and also the last part of this Chapter for justification of the choice.
4. See, Revd. R.G. Slater, "The Story of the College" in Christ Church College Diamond Jubilee Magazine, 1952, p. 23.
5. *Diamond Jubilee Magazine*, 1952, p. 33.
6. Ibid., p. 48.

7. Ibid., p. 84.
8. Christ Church College Society, Kanpur—Memorandum and Rules and Regulations, 1956.
9. For an understanding of the aims and objects of the Arya Samaj and the educational movement connected with it, see, Lala Lajpat Rai, *Arya Samaj*. London: Longman Green and Co., 1932; C.P Upadhyaya, *The Origin, Scope and Mission of Arya Samaj*. Allahabad: Arya Samaj Chowk, 1937.
10. D.A.V. College Kanpur, *Swarna Jayanti Smarika*, 1969, p. 12; hereafter cited as Smarika.
11. Law faculty of the college was separated in the common building as an independent Law College (1958) and the girls section developed into a full-fledged post-graduate Dayanand Girls College (1959).
12. Dayanand Brijendra Swarup College and P.P.N. Degree Colleges were established in 1959 by "loaning" out the Principals and the entire teaching staff as part-timers, being paid salaries from D.A.V. College and allowances from the new "colleges" and later Mahila Vidyalaya cropped up on the same pattern.
13. Subhash National College, Unnao, which had run into financial difficulties was acquired by the D.A.V. College Trust and Management Society, rechristened as Dayanand Subhash National College, secured affiliation for Teachers' Training Classes and Law and overnight turned into a profitable unit.
14. See, footnote No. 16, Chapter 3.
15. Sanatan Dharam College, Cawnpore, Prospectus, 1921.
16. See, Babulal Misra, "Kaalej Ke Mahan Sansthapak" in *Swarna Jayanti Smarika V.S.S.D. College Kanpur*, 1971, p. 38, hereafter cited as *Swarna Jayanti*.
17. Jawaharlal Nehru, *An Autobiography*. London: The Bodley Head, 1955, p. 382.
18. Alexander MacRobert, A.B. Shakespeare, Thomas Smith, etc.
19. Rai Bahadur Bishambhar Nath, Balbhadra Pd. Tiwari and Lala Hardat Rai.
20. Jugal Kishore, Kamlapat and Bankey Behari Lal.
21. See, Address given to Lt.-Governor of U.P. at the foundation-laying of the College on 1.3.1920 in *Swarna Jayanti*, op. cit.
22. See, "Acharya Kul" in *Swarna Jayanti*, Ibid., pp. 44-46.
23. See, Ayodhyanath Sharma, "Ait ka Akalan", *Swarna Jayanti*, p. 15, Sansmaran ke Kshana.
24. *Swarna Jayanti*, Ibid., p. 17.
25. Ibid., p. 39.
26. Principal's Report on the occasion of the First Convocation on 21 December, 1961.
27. Memorandum of Association, Halim Muslim Degree College, registered on 10 December, 1965.

28. See, the *National Herald*, Lucknow, 1 and 9 October, 1973.
29. See, Vidyak Society Annual Report, 1968-69, p. 7.
30. See p. 5, 1972-73—Annual Report of Guru Nanak Vidyak Scciety and pp. 3 and 4 of 1968-69—Annual Report.

CHAPTER SIX

TEACHER'S ROLE : ITS DIRECT CONDITIONING BY COLLEGE MANAGEMENTS

Educational breakdown : Teachers to blame, Teachers' breakdown : Whom to blame?

"THE CLIMATE of irresponsibility that envelops our seats of learning enables teachers to make self-righteous complaints and demands without acknowledging any accountability for the quality of the graduates they produce. If academic standards are low, can they blame anyone else? Their alibi consists of an interesting hide-and-seek game. Whereas academic institutions should ideally be run by the academic community, they lament, non-academic forces dominate our educational system. But do they want it to be otherwise? As of now, when things go wrong, they can sit back and complain, and throw the blame on everyone else, not forgetting meanwhile to draw their pay at the end of every month."[1]

The unmistakable judgement contained in the above rhetoric by V.V. John, a former teacher, educational administrator of extensive experience and a prolific writer on educational issues, is widely shared. Amrik Singh, as if in resonance, declares that the real issue in higher education is the poverty and ineffectiveness of teaching for which no one else except those who teach and to some extent those who are taught are responsible as no non-academic agency can be blamed for coming in the way of reform of the system as it operates today. He notes the absence of professional identity and pride in the academic community, though its relatedness to the way the teachers are recruited and promoted at the colleges and university level is recognised.[2] Edward Shils has attempted to analyse and explain the failure of university and college teachers in India by referring to the academic tradition being exogeneous to the Indian tradition, the low attracting power of the teaching profession with its internal hierarchy working as a handicap to achievement, resulting in frequent and intense conflicts and a tradition of concern with undergraduates as well as a disregard for research.[3]

One can disagree with the specific judgement of these writers but not with the general statement "that the college teacher is a key element in the academic equation and perhaps the key to the improvement of quality and it is therefore clear that he must be understood."[4] But the key to understand the teacher may in turn lie in understanding the control mechanism of the colleges and the universities.

Four determinants of social roles

For every role in society related and complementary role-sets provide prescriptions of dos and don'ts which do not always run on the same lines. The sanctions attached to the discrepant prescriptions may also vary in strength and severity. A role may also arouse dissimilar expectations in different sections of the community. Absolute symmetry between prescription and expectations on the one hand and acceptance and enactment by the role-position occupants on the other is unthinkable. Disparity may exist, even in the role-image carrried by an occupant of a position and his actual performance. Heterogeneity within and between the prescriptions, expectations, acceptances and performances—the four determinants of social roles—keep all roles perpetually in a state of partial flux.

Even the legal definition of the role of college teachers provided by the Kanpur and Meerut Universities Act, 1965 has inspired incompatible interpretations by the Kanpur University authorities, the State Government, managements of colleges and teachers on many occasions. Even when the legality of the appoinment is not in dispute, the prescriptions provided by the University, the Government, the Managing Committees or some sections therein, different students and their parents, are characterized by only a partial overlap. A broad agreement on the synthetic nature of the role of college and university teachers—scholar who acquires knowledge as a life-long learner, transmitter of a body of knowledge, skills and values and the researcher who extends the frontiers of knowledge—does not rule out disagreement about the evaluation of the triple elements and their respective proportions in the mix to constitute the synthesis.

When disagreements arise, not all the contending definitions have equal chances of winning in the contest. I will present some case studies of disputes, to bring out the relatively dependent nature of the teacher's role.

Those who have the power to hire and fire teachers certainly have the capacity to impose their stated as well as unstated definition of the role even on the unwilling incumbents. The students, in whom the teacher seeks the fulfilment of his calling, too reinforce or retract certain aspects of the teacher's role. What the students call out from the teachers too, to a great extent, depends on the management's contribution to the making of their own role. Similarly, the demands put on the occupants of teachers' positions by the University and even the Government in part reflects indirectly the demands generated by the management through their influence with these agencies.

In the complex power distribution that makes the college system, the weak do not always lose the contest. Where legal and open course is found or is anticipated to be unrewarding, extra-legal and subterranean stratagem may be resorted to meet the disagreeable counter-prescriptions by cunning, fraud and subterfuge.

The absence of the exact predetermination of the outcome in each case makes the role determination not only precarious but its investigation an interesting process? But does this mean an absence of any over-arching pattern? What follows would hopefully bring out the patterning of the teacher's role by the control mechanism binding the college system.

Recruitment and promotion of teachers

Appointment of teachers in colleges is governed by the University Act pertaining to the University to which the colleges may be affiliated. The University lays down the minimum academic qualification as a condition for a person to be considered as a candidate for appointment as teacher in an affiliated college; the University also lays down certain conditions to curb the arbitrariness of the Managing Committee in selecting the teaching staff. Within these limits imposed by the University, to maintain a minimum academic standard and ensure the appointment of properly qualified teachers, the Managing Committees, as employers, are free to exercise their discretion in the selection of teachers for appointment in their respective colleges. The regulative role of the University, assisted by the University Grants Commission, has been steadily growing but not without meeting resistance on the part of private managerial interests with diverse strategies.

Since the establishment of Kanpur University, the appointment of teachers in the colleges under study had been governed by Chapter 6, 26(1) and (4) of the Kanpur and Meerut Universities Act, 1965. The Management was required to report to the Vice-Chancellor within fifteen days of the appointment together with all the applications and connected papers. The continuation of the appointment was subject to the approval of the Vice-Chancellor who might either approve the appointment or with the concurrence of the Selection Committee of the University in the subject concerned disapprove of the same, in which case it shall be terminated as soon as may be but not later than the date of expiry of the period of probation. Section 28(1) provided that every teacher, in an affiliated college, shall be appointed under a written contract, which shall contain such terms and conditions as may be prescribed, which shall be lodged with the University, with a copy each with the Management and the teacher concerned. The Act also stipulated that dismissal or removal of a teacher, by a decision of the Management, shall not take effect unless it has been approved by the Vice-Chancellor. Later the Uttar Pradesh State Universities Act, 1973 (President's Act No. 10, 1973 enacted on September 2, 1973) came into force. An important change was incorporated in Chapter VI, 31(4) (c) and (d), providing for selection committees for the appointment of the Principal and other teachers of an affiliated college. With two experts to be nominated by the Vice-Chancellor and the Dean in case of the Principal and the Principal and his nominee teacher in the case of teachers' appointment, the academics constitute a majority in the selection committee and are directly in a position to control or at least report to the University against unfair appointments.

In the case of colleges established and administered by a minority referred to in Clause (1) of Article 30 of the Constitution of India, the experts shall be nominated by the Management from out of a panel of five experts, suggested by the Management and approved by the Vice-Chancellor.

The control over the appointment of teachers and Principals in the colleges is sought to be further strengthened by the conditions (vii) and (viii) of Conditions for Introduction of the Revised Pay Scales by the U.G.C. Apart from the stipulated constitution of the selection committee, it is laid down that "all appointments of teachers in colleges shall be made on merit and on the basis of all-India advertisement."[5]

All this indicates that the existing provisions of statutory control over the appointment of teachers in the interest of "determination and maintenance of standards of teaching, examination and research in Universities" is still considered to be soft by the U.G.C. The managements, on the other hand, consider these regulations as too harsh and suffocating, abridging their right to administer these colleges. The managements' strategy is multi-pronged and flexible, to have it all one's own way—legal resistance, circumvention, compromise, false promises and even confrontation.

Biases: Recruitment and promotion processes

Sansthan colleges

Of the seven colleges studied, D.A.V. College, D.B.S. College and Dayanand Girls College are under the management of the Dayanand Shiksha Sansthan whose boss, Sri Virendra Swarup, is the Chairman of the U.P. Legislative Council and member of the Executive Council of Kanpur University. As we have already discussed, the management represents the "pure" type. The educational resources are controlled, for using them as a springboard to corner still more, converting them into political inputs, deriving economic benefits by manipulating the huge complex of funds and control of colleges is used for berths on the Executive Councils of the universities, bagging the Graduates Constituency of the

Legislative Council, and acquiring a controlling share in the governance of Higher Secondary education and examinations. The educational resources, the political power positions and the manipulative control of funds are seen as inter-convertible currencies. Teaching capabilities are given a weightage after calculating the contribution that a candidate can make in winning elections, extending control over other educational institutions, securing patronage from political or administrative bosses or is prepared to work on lower emoluments without complaint.

Within these overall policy considerations, variations are found from college to college. In the D.A.V. College founded in 1919, a large number of teachers (about 35%) are on the rolls whose appointment predates the emergence of the "pure" type of management. With more than five thousand students and three hundred approved teachers, the college is a paying concern. As reported earlier, the savings from this college and the technical knowhow have been used in the past to export capital and technology to newer colonies.

The indulgency pattern

I could not come across any case of employment below the U.G.C. grades in this college. In fact the college management has followed the "indulgency pattern" in dealing with its teachers at D.A.V., in case they do not oppose the boss and his policies. At least ten teachers could be spotted who could absent themselves from teaching duties for months together and might not be seen on the campus at all even in normal times.

Since 1969 the Sansthan had been recruiting teachers in contravention of the University Act. On a promise by the Management that in future they would abide by the University rules, the university agreed to approve these irregular appointments from 14 February 1973, in case they fulfilled the minimum qualification. There were 93 such cases from the D.A.V. College. Each teacher from the college was asked by the college administration to send in his individual application. The number of applications received was one short of the total number of cases. On inquiry it was found that this person had taken up an appointment elsewhere, being uncertain of his future in this college; but the salary was being accredited to his account in the bank for the past three months, after he had taken up the new job.

The "indulgency pattern" is further exemplified by the fact that a large number of teachers of the college (estimates vary from 70% to 90%) spend their time and energy in other part-time remunerative activities, like private coaching classes, writing examination aids, farming, running publishing concerns, printing presses, managing properties or other business concerns, etc., without any hinderance by the Management, though this work is in contravention of the rules. The Executive Council of Kanpur University had condemned these practices through a strongly worded resolution, drawn the attention to the Statute 10.02 (3A) and called upon the managements to abide by this Statute to the very letter and within a fortnight send the names of teachers who in some way may be contravening the Statute.[6] The managements just slept over it.

Off and on some teachers, including very senior ones, are provided by the management itself, over and above the regular work in the college, part-time teaching assignments, which carry Rs. 50 to Rs. 200 p.m. as allowance. Two teachers had secured better teaching jobs elsewhere but they preferred to remain in this college because of the advantage of the "indulgency pattern."

That the "indulgency pattern" works to defraud the students of the college of their legitimately earned chance of benefiting from the teachers' guidance is another matter to which we shall revert later. But suffice it to say that it disorients the teacher away from teaching in the college.

More than a hundred teachers have been appointed in the college since the establishment of Kanpur University. An overwhelming majority (90%) consists of those who passed out from the same college and had shown no dangerous signs of questioning anything that "the boss", the Principal or the Head of the Department may have done. Those who intend to seek a teacher's job in the college practise anticipatory socialization projecting their timidity towards all proximate and ultimate authorities, otherwise they are screened out. Ten cases could be traced owing their appointments to their kinship with the elders who were already accepted on the staff. Two could be traced owing their appointment to friendship with a son of "the boss", and another to a promise of a disruptive role in the Teachers' Association. Three teachers owed their appointment to the services they had rendered to "the boss" in the Legislative Council elections, while they were serving in other Intermediate Colleges.

This should not convey the idea that all these teachers were under-qualified. The point being emphasized is that the process of their recruitment and the extra-qualifications sought in the candidates instills in them a desire to play court at the "*Bangla*" (residence of "the boss") rather than devote to study and research or teaching or organizing co-curricular activities of students.

One of the teachers is a brother of a Muslim M.L.A. of the city; another, a temporary appointee, happened to be recommended by the wife of a former Chief Minister. The importance of the appointment of people who can help pull political strings lies not only in collecting votes, which all teachers with a few notable exceptions do, but in softening the arms of law. One more teacher was appointed because he was the manager of a Higher Secondary School and as such was influential in that area.

When the teachers know that the source of their strength lies outside teaching, they strive to augment that rather than teaching.

The carrot and the stick

It is not only through recruitment of fresh teachers that the role of teachers is moulded. The successive transfers of two Principals to Dehradun and back in the 1956-58 period, and the appointment of three other senior professors as Principals in other Sansthan-managed colleges helped in orienting even older teachers towards exhibiting serviceability and subservience to the "boss" rather than excellence in teaching.

One of them, after rising to become the Principal of a Sansthan College, showed symptoms of independence and was immediately cut to size by the "boss". His services were terminated, illegally. He went to court, and there was endless litigation. When finally he won in the High Court, as reported by him, the Management went in for appeal to the Supreme Court. In the meanwhile he reached superannuation age and preferred a compromise, whereby the Management paid him a year's salary instead of for five due to him and helped him to be eligible for State Government pension by reinstating him.

In another case of Reader-Headship in Zoology, the college management encouraged three rival claimants to go in for a time-consuming and costly luxury of a civil suit, after appointing an under-qualified person. One of the contestants complained to me that he has already spent a half year's earnings on the suit. Surely contesting court cases and occupying academic chairs under court injunctions retracts quite a little from the aura built around a teacher's role. But do the managements care?

Extraneous factors enter each recruitment

In the Dayanand Girls College the recruitment policy of the Management, within the broad framework of the interests of the Sansthan Kuladhipati, takes a different form. The college, as an outgrowth of D.A.V. College, had some teachers who were initially recruited for D.A.V. College. For the session 1973-74 the college had fiftyfive teachers on the list of the University and about six more.

The appointment of the teachers of this college could be analytically divided into four classes, though in practice the categories overlap. In the first would fall a small coterie including the Principal who were said to have been provided jobs to repay some old debts, two of them having already been helped to become principals in other colleges. The second category consists of those who, either through ignorance or through weakness were agreeable to work without demanding full salary, dearness allowance, provident fund, interim relief, etc. Almost everybody falls in this class. The third would include the wives and daughters of "trusted" teachers in employment of the Sansthan, of teachers of other colleges who could be pressurized to gather support in the Council elections or to control University Teachers' Association to keep it in good humour and of helpful officials. A full two-thirds of the teachers come under this category. Then we have those youngsters who are helpful in elections, are prepared to work under worst humiliation, are engaged part-time or on a temporary basis or have passed out from this very college. The college has quite a few competent teachers but no teacher could say without fear of contradiction that extraneous factors had not at all entered in her recruitment.

The alienation of the present occupants of the teacher's position in the college from the teacher's role could not be better illustrated than by the nerve-racking struggle that they had been pushed into, since their petition to the Kuladhipati (dated 18 August, 1973) when salaries were not paid to them, for the months of May, June and July, 1973.

They wrote in their 8 September, 1973, petition: "This (non-payment of salaries) has caused great inconvenience to us because we are being thereby deprived of means of our livelihood and incomes urgently needed to run our domestic budget, especially in times of rising prices, increased cost of living and scarcity of essential commodities. More agonizing is the fact that this situation of postponement of regular payment of salaries for several months and then making a partial payment thereof and that too only after being repeatedly requested by the teachers, is not new but a chronic feature of the salary disbursement policy of our college. We may have often been forced to silently bear the hardship in the name of 'loyalty' to the College authorities." The teachers threatened to forward their case to Kanpur Teachers' Association (KUTA) and mentioned in their petition a news item in the *National Herald* of 5 September, 1973, stating that the U.P. Government had decided to shortly take over the management of all "sick" or mismanaged degree colleges in the state and that their college had been ailing for a long time.

Threats, cajolery and appeals to traditions of loyalty having failed, Virendra Swarup, the Kuladhipati, signed an agreement on 14 November, 1973, admitting (i) Rs. 57,877.10 as salary arrears from March 1972 which were promised to be paid on or about 15 November, 1973, (ii) the arrears of interim relief from March 1972 amounting to Rs. 14,310.62 to be cleared latest by 15 January, 1974, (iii) D.A. arrears from July 1971 to July 1972 to be cleared by 31 January, 1974, amounting to Rs. 70,000 and (iv) Provident Fund arrears of

Rs. 78,438 from March 1971 may be deposited by the management not later than the end of the current session. The agreement also provided that the P.F. contributions from the salaries from November 1973 onwards would be regularly deposited and salaries in the revised scales (1966 U.G.C. scales) would be available to all teachers from November 1973 onwards.

It may be added here that elections to the U.P. Legislative Council were due in April 1974 and the General Secretary of the KUTA had declared his intention to contest Virendra Swarup. Therefore, Virendra Swarup could not afford a conflict with his own entourage. After making part payment according to the agreement the management advanced a number of excuses for gaining time.[7]

It is revealing that the memorandum dated 8 September, 1973, was signed by the teachers alround the margin on the left and the bottom. What role can such terror-striken persons play? When interviewed, three of the teachers expressed grave apprehensions for the safety of their person and possibilities of scandal stories being concocted. Much of their fears were imaginary, but the climate could scarcely be conducive to their discharging duties as teachers.

Another illustrative case is that of a lady lecturer in Geography whose appointment on 9 September, 1968, was duly approved by the University.[8] She was paid a salary of Rs. 140 p.m. only in 1968-69 gradually rising to Rs. 265 p.m. in August 1972 whereas the mandatory pay scale was Rs. 300 with an annual increment of Rs. 25. Even after the whole issue came out in the open with the teacher's petition and memorandum of 18 August and 8 September, she was paid only Rs. 350 p.m. in November 1973 whereas she should have been paid Rs. 400. Thus the total money that was due to her because of illegal underpayment by the management inclusive of salary, dearness allowances and interim relief amounted to Rs. 11,794 by the end of November 1973.[9] Her representation to the Management, the University and the KUTA brought the abortive attempt to prove her original appointment itself as a "clerical error", thus threatening other confirmed teachers as well, that any appointment could be cancelled with retrospective effect.

On the other hand, some other favoured teachers, who initially were appointed on a part-time basis but worked full-time, were shown as proper full-time appointments in the returns sent to the University, thus gifting them the benefit of University seniority in return for not preferring their claims to full mandatory scales or other allowances, the grants for which were procured from the Government.

All this defrauding and keeping the teachers in a precarious condition, by threats of rewriting history by the Management, is made possible because the proceedings of the Managing Committee meetings, financial returns sent to the State Government and the statement about teachers and students to the University and the bank accounts in the U.P. Cooperative Bank housed in D.A.V. College are allowed to remain secret documents. Neither the teachers concerned, nor the accredited KUTA office-bearers are allowed access to the information and the Government and the University authorities do not compare the returns to punish the discrepancies.

Even the signed agreement by Virendra Swarup admitting huge underpayment did not result in any adverse governmental action.

Those who were promoted Readers were also not paid in full and were under a constant threat of "derecognition" if they asserted their rights. The whole development erupted in a complete breakdown of teaching in the Sansthan Colleges in April 1975, which would be discussed later.

Recruitment of Riffraff : The Case of D.B.S. College

In D.B.S. College, the recruitment policy of the management, to start with, was to have the entire staff including the principal on a part-time basis. The Principal received an allowance of Rs. 100 p.m. and the teachers Rs. 50 p.m. while drawing their full salary and allowances from D.A.V. College, as if they were working full time in D.A.V. College where they had their substantive appointment. One of the teachers was a close relative of the head clerk of D.A.V. College and the suggestion to appoint him as a lecturer in D.A.V. College was unacceptable to the Head of the Sociology Department on account of his poor academic record and total lack of teaching experience or aptitude. Another teacher, prior to his appointment at D.B.S. College, was teaching classes VI and VIII in the untrained teacher's scale for Junior High School. He had earlier worked for Virendra Swarup in the Council elections. Both these teachers, engaged on the paltry salary of Rs. 50 p.m. as they were not teachers at D.A.V. College, are now Reader-Heads of the Post-Graduate Departments at the College.

As the Principal of the college was a former teacher of Virendra Swarup at D.A.V. College and for long was "managing" the games fund of the college for the boss and was an important Brahmin canvasser in the elections, who could do anything for the boss, he was given a greater say than any other Sansthan Principal in recruitment of the staff in the new college by the boss.

B.Ed. and M.Sc. admissions were made in the college after charging huge donations, without issue of any receipt and passed on by the principal to the boss, which fact would be dealt with later. This fact also made the principal of the college more important than any other principal under the Sansthan management. Later appointments to the teaching staff were made either by the Principal with the concurrence of the boss or by transfer from D.A.V. College, when science classes were opened.

The qualifications sought for in the candidates were that they should not mind working in less than the mandatory grades, help in collecting illegal fees and donations from the students, help or at least not obstruct open defiance of University stipulations about minimum attendance to be put in by students, for being sent up for University examinations and even help favoured examinees in the examination rooms and afterwards to secure good marks and not to complain about substandard laboratories and empty libraries.

If some persons have managed to be recruited as teachers in the college who value academic work, study, teaching and at least a semblance of research, it is so in spite of the deliberate discouragement of such tendencies at the recruitment level.

A former president of the Students' Union of D.A.V. College, who is at present a secretary of the Kanpur City

Congress Committee, got recruited as a teacher here. He does not participate in the general "loot" that has been going on in the name of the college but comes to the college once in a fortnight. Incidentally in the Congress Committee he is said to help bolster up the boss's interests. Another teacher happened to be the son of a Congress corporator, in-charge of allotting housing sites on behalf of the Municipal Corporation. The college could help him get the top position in the post-graduate examinations, though as an under-graduate (first year) he could just manage to get through, after repeated attempts. He could manage the later laurels while running a well-known liquor bar of the city. Both father and son are indispensable in the Council election work. It would be no exaggeration to say that the teacher attends more regularly and dutifully at "the bungalow" than at the college. Many people depend upon his helpful nature to get things done by the boss.

Some of the teachers who were collecting illegal donations, to be passed on to the boss through the Principal are alleged to have started taking their slice of the cake. So also the principal could not be expected to be honest with dishonest money.

Indulgency pattern breaks down

The goings-on in the name of the college are well documented in the Pande Commission Report as a result of an inquiry under the Kanpur University Act.

Some teachers were recruited and pampered by the Principal and the management for their skill in squeezing out donations, mastery in managing the unmanageable toughs amongst students, craft in curbing protest and stratagem to outsmart University officers' vigilance against unfair means in examinations. Soon they became conscious of their importance and began to appreciate their value much beyond the one willingly paid by the Principal or the boss. As a consequence the tripod fell apart, each leg declaring the other two not only superfluous but on whom the law must fall with a heavy hand.

As long as the "indulgency pattern" was acceptable to the management, the Principal and the teachers, everything was "peaceful". "The teachers did not teach, the students did not study and the management had no education to manage", in the words of a former Principal of D.A.V. College. Here was a degree-spinning factory with Government aid, guardians' money and people's good faith turned into private gain for those who had appropriated the status of Management, Principal and Teachers.

When, back in 1970, the teachers of the college represented to the principal and the management that they should be paid the full grade according to the U.G.C. stipulation of 1966, the Principal is credited with the classic remark: "What makes you demand full grade; I have never demanded of you full teaching?" A queer appearance of exchange-equivalence principle governing educational enterprise! The breakdown of the "indulgency pattern" resulted in the institution of an inquiry into the complaints of widespread financial irregularities and other serious lapses and irregularities regarding examinations, etc., under Section 40 of the U.P. State Universities Act 1973.[10]

An interesting case of "indulgency" is that of a Reader in Hindi whose recruitment basis has already been referred to. He had some quarrel with the Principal and was thrashed in a public restaurant by some student toughs, egged on by another teacher. Since then he did not go to the college for more than three years, till the Pande Commission was appointed but continued to draw his salary. He used to mark his attendance at the "bungalow" and worked in the Council elections.

As the recruitment of teachers in this College was partly influenced by the Principal, he was able to recruit half a dozen trusted lieutenants amongst the 102 approved teachers of the college. The Heads of the Departments of Sociology, English, Education and Chemistry and a lecturer in Economics along with the office incharge formed a coterie which ran the college as a pocket borough of the Principal within the educational empire, presided over by the Kuladhipati. Except the office incharge the rest of them happened to be Brahmins, the Chemistry head being a close relative of the Principal. This closeness to the Principal and differential monetary benefits derived by different teachers and the existence of independent channels to the boss created conditions of jealousy and divided authority.

The lecturer in Economics, who played for high stakes, building a minor Mafia-like organization, used "unity-struggle-unity" tactics in the relationship with the Principal.

Another important actor in the drama was a lecturer in Political Science who was a Ph. D. student with the Principal. He was recruited because he gave a deceptive appearance of docility and they needed at least one person, in the Post-graduate Department, who would engage classes. He took his teaching role rather religiously and was able to band together from three to eightythree teachers at different times to clean the Augustean stable, so that it may have some resemblance of a college.

Even in this college whatever the recruitment policy and reinforcing demands from degree seekers, there are teachers for whom pecuniary allurements are infirm incentives and threats of bodily injury not menacing enough. The fact reasserts the impossibility of absolute conformism.

The evidence given by a number of teachers before the Pande Commission to expose the fraudulent practices of the management, the Principal, their own colleagues and their "student" accomplices shows that money does not talk with equal ease to every body.

At the end of the 1973-74 session the Principal and many teachers, who were suspended by the management on charges of gross irregularities in the University examinations of 1973, were reinstated allegedly to bolster up the chances of Virendra Swarup in the Legislative Council elections. The Principal and the management jointly sensed that the local KUTA unit was proving a thorn in their side. On the eve of the elections of this unit in 1974-75 session eleven temporary teachers were given appointment to sieze control of the organisation. The attempt did not succeed as a majority of the new entrants, in secret ballot, betrayed the trust placed in them, again providing that wrong recruitment policy does not always succeed in its objectives. The overall effect on the recruits however, is to get bogged up in issues other than teaching.

Teachers compelled to resort to street pressures

We have already seen that the Sansthan Management had refused to abide by the University rules about the recruitment of teachers in the affiliated colleges from 1969. However, through a compromise with the Vice-Chancellor on intervention by the KUTA and the Management's assurance that in future it would appoint teachers according to Schedule VI(1) of the University Act, 92 teachers of D.A.V. College, 33 of D.B.S. College and 26 of Dayanand College (Girls) were approved by the University on 1 March, 1973. But they lost their seniority in comparison with teachers of other colleges, as proper appointment letters, confirmation letters and agreement forms are not in the tradition of this Management.[11] When the teachers of D.A.V., D.G. and D.B.S. Colleges started making representations about huge defaults in salary, provident fund, dearness allowance, interim relief and irrefutable defalcation charges were made, the Managements on March, 1975, in violation of the University Act, Chapter V, 3F(2)(c) and 35(2) issued orders of termination of service, confirmation deferment, withdrawal of confirmation, extension of probation, demotion from Readership to Lecturership in all conceivable combinations, covering fifteen teachers of D.A.V. College and five of D.C. College. The policy sent all the Kanpur College teachers on strike and *dharna* from 1 to 13 April, 1975. Consequently the management had not only to withdraw the illegal punitive orders but also agree to a number of other demands of the teachers.

Thus the policy of the Management clearly added an agitator's role to that of a teacher, just at the fag-end of the academic session. On 9 April, 1975, however, the management got some 25 blacklegs and some other outsiders assembled at "the bungalow" who had marched to the College campus to break the strike, so that the management's right to hire and fire at will may be established. Three teachers, who participated in this procession, wept profusely at the college gate, as their humiliation on the street in front of the college hostel gate by students and their losing face with other teachers had proved emotionally shattering.

Sanathan Dharma Mahamandal College

The V.S.S.D. College is governed by S.D. Mahamandal but the actual governance is done by Sri Narendrajit Singh, President of the Mahamandal and Secretary of the College Managing Committee, who inherited these positions from his father, late Rai Bahadur Vikramajit Singh. Narendrajit Singh is the Chief of the Rashtriya Swayam Sewak Sangh (R.S.S.) in U.P. who went to jail in connection with the Gandhi murder arrests of R.S.S. men in 1948 and was again detained after the declaration of Emergency on 26 June, 1975.

R.S.S. bias disturbs harmony

The recruitment policy in this college has a number of elements, the most important being the R.S.S. bias. The college had in all one hundred and thirtyeight teachers on its rolls. In the case of 34 teachers, undeniable R.S.S. links could be traced. Most of them continue to lead the R.S.S. on the campus, in daily parades, in organising Akhil Bharatiya Vidyarthi Parishad (R.S.S. Student Front) and holding offices in the City Jan Sangh or contesting for the Legislative Assembly as Sangh candidates. As the college has a large number of non-R.S.S. and even anti-R.S.S. students and teachers, the R.S.S. and anti-R.S.S. division has created high tension and even a break-down in the teacher-taught, teacher-teacher and teacher-administration relationhip.

One teacher had gone out as Pracharak of the R.S.S. to Bulandshahr for one year but was given seniority and increment, which was formally protested against by another teacher but to no avail. In the 1973-74 session nine teachers went out to attend the R.S.S. camp at Bithoor without proper leave from the Principal.

As the recruitment and promotion policy is perceived to be pro-R.S.S., teachers take partisan attitudes in student politics and, as a consequence, cannot command universal respect of students. At the end of the 1973-74 session there was a shooting incident in a students function on the campus. It is said that the alleged culprit, a non-R.S.S. former student, was whisked away, with anti-R.S.S. teachers conniving at it. In the union elections on 1 December, 1974, anti-R.S.S. students objected to the association of an R.S.S. teacher as an election officer, which was over-ruled. When the Bharatiya Lok Dal candidate won the elections, the victory procession hurled abuses at the hostel residence of the Warden, the impugned R.S.S. teacher. Incidentally all the Wardens in the college hostels are R.S.S. men. A violent clash took place in which lathi blows, brickbatting and even a gun shot were reported. The college had to be kept closed by the District authorities for four days to avoid further violence.

A lady lecturer informed me that on an earlier occasion anti-R.S.S. boys had made a false allegation against her, that she helped R.S.S. candidates in elections as she formerly belonged to the A.B.V.P. Her own appointment was made in preference to another R.S.S. candidate and a son of the Principal, because she had passed in the first division from the same college, had good academic career and was adjudged better by the Head of the Department; though her father had gone to jail for an R.S.S. cause and was known to Narendrajit Singh. She said that many Sangh-minded teachers openly help the R.S.S. in elections.

In the 1973-74 session when a non-R.S.S. faction organised a strike, the Head of the Commerce Department prevented Commerce students from joining it and was involved in an ugly incident with the strikers. When the R.S.S.-controlled Union organized a strike he was with the strike. It may be a mere apprehension in some cases or trumped up charges in others or by and large a genuine field view, the preference shown to R.S.S. men in recruitment creates a psychological barrier in the minds of students against accepting teachers as acting without fear or favour.

A teacher in charge of the time-table of his Department said that an R.S.S. lecturer told him that he would ignore any class assigned to him at 7.30 a.m. as he had to attend an R.S.S. parade at that time. Eventually the time-table had to be recast to accommodate the R.S.S. parade. The time-table incharge realized that some teachers were more equal and extra academic considerations could not be brushed aside.

Obsequious flattery further disorients teachers' role

Another policy orientation in recruitment that disorients the teachers away from teaching is the weakness of the management boss for obsequious flattery. At least 31 teachers stood out with this behavioural trait, that cut across politico-ideological divisions. The group includes family priests, poor people helped by Narendrajit Singh's family charity, teachers with a political ambition in the Sangh and weak and corrput teachers who substitute sycophancy for work in the college and also those who do not want to be outrun by others in the careerist rat race. This has created a climate of competitive coquetry.

All is not lost

Another factor, in determining recruitment, was found to be the relationship with Managing Committee members, principal or other teachers. Only nine teachers came in this category. Moreover, none of them was considered substandard by prevailing norms.

A large number of teachers have been recruited on the basis of meritorious academic record and also because they were former students of the college. The existence of the R.S.S. and the sycophancy bias in selection has not always resulted in recruitment of academically poor staff. Moreover some have gained entry through these dubious channels but have tried to find satisfaction in living up to their own conception of a teacher's role. Others have moved in and out of these categories for other reasons. I did not come across a single case where a teacher was harassed if he did not positively oppose Narendrajit Singh personally or R.S.S. activities in the college or was not too outspoken.

A weak 'indulgency pattern' and other mitigating factors

I was told that in the selection of teachers in the newly opened Education Department, the Secretary wanted a specific candidate to be appointed. The experts put this candidate low in the order. So more candidates than the required number got appointed, but those who were high on merit did not get excluded. The Principal and the Secretary had exchanged some letters in this connection.

When the former Head of the Commerce Department retired the seniormost teacher was bypassed and one, who is Secretary of the City Jan Sangh and devotes quite some time to running a private factory, chosen.

The "indulgency pattern" in this college is nothing as compared to Dayanand College but the fact that ten of the eleven teachers of Commerce other than the head were engaged in private coaching in the period when I was gathering information there speaks for itself.

Serious charges and counter-charges were made by Chemistry teachers supporting the head and opposing him, about engaging in private tuition, helping examinees in practicals to secure high marks for money and receiving commission for purchases for the Department. R.S.S. supporters are involved on both sides and the management has taken no notice in spite of the realization that the factional fight for private gains is spoiling the image of the Department.

Educational resources converted to Sangh's advantage

Because of the recruitment and promotion policy of the management, teachers are encouraged to carry on R.S.S. propaganda through the official platform of the college. The college has an institution of prayer at 10.15 a.m. every day. On 21 December, 1974, a lecturer in Commerce informed the prayer gathering that in Banda District the Christians were converting Hindus, so to counteract this evil influence a camp was scheduled to be held there in the winter vacation and he appealed to the students to join this camp. Two teachers complained that they were reprimanded for not attending these prayer meetings, even though they were present in the college. Such exhortations in favour of R.S.S. ideology are quite common.

This management has tried to convert control over educational resources to politico-ideological resources for the R.S.S. but personal profit is ostensibly not sought and no scandals of Dayanand Sansthan type were heard. In fact, the stories of Narendrajit Singh going out of his way to help some needy students out of his own pocket and inquiring about the performance of students in the examinations and preaching of ethical conduct discourages dereliction of duty on the part of average teachers.

There has been no open defiance of the University Act regarding appointment of teachers. The President of the

Managing Committee, the Principal and the Head of the Department are given a say in the selection though Narendrajit Singh has generally the decisive voice.

Christ Church College Society: Distinctive subculture of liberal Christian values

As we have seen in Chapter 5, the Managing Committee of the college has by and large followed the liberal British tradition and has not constructed any narrow meaning on Christian values. These are understood as "more a questioning faith than an orthodoxy". The rules and regulations as they stand have ensured a perpetual and absolute control by the Bishop of the Diocese. The Bishop has exhibited no signs of deriving monetary or political advantage out of the college. In practice the principle of vesting all power and responsibility in the office of the Principal has generally kept out extraneous considerations of the management from disorienting the teacher's role. The college by all standards is comparatively the best college in the city, recognized as such even by rival colleges. It has attracted the best students and teachers. Disaffection resulting in the breakdown of teaching is the minimum, specially breakdowns due to endogenous causes. But here too it cannot be said that private control of the recruitment process has had no adverse effect on the teachers' role.

The traditional subculture under strain—reassertion

The object of the Society stated as "to maintain sufficient staff to preserve and strengthen the Christian character and purpose of the Institution" can take on a narrowly constructed meaning verging on communal discrimination in appointment and promotion of the staff, to the detriment of educational norms. As and when the Principal feels cornered, he is likely to take recourse to this diversionary tactics.

When the present Principal was appointed in 1958, he had to function in a difficult psychological milieu. He was a Malayalee not knowing a word of Hindi, younger in age than a large number of teachers, four of them Christians, and the teachers had earlier passed a resolution in support of the Vice-Principal being promoted Principal. To strengthen his base and to break his real or imaginary isolation and under malicious advice he embarked upon a policy of discriminatory recruitment and idiosyncratic allocation of remunerative work.

He followed "a policy of favouritism based on sycophancy and even communal preference. The irrefutable fact remained that since his writ began to run in the college, he made seven appointments in the teaching staff where members of a particular community were appointed either without the minimum requisite qualification or against better qualified and experienced candidates from communities other than this. . . He (has) appointed four new incharges of Games and Sports and all of them may be by a queer stroke of luck belonging to the same community".

This policy did not specially endear the Principal to the teachers including some Christians. This resulted in his isolation which led him to take some other false steps like denying Janmashtami holiday, refusing casual leave, demanding explanations in rude terms and disbanding the Staff Club and the Staff Council. An ugly incident also took place between the Christian Warden of the college hostel and a brother of another teacher. The Principal took no action and the matter went to a criminal court.

Finally the Principal took the ill-advised and illegal step of dismissing the President and the Secretary of the Teachers' Association on 30 May, 1966, on flimsy and trumped up charges. Though the college was closed for the summer vacation, the action aroused spontaneous mass protest among former students and teachers of the college. As the dismissal order had contravened Statute 29A(8) and 30(4) and (11) as given in the Agra University Hand Book 1965-66, Ch. XVIII, the Vice-Chancellor of Agra University as well as the Vice-Chancellor of Kanpur University which was just formed disapproved of the management's action. In view of the illegality and the storm of protest that the action aroused, the Principal had to take back these two teachers.[12]

From then onwards the Principal rectified his erroneous policy and with the good offices of some well-wishers of the college, amicable relations were established between the management as represented by the Principal and the teachers.

Nomenclature itself disorients

Still it cannot be said that the sectarian nature of the college management, even when no narrow view is taken by the management, does not disorient the teachers. Whenever a non-Christian teacher feels rightly or wrongly let down he has to struggle hard to keep off a feeling of communal discriminations. In some cases even a wrong done by a teacher may go unpenalised, for fear of the action being dubbed as communal vendetta. A teacher was apprehended while helping a student in the University examination. As the senior teacher who caught this unfair practice was a Christian, the whole episode got buried under the communal debris. The management developed cold feet and the accused teacher dragged the other teacher into the civil court for defamation.

'Minority' status evoked against academic democratization

As the college is a minority college the management has tried to seek exemption under Article 30(1) of the Constitution of India.

The Principal of the college wrote a letter to the Registrar of the University dated 27 June 1969, conveying the resolution of the college Governing Body that Statute 6.05 of the First Statutes of Kanpur University were not applicable in the case of appointment of the staff of Christ Church College. This was rejected by the University[13] but the college continued to make appointments without the University experts.

When in February 1973 these appointments (17 in all) were approved they were done so from the date of their appointment as appointment letters, agreement forms and confirmations were all done properly, unlike in the Sansthan colleges.

Earlier the State Government had also thought Christ Church College or such other minority colleges should not be given exemption from the regulatory Statutes of the University, which were aimed at ensuring appointment of good and able teachers to maintain teaching standards.[14] Now the U.P. Universities Act 1973 has given some concession to the minority colleges to select experts out of a panel suggested by the management itself and approved by the Vice-Chancellor.

The college is making efforts to become an autonomous college but some non-Christian members of the staff have developed apprehensions that the management might become more arbitrary in selecting teachers and their services might become insecure. In point of fact, the U.G.C. conditions for granting an "autonomous" status make such apprehensions unfounded. But the private control of management is hardly assuring to the teachers.

'Self-fulfilling' norm has positive consequences

The differential effect of the recruitment policy of the colleges can be observed by the following incident.

Students of D.A.V. College and D.B.S. College had walked out in one paper each in the University Examination of 1974. The University decided to declare their results awarding average marks, secured by a candidate in the papers he took, for the skipped paper. Some teachers in Christ Church College staff meeting protesting against this unacademic decision of the University suggested that they should approach the Vice-Chancellor for higher marks to their college students in cases where the total went down because of the papers they took and did not walk out like the Dayanand students. The suggestion for securing an unacademic concession for college students was scorned upon by the overwhelming majority of teachers. The teachers went en masse to the University office some 10 kilometres away to protest against the unacademic decision *only*. Gresham's Law is not infallible, after all.

The prevalence in this college of malpractices, of taking up private tuitions, and even of students whom a teacher may be examining as internal examiner in practicals or of almost full-time involvement in business or writing guide-books or examination help books and neglect of work with students inside and outside the class room, indicates that the disorientation of the teachers' role is not effected by the management policy alone. On the other hand the discouragement of certain practices by the management does create a healthy climate and keeps down the disorientation.

For example, it was learnt in the 1974-75 session that a certain teacher agreed to give private tuition to a group of students who were likely to be examined by him. Senior teachers intervened and the teacher, accepting the good advice, returned the advance fee that was earlier collected. In another incident reported by a senior teacher a dealer in scientific material complained to him against another junior-appearing teacher in a different department that he had turned down the dealer's offer of commission if material was purchased from him. The dealer was shocked at the "innocence" of the young teacher.

This does not mean that unfair practices do not exist in this college. They are there but the quantum is low and one who indulges in them if found out would lose face. The teachers here are as much affected by the college climate as by the larger milieu of pecuniary culture and cut-throat competition.

Halim Muslim College : Weak communal character

Sixty per cent of the teaching staff of the college is Muslim. Senior non-Muslim teachers were unanimously of the view that there is no discrimination in appointment or promotion. One of them had even acted as principal when the permanent principal was on long leave to the U.S.A.

Three Muslim teachers when asked to explain the ways in which the Muslim character of the college could be discerned answered: (1) name of the college, (ii) the founder and (iii) the founding body, i.e. the Muslim Association. Theology classes are not held even on a voluntary basis. About the non-Muslim appointment they said that competent Muslims were not available and moreover seeing the present times (Zamane ki Hawa) such distinctions are difficult to maintain.

Low academic profile: Dialectics of 'indulgency'

As has already been mentioned in the preceding Chapter, the college was raised from the Intermediate College and its principal became the first principal of the degree college. He did not possess the minimum qualifications to be so appointed but got exemption from the University rules because the then Vice-Chancellor of Agra University believed in "indulgency pattern". Moreover, this principal was helpful to Virendra Swarup in the Council elections and the exemption could be considered an obligation returned. Other teachers that the principal recruited from among the Intermediate staff were equally underqualified. One teacher was foisted by the Vice-

Chancellor and as affiliation of the college and exemption of the underqualified staff depended upon him, it was considered no great concession.

The management started with the assumption that the college would get only second-rate students even from among the Muslims as good students and affluent parents prefer Christ Church College.

One teacher, who runs a number of private schools for children as a business proposition, does a lot of insurance work and has some other business interests as well, informed me that he got in because he knew some important members of the management and he could teach both Sociology and Commerce.

Thus the picture that emerges is that the management from the very beginning never aimed at excellence in recruiting teachers.

The only exception was the appointment of the new Principal after the retirement of Principal Rizvi. The half-educated management thought that appointing a U.S-educated Ph.D. and giving him a free hand would be a good service they could do. But the gentleman had only one foot in India. Of the three and a half years of his principalship, for full twenty-four months he was in the U.S.A. and for all practical purposes the college functioned without a Principal.

The management confined to hide merchants could recruit only second-rate teachers to teach second-rate students. The lack-lustre character of the college was built in the recruitment policy of the management.

Guru Nanak Girls College : Another case of low academic profile

Like the Halim Muslim College, this institution is also an outgrowth of an Intermediate College. The Principal and seven more teachers were promoted from the Intermediate Section. She too was not qualified for appointment in a degree college and exemption had to be sought.[15] Other teachers were recruited on the recommendation of some member of the management, the Principal and later, when the University rules were amended, even of the experts. Neither the teachers nor the Managing Committee members interviewed disagreed with this description of the recruitment practice. Again, like the Halim College, the management, the Principal and the teachers thought that they would get only second-rate students as the better ones would join the Municipal Corporation College for girls which was not very far.

Teachers' role and Sikh rituals : Muted misgivings

Though it is a Sikh college, in the recruitment policy there has never been a bias in favour of Sikhs. The Principal herself is a non-Sikh and so also other 13 teachers. Only three teachers happen to be Sikhs. Baba Mohan Singh is supreme in the Managing Committee. His presence and the Sikh make-up of the Managing Committee has brought in the institution of daily prayer after the fourth period. Sikh devotional songs (Shabad) are sung in chrous at this time, led by the Music Teacher (a non-Sikh). All teachers have to attend this. Sikh festivals are also celebrated. The staff is made to participate in Sikh religious processions. Students were also taken to attend the All India Sikh Educational Conference held in the city in 1974. Most teachers did not object to this but some grumbling has already started. In any case these activities are extraneous to the teacher's role. The new manager has already expressed his regret that the Sikh character of the college has not been maintained in the appointment of the principal and the teachers.

Some teachers complained that the ad hoc pay of Rs. 100 per month was paid irregularly, after three to six months of delay. One teacher's services were terminated, but her salary was being distributed between two lecturers' one getting Rs. 200 and the other Rs. 300 per month. This unauthorised utilization leaves room to suspect other mal-practices. It is also observed that large amounts were kept in hand. The manager of the college changed the bank which used to handle college accounts earlier. The college banking work given to the new bank gave a leverage to the manager to ask for favours from the bank for his private business interests.

These facts indicate that the struggle for control of college resources may lead to similar difficulties as have erupted in Dayanand Sansthan Colleges. But the presence of Baba Mohan Singh, a non-profit-seeking religious man, was reported t have served as a positive check.

Dull and drab management

Teachers regularly engage the assigned classes and this to some extent compensates for their low academic attainments. There are no noticeable negative features but so also is there nothing in which one could take a legitimate pride. In this college like the Halim Muslim College, the promotion of an underqualified Principal from the Inter College and non-academic businessmen controlling the Managing Committee have resulted in fixing a dull and drab role for the teachers.

REFERENCES

1. V.V. John, *Misadventures in Higher Education.* New Delhi : Young Asia Publications, 1973, p. 124.
2. Amrik Singh, "Examination : The Strategy of Change" in Amrik Singh and Philip G. Altbach (eds.), *The Higher Learning in India.* Delhi: Vikas, 1974, pp. 291 and 293; Amrik Singh, "The Fallacy of Mo(e)re Funds" in *Profiles fo Indian Education.* Bombay : Parle Tilak Vidyalaya, pp. 69-96; and Amrik Singh, "Higher Education in the Seventies", *Quest*, September-October, 1971.
3. Edward Shils, "The Academic Profession in India", in Singh and Altbach, 1974, op. cit., pp. 202-236.
4. Singh and Altbach, op. cit., pp. xiv.
5. Appendix "ख" attached with स०शि०(११)-६०४५/१३-१४(७)/७४ dated 28 December, 1974; issued by the Commissioner and Secretary, Education Department, U.P.
6. Kanpur University Executive Council Minutes, 26 May 1970, Item No. 11, hereafter cited as KUEC.
7. Refer to KUTA files : Virendra Swarup's letters to the Principal dated 21 January, 1974, to the Secretary, Staff Association, dated 31 January, 1974 and an other dated 6 February, 1974, and the strike resolution of the D.G. College teachers dated 21 March, 1974.
8. Reference Kanpur University letter No. 7745/56 dated 23 June, 1969.
9. Reference KUTA files : Santosh Rohtagi's representation of 6 December, 1973.
10. See, शिक्षा (ii) अनुभाग शास्नोदश संख्या 4052/15-3(25)/73 dated 26 June, 1974.
11. See, Kanpur University Executive Council Minutes 1971, p. 6, item 33 and follow up records of the Affiliation Section.
12. See, *The National Tribune*, Vol. 1, No. 10, 18 June, 1966, Kanpur.
13. See, Kanpur University Executive Council Minutes, 1969, p. 190, item 15, and pp. 192-203.
14. See, Kanpur University Executive Council Minutes, 1971, p. 401, item No. 3 and pp. 409-10 for the Government letter.
15. See, Kanpur University Executive Council Minutes, 1967, pp. 37-38, for the meeting of 16 September, 1967.

CHAPTER SEVEN

TEACHER'S ROLE : ITS INDIRECT CONDITIONING BY COLLEGE MANAGEMENTS

Control of the University

THE EDUCATIONAL entrepreneurs' popularly known as managers of private colleges, manage to get into the highest control points of the University and pursue their objectives of controlling education from this centre as well.

As employers of teachers, in the colleges under their control, they mould the teacher's role and are able to produce some senior teachers who can work as fronts for the real controllers, especially after their retirement. Attaching themselves to the apron-strings of the managers can put them formally in the prestigeous positions of presidents or some other innocuous offices in managing committees, where they can pocket some extra money and provide a pleasing facade to the ulterior objectives of private managers.

In the first adhoc Executive Council of Kanpur University, consisting of 17 members excluding the Vice-Chancellor and the Registrar, we could spot out Sarva Sri Virendra Swarup, Narendrajit Singh, Jawaharlal Rohatgi, Inder Singh and R. C. Gupta as pure managers, whose only connection with education was managerial control and Sarva Sri Satguru Saran Awasthi, K.P. Bhatnagar and P.L. Srivastava as retired teachers, who were playing the subsidiary role in the private management of college education. Thus the private managerial Interests had a controlling representation on the Executive Council (E.C.), if we add Ninan Abraham and S.S. Sharma, the two Principals who were acting as "Managers on the Campus" for Christ Church and V.S.S.D. Colleges. Their domination in the successive Executive Councils of Kanpur University continues, with the Vice-Chancellor, the Registrar and other members changing; but Dayanand Sansthan and Sanatan Dharam Mandal bosses continue to adorn all the Councils along with their satellites.

Subversion of teacher's role

As we look into the minutes of Executive Council we find an incessant effort on the part of management interests to circumvent the U.G.C. and University stipulations of the minimum educational and experience qualifications required for appointment as teachers of various categories in the affiliated colleges.[1]

Principal Mathur writes: "Today one can be awarded the highest degree by the University, if one is capable of purchasing it. This change in the values of life has lessened the importance of learning."[2] The statement has a grain of truth, but if we give up the only available criterion—the University degrees—could we tell a college principal from a ring-master or college teachers from circus clowns without a prolonged evaluation by competent experts in each case?

One should make a distinction between an honoris causa degree, as the one awarded to the half-educated millowner Sir Padampat Singhania in 1969 by Kanpur University on a proposal by Sri Virendra Swarup or the one given to the management boss Sri Virendra Swarup himself by Agra University the following year and the degree, earned after years of research.[3] If the managements seek appointment of teachers without degree or third-class degrees or without adequate teaching experience or the right to select persons with inferior qualifications when better qualified persons are available they undermine teacher's position.

There are cases of teachers without Master's degree in the subject, third divisioners and without adequate teaching experience. Then there is an effort to reserve the right of the management to appoint teachers with lesser qualifications than those of other applicants without any hinderance from the Vice-Chancellor. In fact the decision of the University to appoint experts on the Selection Committees of teachers in different colleges and appoint University representatives on the Managing Committees is resisted at three stages. First at the stage of the enactment of the Statutes and Ordinances, secondly, by managers' representatives sitting on the Executive

Council sub-committees to suggest panels, delaying its consideration by the Council and giving long legalistic notes of dissent, thirdly, defying the University orders and again using the position on the Council to effect a compromise. It is interesting to observe how Virendra Swarup switches or confounds his position of Chairman of the U.P. Legislative Council, Member, Executive Council of the University, and Chief of the Dayanand Shiksha Sansthan as exhibited in E.C. proceedings.[4]

Management's student policy and its consequences for teachers

The policy that a management follows towards admission of students, control and manipulation of their activities and organisations for academic or non-academic purposes contributes towards moulding of teacher-taught relationship round curricular teaching, as well as teacher-student relationship round co-curricular and extra curricular activities. Thus it has consequences for the making of teacher's role.

We have already seen that the recruitment of second-rate students in Halim Muslim College and Guru Nanak Girls' College has reinforced the humble status and moderate expectations from the teachers of these colleges. These teachers were recruited from among the Intermediate College teachers, led by the principals of the same calibre and from among recommendees of the Managing Committee members or University officials. Both the expectations and the performance here are only marginally different from those of unrecognised and unaided private coaching institutes preparing candidates for public examinations, with considerably secure jobs.

The case of D.A.V., D.G. and D.B.S. Colleges on the one hand and V.S.S.D. College on the other reveal important similarities as well as some dissimilarities. These cases, as contrasted with the Christ Church College, would show the differential consequences of student policy of the managements for teachers' role-position.

Prolonged student strikes

On 9 March, 1974, a lecturer in Hindi at D.A.V. College informed me that he was able to meet his classes only on 22 days in the whole session as the College had remained closed for long periods for various reasons, the most common and recurrent occurrence for the past four years in a row being student strikes. Now on verification, it was found that this lecturer's performance was not atypical. The range appeared to be between 20 and 26 days, depending on the time-table arrangements. Nobody seems to have lost his night's sleep over this fact. The "teachers" continued to be paid their salary as usual, the management got the Government grant and the students' fee without any cut but with only a drastically reduced expenditure on day-to-day consumption and 309 post-graduate and 295 undergraduate students drew Central Government, State Government, Kanpur University and other scholarships and another 551 got non-recurring assistance from the same sources for the session 1973-74. To cap it all the University examination results were not particularly discouraging.[5] The teachers' worry began late in the day when they found that the student policy of the management and recurrent trouble at the college had led to an exceptional fall in Dayanand College's enrolment in Science especially Physics sections, which might mean teachers' retrenchment.[6]

Equivocal attitude of management towards activists

A slight cause for discomfort was the release of the College Union President from jail in early March 1974 and his declared intention to take the University examination as a regular candidate. The principal was not prepared to give him a false certificate that he had put in the requisite attendance, as he had abused the principal publicly in the choicest North Indian style.[7] The via media suggested by the college authorities, that the student take the examination as a private candidate, was not acceptable to the president, as that would legally debar him from being a regular student even in the following session. Trouble was apprehended on the campus after the Holi holidays and elections to the Legislative Council, where Virendra Swarup was a candidate from Kanpur-Jhansi Graduates Constituency, were due at April end.

On 24 March, 1974, the *National Herald* of Lucknow and other newspapers reported the assassination of Mahesh Pratap Singh, D.A.V. College Union Secretary in 1971-72, a close friend of the present president, and a student of D.A.V.College of Law. The murder was alleged to have been committed by Vidyarthi Parishad rivals of the Sanyukta Socialist (S.Y.S.) leadership of the Union. The *National Herald* reported on 25 March : "In an emotionally charged atmosphere in the D.A.V. College hostel where their leader's body was brought, angry students shouted slogans like "Khoon ka Badla Khoon" and "Chandu-Mathur Conspiracy Nahin Chalegi" at the D.A.V. College itself. Some students stoned the chemistry laboratory building after their plea for postponement of today's practical examinations was not initially accepted. The tension however eased when the S.S.P. persuaded the D.A.V. College authorities to postpone the examinations." Now this murder and the events that followed in quick succession brought into bold relief the policy of the management and its consequences for the teachers' role performance.

The murder took place on the 23rd night. On the 24th students shouted slogans and extensively painted the city walls with the allegation that behind this murder stands the conspiracy of Virendra Swarup, nick-named Chandu, and Principal Mathur. On the 28th a brutal assault was made on Principal Mathur "by some of the students of the college and anti-social elements in the city, in the College Campus".[8] On the 31st a largely attended public meeting was held at the Parade Grounds, Raj Narain Singh, the Socialist leader, alleged the involvement of Mathur and his employer, Chandu, in the murder. On 2 April, D.A.V. College Union presented a memorandum to Virendra Swarup detailing the Principal's involvement in the murder and Virendra Swarup, according to the Union Press note, asked the students to peacefully wait "till April 5". On 5 April the Board of Management, according to the *National Herald* report on the 6th, suspended the Principal in fulfilment of the students' demand. On 24 April, Virendra Swarup denied this Press report and asserted that "Mathur on his own request had been relieved from the post of Principal till the investigations in the murder of Mahesh Pratap Singh, ex-Secretary of the Student Union were over".[9] The Principal continues to draw his salary and is not likely to be back in his seat till his superannuation after about a year and a half.

Management's policies led to the murder

A senior teacher of the college said that he did not suspect direct involvement of Chandu or Mathur in the murder but their policies have led to this incident. The facts were corroborated by other sources also. In 1967 when the Sanyukta Vidhayak Dal came to power in U.P., no union was formed as the State Government had made unions voluntary. A Notification for the withdrawal of union fee was issued but the college could save some ten thousand rupees. The following year an R.S.S. boy backed by the management got elected and though a strike was organized after the elections, he signed Rs. 20,000 of the Union for some construction in the hostel. He along with some other R.S.S. boys was allowed to grab a room in the hostel, without being a formal resident student, informally by the Principal.[10]

The pampered Union President accompanied by some other toughs raided the Resident Warden's quarters in the hostel, insulted the aged teacher and his family members. Teachers of the college protested against this indiscipline and as the Principal and the Management wanted the matter hushed up, the teachers struck work demanding definite disciplinary measures against the miscreants. A show-cause notice was issued after seven days but no further action was taken.

In 1969 again the elections could not take place and the "return" of the collected fee resulted in huge savings for the Management. In 1970 the election to the Union and its functioning was involved in a court case encouraged by the Principal and the Union could not function. In 1971 Mahesh Pratap Singh, an S.Y.S. candidate, got elected against the wishes of the authorities. The Principal asked him to transfer Rs. 32,000 from the surplus Union Funds for some construction in the college in keeping with the "tradition". The Union leader did not comply and in spite of mobilization of some other Executive Committee members by the Principal for the proposal, it could not be made effective without the General Body's approval. The group mobilized against Mahesh Pratap Singh included the R.S.S. boys, who are now suspects in his murder. The following year Mahesh was refused admission, though he had passed in good second division.

The 1972-73 session saw strikes, three to four months in

jail for a number of Mahesh supporters and other students got elected to the Union but it could not function. In 1973-74 an S.Y.S. candidate again got elected in spite of the establishment's efforts to get him defeated. He stormed into the counting office with his supporters to ensure that no rigging takes place. The teacher incharge of counting confirmed in an interview that he was approached by the establishment to see Rana, the S.Y.S. candidate, defeated; a number of teachers were also involved on behalf of the establishment. After the election, Principal Mathur got distributed through the College machinery a pamphlet alleging misuse of Rs. 6000 by the President. In the budget session this pamphlet by the Principal and a pistol shot by the R.S.S. distractors successfully collaborated to prevent the passage of the budget. No action was taken against those who fired the shot, as the result was welcome to the establishment.

Teachers as policemen, strike breakers, agent provocateurs etc.

The policy of the Management is to maximize earnings by admitting as many students as they can. In 1972-73 there were 6,939 students in the college. In the process a large number of toughs, politically-oriented professional students and other discipline problems got enrolled. The management expects the Principal and teachers to control them by bribes, putting one faction against another, favouring one and terrorizing another and making scandalous compromises with shady characters.

Teachers in charge of Union Games and Sports and such other activities have to have policemen's strong-arm tactics, cunning of professional strike-breakers or be agent provocateurs and adroit political agents of the Management.

Prolonged strikes by students only help the Management in saving a lot of money from the Boys Fund account. An effort to control unions is also made to harness student power to the Management's private interests, either of profit making or personal political ends or political party of the boss. Thus in consequence of the Management's policy the colleges get closed for long periods, teachers get involved in student politics and sometimes they use control of the Union to play the game of personal advancement even against the Management. This role of teachers has nothing to do with the studies, teaching or research for which the colleges are ostensibly organized.

D.B.S. college exemplifies dubious roles

The case of D.B.S. College further exemplifies the same distortion. The Management policy of using the college for collecting huge capitation fees, gobbling up library fees, magazine fees, games fees, etc., and not returning the caution money, was well known to the teachers, some of whom were partners in the game or at least had to serve as collection agents. Candidates were sent up for University examination irrespective of attendance at the college and even cheating was organized at the examinations for monetary considerations.

Some teachers thought it good business to organize the racket independent of the Management and the Principal. If the establishment gave them an acceptable share, well and good, otherwise they would do it on their own. The teacher in charge of the Students Union soon became an equivalent of an independent warlord. Those who were collecting illegal donations and capitation fees on behalf of the Management began to decide their own share.

I was informed by a teacher of another Sansthan college that teachers of B. Ed. and L.T. in Sansthan Colleges had entered into an agreement with Virendra Swarup that each teacher could get one candidate admitted in these classes without capitation fee and most of them made money under this agreement. The justification is, "why not make hay while the sun shines" or as they say in Hindi, Behti Ganga Men Hath Dholo. A group of ex-students also joined in the racket.

If a teacher organizes or participates in a Mafia-type organization and it continues for some time, the Management's student policy is directly responsible for it, firstly, by providing a model, secondly, by using the teacher in illegal activities and, thirdly, by failure to expose the whole racket and punish the teacher, as they have many skeletons in the cupboard.[11]

The Pande Commission Report, with its limited terms of reference, makes a harrowing reading of incredible acts of omission and commission. (The page numbers given in parentheses are according to the typed copy sent to the Vice-Chancellor). In 1972-74 the bank accounts of D.B.S.

College were operated by Virendra Swarup and his wife Dhara Rani unauthorizedly (p. 3). The Principal and the Head Clerk indulged in improper money transactions (p.7). It was established that Government grants were utilised for other purposes, for which the Principal was held responsible (p. 9). More money was withdrawn from the Treasury than sanctioned. Money was withdrawn from the bank in the name of the Principal. But Rs. 432 less was deposited with the Treasury, for which the Principal is held responsible (pp. 10-11). If the fact had not been brought to light during the inquiry Rs. 2,563 would have been misappropriated for good. On sample checking the Commission came to the conclusion that some withdrawals of caution money shown to have been made were definitely false (p.12). In 1971-74 Rs.30 per B. Ed. student and Rs.10 from every other student was collected annually as donation for three consecutive years amounting to Rs.11,754 out of which Rs. 10,770 were claimed to have been returned to the students. Out of this Rs. 2,305 seem to have been misappropriated for which the Principal is held responsible. In fact the entire collection was illegal (p.14). Rs. 7,608.25 were fraudulently paid to bogus firms (p. 18). In contravention of the U. P. Universities Act, 1973, "Admission Form" fee of Rs. 20 per B. Ed. student, Rs. 10 per M.Sc. student and further Rs. 30 and Rs. 10 respectively from these students were admitted to have been collected for the commercial shops built by the college (p. 23). A teacher gave evidence that a capitation fee of Rs. 1,500 each from third divisioners and Rs. 1000 each from second divisioners was collected for admission to M. Sc. for which open accounts were not kept. He himself collected this fee up to 1972 and gave the collected amount to the Principal under a code account. The Principal operated the account of these donations. Similarly money was collected from Biology students but no accounts were kept (p. 24). Thousands of rupees are saved from the Magazine fee by spending a small sum for four years and no magazine was brought out for the remaining ten years of the college's existence (p.25). A Reader in History was paid Rs. 400 p.m. but Rs. 700 p.m. was shown in the returns filed. As Games Incharge, this teacher made payments of Rs. 19,485.36 to one restaurant and Rs, 7,400 to another. The Management boss

Chandu's son was married the same year but it could not be established that these restaurant bills were really on the marriage account (p. 30). Examinees found using unfair means were not reported to the University and some apprehended answer-books were substituted by new answer-books. All the detected material used as unfair means was not sent to the University to protect the culprits and possibly to get them the benefit of the doubt. Seating arrangements in actuality were different from the plan submitted to the University and some candidates were sent up for University examinations, even though they were not students of the college. Students admitted as late as 16 December, 1972, were sent up. Money collected from the teachers and students for the National Defence Fund was not sent to the Government and Rs. 21,000 was withdrawn by Virendra Swarup,[12] and another Rs. 6,830.36 transferred to the Budhijiwi Congress Samiti.

The Commission also found that the Union bank account was opened in the personal name of a teacher and there was no way to check if misappropriation had not taken place. There was a theft in the Botany laboratory for which a teacher was suspended for some time but this cognizable offence was not reported to the police. A former president of the Union alleged that there was firing on the Campus by students and some lecturer on 11 September, 1974, to break the students' strike. The fact of firing was admitted by the Principal before the Commission.

Nobody could say that all these criminal and quasi-criminal activities, indulged in by the Principal or other teachers named in the Pande Commission, could be contributing to study, teaching or research. They are the natural outcome of the Management policy.

Teachers' role dependent on management policy

As compared to this high crime sensationalism the report by a young Dayanand Girls' College lecturer would look dull and drab but all the same exemplary of the dependent nature of the teacher's role. The students had been complaining that the Chemistry laboratory and the lecture theatre did not have exhausts or other fans. She had herself forwarded twentyfive M. Sc. students' complaints to the Head and pleaded the case that teaching and study were adversely affected under these conditions.

I was shown a letter written by a lecturer to the Head in January 1975 that the practicals were not being held as the laboratory lacked equipment and so students were suffering. Another letter acknowledged that the ignition tubes were bought for the college laboratory in January only to provide some practice to students.

The Principal, instead of spending some money to help the cause of students, wanted the lecturers to file a general complaint against the Head. When they did not oblige she made the Head write against them and gave them the sack notice, which had to be withdrawn due to mass agitation by the K.U.T.A.

Though the practicals started only in January, when the college reopened on 15 April after a fortnight's strike, the Head gave in writing the order that the laboratories would be closed for the session just after six days. The teachers requested the Head and the Principal to let the laboratories function for some more days but the authorities would not listen, as that would mean use of some more chemicals. Thus interests of a private management discourage teachers' healthy efforts to teach which are themselves a rare phenomenon. The Chemistry laboratory case is exemplary and if we try to be exhaustive the picture would not materially alter.

Pro-R.S.S. policy of management disrupts teachers' role

The student policy of the V.S.D. College Management like their teacher recruitment policy is to practise partiality in favour of the Rashtriya Swayam Sevak Sangh.

The Management does not seem to be interested in making money, charging any illegal fees or asking for donations and also shows some interest in improving teaching. The last objective however conflicts with the partisan political stance of the Management boss.

Those teachers who do not agree with the R.S.S. ideology are harassed by the Sangh boys and many a time ridiculed by the Management in front of the students. In the session 1973-74 the student union led by the R.S.S. presented a 28-point Demand Charter to the Principal and the Management, which included partisan charges of corruption against some teachers. The Secretary of the Managing Committee called a joint meeting of students' representatives and teachers to discuss the Charter. When a senior non-R.S.S. teacher objected to a discussion about teachers in the students' presence, the students did not insist. The Management's Secretary suggested that other demands may be discussed. One of the demands was that the attendance of teachers at the prayers may be made compulsory. A leftist teacher objected to this under the "conscience clause" of the Indian Constitution. The lawyer in the Secretary could not answer this. But he quipped that the college could have Dussehra and Diwali holidays if the "secular conscience" of this teacher permits it. The ridicule is not always so subtle.

R.S.S. students report on teachers to the boss directly. Once objection was taken to the indent of Communist Manifesto by Marx and Engles by the Sociology Head for the college library, as R.S.S. boys had protested. The Management had to be satisfied that it was one of the prescribed readings in the University syllabus. I have already referred to the suspicions of non-R.S.S. students about the impartiality and honesty of R.S.S. supporters among the teachers.

This policy of the Management divides the staff and the students vertically in warring camps, mostly indulging in cold war but sometimes in the breaking of skulls also, as for example the post-election ugly demonstration in front of an R.S.S.-ite Hostel Warden that developed into widespread violence culminating in a shooting incident in March 1974.

The effort to control the Union for the R.S.S. by the Management leads to similar results as in D.A.V. Some teachers in order to be in the good books of the Management begin to dabble in student politics with disastrous consequences for their teacher-role.

The Sangh-oriented student policy of the V.S.S.D. Management resulted in not only a disorientation of the teachers' role, a breakdown of all functioning of educational institutions of Kanpur but a knockout of all normal life in the city on 24 January, 1975, and the following week.

The *National Herald* reported on 25 January, 1975 : "A 48-

hour curfew has been clamped by the District Magistrate in the riot torn areas of Nawabganj, following a clash between members of a Moharrum procession and students of a college. Two persons, including students, were killed and over two dozens, including eight police personnel, were injured in the clash . . . . According to the District Magistrate there was a scuffle between some students and the processionists over eve-teasing. Unofficial reports, however, said the procession was stoned by persons inside the hostel while it was passing the hostel . . . ."

The genesis of this tragedy is that the College Management had been laying claim to some of the land used for the burial of Tazias. Recently too there was trouble here on the Moharrum day. The Principal of the college shielded his students; the teachers of the college demanded Rs. 50,000 as compensation to the students. The Jan Sangh leader in the Legislative Council visited the spot and condemned the administration and the city Jan Sangh demanded change in the route of the Taziadars to avoid recurrence of the trouble.[13]

Thus we see that due to the student policy of the Management, the teachers of the college, even in a case of such vulgar expression of the R.S.S. ideology, either support the communal approach or are silenced. If the Karbala ground is shifted the College Management might gain some land. When trouble could be apprehended due to past history what precautions did the Sanghist Wardens of the College Hostels take? Well, for the Management to ask these questions is to put themselves in the dock.

These facts lend little support to Shah's observation : "But since private managements particularly in bigger towns are generally not involved in politics they leave a considerable degree of freedom to their employees as long as such freedom is not exercised to the detriment of the institutions real or imagined interests. . .teachers have better opportunities for experiment and innovation.[14]

Christ Church College: Education the supreme aim

The Christ Church College Management in contrast has no private profit motive, personal or sectional politics and the minority whose interests it might like to champion is small in number in the city and among the students. The Management seems to have only educational considerations in dealing with students. Back in the 1963-64 session the Union President had misbehaved in a college function. The teachers wanted a firm action against the miscreants but the Principal under wrong advice developed cold feet. The Principal funked and got isolated from the staff and the staff in turn got alienated from its own responsibilities in the college. The process culminated in the traumatic events of the summer of 1966 already described earlier. But correct lessons seem to have been derived from past mistakes precisely because the Management had no private interests to defend.

In contrast with the above discussed cases, in the 1973-74 session when the leaders of the Christ Church College Students' Union tried to be clever and raise a communal bogey by demanding installation of the image of Goddess Saraswati, the symbol of learning, in the college premises, the mischief was nipped in the bud.[15] The teachers stood as one man with the Principal and when some Union officials indulged in vandalism it was swiftly and firmly controlled as the trouble-makers were isolated and expelled.

There has been no case of inferior candidates being admitted into much-sought-after courses and the formal rule of the Principal's right to admit some students outside the merit list has remained a paper rule. This student policy of the Management throws a damper on the teachers who might otherwise like to use their influence to help their friends or relations.

During my field investigation a number of cases of unfair help given by some teachers to the wards of other teachers especially in the science faculty were discovered. Some of them have been suspected of indulging in the unfair practice for money also. But due to the Management's students policy being just the opposite, the attempt is sabterranean and as such does not find a congenial climate for growth. But it would be idle to believe that the teachers' practices in other colleges and even Universities do not find an echo in some hearts in this college. There is no quarantine that works and that is why the distinction between private and public remains blurred. One can always "prove" the ills of private gain in public undertakings and vice versa. But the distinction is worth while for analytical purposes.

The person to get the First Class First in Law in the 1974 examination was an Income Tax Deputy Commissioner. He was a "regular" student of Dayanand College of Law. No student of the class could be contacted who had ever seen him attending any class. It is said that the examination process was made "soft" for him by the college teachers at the boss's behest. Such a thing is unthinkable at Christ Church College. For the purchase of games material, the dealers, the student players and staff incharges are brought together and the best and the lowest cost material offered in competition is bought. Thus the incharges may be deprived of a free blazer or a racket or the student captains some personal advantages, but the students' money is spent economically on students' sports. This is made possible because the Management does not want to save money or promote one group against another and, as a consequence, the teachers do not get bogged up in petty squabbles.

Outstanding sportsman and successful teacher resocialized by 'pure' management into crime suspects

It is well know in the educational circles of Kanpur that Principal Pandey of D.B.S. College, who gets so frequently an adverse judgement of the Commission of Inquiry referred to earlier, received his early socialization into making business ethics the basis of educational enterprise, while managing the Games and Sports of D.A.V. College. Similarly, Seth, a partner in the "Killer Glucose" firm[16] which made the headlines in the national dailies and consumed quite some time of the Indian Parliament in April 1974 was an under-study of Pandey in sports management of D. A. V. College. Seth took independent charge of this onerous duty after Pandey got promoted as Principal. Both Pandey and Seth were good students and outstanding sportsmen of their days. Earlier students of Pandey say that he was a conscious and successful teacher in the classroom and Seth represented the State in more than one game. The student policy of the "pure" management was the undoing of both and many more. In contrast Christ Church College has produced their own but very different from Seth and Pandey as Teachers Incharge of Games and Sports for decades.

Subversion of the examination system

In the U.G.C. suggested code of conduct for teachers, the academic duties recounted are preparation of lectures, demonstration, guidance, invigilation and assessment and failure to perform them or gross partiality in assessment are specifically mentioned as lapses constituting improper conduct.[17] Thus invigilation and impartial evaluation in examination is recognized as legitimate part of teachers' duty.

Most writers on education and leaders of public opinion have rightly criticized the educational system as being examination-centred, rather than teaching-centred and a large number of evils of the prevailing system may be logically and empirically traced to this lopsidedness. A good evaluation system cannot create good teaching as good teaching, on its own, does not assure good evaluation system. Amrik Singh may be right in pointing out that to regard examinations as the central issue in education is to start with wrong premises and therefore arrive at wrong conclusions.[18] But who can deny that corruption of the examination system is the surest and quickest way to damage the system beyond repair from within? Its improvement may not be very effective but its depravation certainly is. Jobs including those of teachers are obtainable on the basis of examination results. So also admission to higher classes and to various courses of education and training are decided on evaluation of the candidates. If this process is corrupted, nothing remains of education, unless one imagines that corrupt examination practices are necessarily confined to some levels. We wish to examine here the role of the Management in contributing to the making of the reality of the teacher in this arena.

Special examination: A slur on the system

A committee to consider the reports of the Inspectors who had conducted surprise inspections at the various examination centres formed by the Vice-Chancellor, under authorization of the Executive Council of Kanpur University, met on 7 June, 1970. The committee "was convinced that the sanctity of University examinations was vitiated in the aforesaid four examination centres and was of the view that unless severe action was taken against those centres it would be impossible for the University to conduct fair examinations. The reported mass copying and mob rule in the examination halls on account of the fact that the invigilators and superintendents were not doing their duty, outsiders had free entry into the examination halls, armed miscreants were outside, signatures of many candidates at some centres were not taken on the examination forms to ensure that no impersonation was done, written material, books and guess papers were freely coming to the examination halls from outside, there was no proper seating arrangement had to be viewed seriously and it must be curbed forthwith to restore faith in the examinations." The Executive Council, on June 12, fully endorsed the recommendations made and the findings arrived at by the aforesaid committee. It decided to cancel these examinations and hold Special Examinations at Kanpur. Against the overwhelming evidence with the University of total vitiation of the examinations at these centres, no straightforward action was possible in defence of these criminal corrupt practices. Behind-the-scene efforts were made, agitation by the involved examinees was mounted and political strings were pulled.

All in all, two colleges under Virendra Swarup's management, one of them D.B.S. College, two from Fategarh district, one from Sitapur and Feroze Gandhi College, Rai Bareli, were involved. On 7 July the issue was again brought up in the Executive Council to let the Special Examinations be held in the old centres. As this would have nullified the very purpose of a fresh examination, the Council turned it down but with a note of dissent by political heavyweight, related to one who was the Secretary of the D.A.V. College Society for decades. On 12 July the Council considered another resolution to cancel the Special Examination and instead declare the results, after screening and scrutiny of the answer books. After the discussion, when vote was taken only one vote was cast in favour of the move; but it was not considered sufficient to close the issue and after a short adjournment three more votes switched over to support the resolution but still six votes were cast against it. The attendance in the meeting was fourteen. The mover of this not-yet-successful resolution was a member of the U.P. Legislative Council. When these attempts proved abortive at the Excutive Council level, Sri Virendra Swarup, Sri Raja Ram Shastri, both M.L.Cs. and Smt. Sushila Rohatgi, M.P., all members of the E.C., met the Chancellor on 13 July and "pleaded for a reconsideration of the University decision on the ground that the contemplated re-examination would cause great inconvenience to such a large number of examinees". I was told that Yashpal Kapoor, associated with the Rae Bareli College Management and Election Agent of Indira Gandhi, had also interceded with the Governor. The V.C. was called to Lucknow, the Chancellor through a D.O. to the V.C. dated 14 July, 1970 suggested: "The screeners should scrutinize and look for positive evidence of the use of unfair means *in individual script*. Candidates against whom no such evidence is available should be given a clean bill and their results announced" (emphasis added—N.S.). He also wrote, "Pending decision of the E.C., since we are racing against time, I am taking the liberty to announce through the Press and radio that the special examination be treated as cancelled." Through another D.O. of the same date it was written that this may be read as "and as such the E.C. may consider cancelling it and announcing the decision through the Press and radio." Legal niceties apart, those who debased the University examination system got a shot in the arm. The V.C. resigned and so did the Dean, Faculty of Science. The E.C. met on 15 July, 1970, under the chairmanship of Virendra Swarup, resolved that the said examination be not held and assuring the V.C. of "implicit faith and confidence in him" and urged him to withdraw his resignation. The next meeting of the E.C. held on 26 July adopted a long resolution moved by Virendra Swarup "maintaining that the decision taken by it earlier to hold the special examination was fully justified" and at the same time provided justification for the reversal of the decision.[19] Private control trampled the examination system under its feet and bemoaned the tragedy. Here private management certainly did not work for autonomy of the educational system.

The special examination was cancelled and a large number of students were awarded University degrees in spite of the examination being unanimously declared a farce by the E.C., thanks to the presence of Virendra Swarup, the educational entrepreneur and a political actor of no mean order.

Should the teacher apprehend the practice of unfair means in examinations and risk public humiliation and a maimed body and be at peace with his own conscience and the U.G.C. code or should he please his employer, help in the business growth of his privately managed college and secure a little monetary advantage to himself in the bargain? The context of the control mechanism in colleges, universities and society at large is heavily loaded in favour of the latter course.

When the questions of continuation of the examination centres at the four colleges and D.B.S. College where the University examinations were polluted in 1970 and of giving further remunerative work to teachers of these colleges was raised in the E.C. meeting of 25 January, 1971. A sub-committee with Virendra Swarup on it was formed.[20] That Virendra Swarup was head of the management running D.B.S. College and the Unnao College did not debar him. The E.C. in its 4 March meeting decided to continue the centre at D.S.N. College, Unnao, with an amiable retired official of the Education Department as senior superintendent. From D.B.S. College, the regular students and ex-students were transferred to appear at D A.V. College and P.P.N. College. The management of P.P.N. College was headed by Virendra Swarup's elder brother and the private candidates of D.B.S., D.A.V. and P.P.N. Colleges were to appear from the D.B.S. College centre. The debarred centres were allowed to continue with additional superintendents.[21] Why this shuttling was confined within the Chandu (Virendra Swarup) empire is anybody's guess.

Recidivism

D.S.N. College, Unnao, and D.B.S. College, Kanpur, can be labelled as "history sheeters" in many respects. Back in July 1967 the E.C. had to consider the question of continuation of the examination centre on the basis of the report of the outside superintendent about malpractices in the last year's examination.[22] The centre was decided to be transferred to Government Inter College with an outside superintendent and invigilators due to the extremely adverse report given by the Examination Superintendent on 16 September. But this was not to be and on 22 December the E.C. considered a letter of Virendra Swarup, "Member, E.C. and Vice-Chairman, U.P. Legislative Council" and decided to continue the centre on an assurance by Virendra Swarup, "President, Managing Committee", that the employees of the college and the Managing Committee would cooperate with the outside superintendent nominated by the University.

Both D.B.S. College and D.S.N. College again occupied the attention of the E.C. on 10 June, 1973, for the outrage of the sanctity of examinations. The Registrar's Memo on the Conduct of Examination for 1973 reported that at the D.S.N. College Centre an attempt was made to terrorize the Flying Squad members by firing and twice their taxi was chased by outside elements. The information about Inspectors Squads was given in a well-planned way to the examinees by exploding crackers and other means. A crowd of outside elements to help the examinees was always present at the centre. At D.B.S. College reports were received that answer-books written outside were smuggled daily into the examination hall before the end of the examination time. Mobile Inspectors Squads were sent to this Centre every day, sometimes twice or thrice a day. Here too the information about the arrival of these squads was given by outsiders and invigilators in a regular way. Special arrangements were made to seal the post-graduate and B. Ed. examination answer-books by University officials as reports about change of answer-books in some cases before despatch of the parcel to the University had been received.[23] On the recommendation of the Examination Committee the D.S.N. College Centre and a few other Centres were cancelled, the Central Superintendent, invigilators and all teachers were debarred from all remunerative work for three years in the first instance. A similar decision about D.B.S. College was for five years in the first instance and the management was urged to take disciplinary action against teachers who actively assisted in the use of unfair means. We have discussed the D.B.S. College case earlier also. The attempt of the Management to have an eyewash of an inquiry by a retired judge was not accepted and finally Pande Commission was appointed by the Government on the E.C.'s request.[24]

These cancelled Centres were again restored and almost all of the teachers who were earlier debarred were exonerated and sympathetic consideration of other requests was promised by the V.C. in the E.C. meeting on 23 June, 1974 which began with the V.C.'s motion congratulating Virendra Swarup for his unanimous election as Chairman, U.P. Vidhan Parishad, for another 6 years. This detailed description of the making of a delinquent role for teachers in relation to examination establishes beyond reasonable doubt that forces other than teachers and students also help in this making.

"Indulgency pattern" continued, examination subverted, honest examiners demoralized

Some disjointed but significant facts need to be recounted. The committee to appoint paper-setters for 1968 included both Virendra Swarup and Narendrajit Singh[25] and I learnt that similar arrangements continued for other years. The report of the meeting on 31 March, 1971, of the Board of Studies of Sociology is self-explanatory. Para 3 reads : "In the absence of knowledge of the University's proceedings and conditions of appointment of examiners as practised from time to time, the Board expressed its inability to prepare the panel of examiners. The Board was critical of academically unsound practices resorted to in the matter of appointment of examiners." The private-management-infested University continued in its old grooves, the stinker notwithstanding.

Whenever students in the colleges of strong private managements find themselves in trouble because of the strictness of examination, they can depend on the management bosses to get the rules softened for them. Naturally those who stand for academic consideration and impartiality are proved to be living in an unreal world. For example, in the 1970 examinations, M.Sc. (Final) Zoology III Paper and M.Sc. (Previous) Statistics II Paper examinees had walked out at

D.A.V. College, Kanpur. In view of the fact that the students expressed regret at the walk-out the Committee (appointed by the E.C.) unanimously resolved that a special examination be arranged by the University.[26] The Committee had also observed after interviewing the examinees and teachers : "On the whole it was gathered that the teachers used to give lectures only on some important topics and the whole course was never covered. The laboratory and the library are ill-equipped, so much so that the students could hardly be benefited by their being in the college. Most of the prescribed practicals were not undertaken by the teachers."[27] In another case two senior teachers of Zoology and Chemistry in D.A.V. College were found guilty of malpractices in the Pre-medical Examinations and debarred by the University for five years from examination work but the Management at its end took no action.[28] The impunged conditions of work, style of work and the "teachers" continue with impunity thanks to their loyalty to the Management.

A candidate with six others approached an invigilator to give facility to cheat or be shot. On reporting another invigilator was deputed to reinforce invigilation. When the examination was on, some pages of a book were found with the candidate. The candidate refused to give any statement and ran away. The Principal reported the case as a "hardened case", "needing a deterrent punishment". The examinee was allowed to appear again as an ex-student the following year[29]. When the Principal wrote to the V.C. that it would not be possible for him to conduct the examination at the Centre when such candidates are treated leniently the E.C. decided to postpone discussion of the letter. The case was of D.A.V. College and Virendra Swarup attended the E.C. meeting. Is it any wonder that only a very insignificant part of unfair means is apprehended and still a smaller number reported?

Abortive efforts at central evaluation

In order to curb malpractices in evaluation the Examination Improvement Committee, on the advice of academically minded teachers and on the insistence of the Kanpur University Teachers Association and their pledged support, decided to have Central Evaluation of Scripts of Postgraduate and Faculty of Education examinations after duly coding them. It also decided that no exception should be allowed.[30]

In the next meeting of the E.C. Virendra Swarup, who was not on the Examination Improvement Committee, opposed the proposal on legal grounds and said that it required prior sanction of the State Government and the Academic Council. In spite of his note of dissent he was put on the Committee to implement the scheme to prepare the plan and for general supervision with his consent. Later the Chancellor's order quashing the Central Evaluation Scheme vide letter No. 616/GS of 29 March, 1972, was procured through representation. When the E.C. wanted to send a representation to the Chancellor, Virendra Swarup gave recurrent notes of dissent[31]. The next Chancellor replied to the E.C. resolution of 2 July, 1972, on 7 April, 1973, stating that the 29 March, 1972, order by the former Chancellor being quasi-judicial it cannot be reviewed[32]. Thus comes to an end another valient effort to root out corruption in examination by striking one's head against the solid rock of private interests. Direct opposition, subversion and delay by agreeing to serve on implementation committee on failure of direct opposition and use of influence, with higher authorities—all tactics are used.

Many a time the University decided to cancel some papers but allot marks to candidates in these papers on the basis of the average marks.[33] In some cases the E.C. decided to condone shortage of attendance for being sent up for University examination if the student withdrew court cases against the University.[34] Such horse trading on the part of those who control education cannot but demoralize those teachers who maintain honest records.

Auxiliary force to entice the teacher

Apart from the Management as employers or as a dominant part of the University bodies, there are quite a few agencies who entice the teacher away from the path of virtue, only a few escape capitulation to capitalistic coaxing. We have already referred to "scientific" suppliers and fictitious firms who make Managers, Principals and other staff incharges rich in the process of making a little money for themselves. Now, we meet an institution that has spread throughout the educational centres in India to fill a functional gap. I mean the "Guess Papers." They serve multitudes of examinees who have neither the will nor the capacity nor time to study but are in a dire need of a degree. They also cover the gaps in the teaching of such "teachers" who may have been recruited from the above category or those who can do and therefore remain busy in better business.

When I started my field work in Kanpur in March 1974, General Elections to the State Legislative Assembly were just over. I counted on the walls of one of the busiest 8-kilometre-long route the space occupied by "educational" and other advertisements discounting the space paid for by publicity concerns. To my surprise almost one-third of such writings on the walls advertised coaching institutes and "guess" papers slightly out-flanking political publicity. Out of these "educational" advertisements half were about "guess papers". All the book-stalls were fully covered by these same advertisements. It was in November that I chanced to meet the King of "guess papers" in the staff room of a college under study. He has almost the monopoly over "guess papers" especially for the University examinations, with a tolerated competition from four other local publishers and three from outside Kanpur. He claimed that the only loss that he ever suffered was when he took the wooly-headed decision to publish some Ph.D. theses. Now he has earned enormous profits by his "guess papers". Students have learnt through experience, according to him, that reading standard prescribed texts does not pay in the examinations. Teachers have learnt the lesson that to write textbooks requires great effort and then they will not sell. His modus operandi is to approach first those who are paper setters, then other people in the department in the same college who can know or guess correctly. If he is to be believed, he got a determined non-cooperation only in two cases. In one case a senior teacher of Chemistry in D.A.V. College set a paper for B.Sc. taking special care to avoid all "guess" questions. Though the paper was perfectly within the syllabus only 9 per cent passed and the University first increased the allotted marks to increase the pass percentage to 18 but even this was not satisfactory and therefore more concessions had to be made. He termed the teacher "callous" towards the students. In another case a setter for two continuous years set unexpected questions. He, with the help of some considerate teachers, got the examiner changed by the University. Most scandalous (!) of all, an examiner in Indian Social Thought, 1974, set questions on recommended readings. Three Sociology teachers, present there, agreed with him in criticizing this "show-off". One of them was writing for the publisher. Half the payment is made when the "guess papers" with answers are handed over to the publisher and the remaining half if the guess clicks. No formal agreement, no receipts, the earning is tax-free. Teachers confirm that there is no cheating in these transactions though some of them have been grossly cheated by text-book publishers. The publisher appears as a powerful factor, out to "help" students and teachers alike. It is a business that has made business of education for all.

The Principal as the first among equals?

The Principal is in any *formal* description of the college system, as Shukla points out, the central figure and role. He is a teacher of some experience and in many cases attainment.[35] Shah, discussing the "Role of Private Colleges"[36] says that if the Principal of a private college perceives his role as the first among equals instead of as the manager of a commercial establishment, he can provide the kind of leadership that will inspire his colleagues to look upon their work as a calling instead of a mere job. But what can he do if the college managements "thwart him at every turn unless he is willing to be a rubber-stamp and functions as the instrument of their own petty egos and mean ambitions". Most private college managements are of this kind, according to Shah.

The long history of the seven colleges of Kanpur studied by me has seen few Principals who live up to the formal description of the college system given by Shukla or the ideal wish of Shah. A senior teacher of Physics who had a short excursion into principalship, which he voluntarily relinquished, said the plight of a Principal is similar to that of Draupadi with the Management, Government, University, Teachers and Students together constituting the

Pandavas. The difficulties of the polyandrous living, that compelled his decision to come back to teaching after a year's thrill-filled life, are really not that insurmountable.

All the principals that I interviewed including four retired ones had a clear understanding as to who was the functional husband and who had won "her" in the Swayamvar. The Government, University, the Teachers and the Students are allowed to torment the Principal or even egged on to tress-pass and harass, only if the conjugal fidelity is suspect or favours begin to be withheld. The thrashing of Principal Mathur by students on the Campus and University action and Governmental inquiry against Principal Pandey already mentioned are clear examples of the wrath of the Management due to its suspecting faithlessness on the part of the Principal. The promotion of two ex-Principals to the Presidentship of the Managing Committee of Sansthan-run colleges, even at the senility stage, shows that youthful favours do not go un-rewarded.

In all the colleges studied except Christ Church College the Principal is assigned and by and large he/she accepts the role of "Manager on the Campus", willing to be a rubber stamp, as the instrument of the "management's petty egos and mean ambitions". Attempts at non-subservience are immediately suppressed at the first signs of their appearance. The case of Christ Church College is of the Principal being the Management and for the time being in command of stable support from a sizable section of the teachers. In Sansthan colleges, the selection of teachers, the admission of students, operation of boys funds, award of freeships and scholarships and even framing of time-tables are effectively carried out by the Management. In V.S.S.D. College, the details of admission of students and the time-table are left to the Principal, with important cases being decided in consultation with the Management boss. The allotment of hostel wardenships, inchargeship of games, magazine, etc., are also made from amongst the members of the teaching staff, by the management in both cases The case of Halim and Guru Nanak Principals is more near the Sanatan Dharma case than the Sansthan case. The only role left to the Principals is that of a watchman for the Management.

Compendium

In the words of Principal Bhanage, "Only teachers who are enthusiastic and cheerful and who have a sense of duty and love towards the young boys and girls can do their job well. Not others, certainly not others."[37] The present study has shown that the recruitment and promotion policies followed by private managements unfortunately sieve out those with precisely these honourable qualities and retain their opposites. However, the few who escape the sieve find the going touch because the same individuals and allied forces control the University as well as subvert the teachers' role.

The student policy followed by the managements to maximize political, personal and economic advantages to the Management bosses feed back into the college system demands on the teacher that further debase the role.

The examination system is systematically corrupted by the bosses to dampen any sense of duty among the teachers that may have survived other assaults. In some cases the teachers become shareholders in the corruptive companies.

Even in the cases where the local management is not all that dysfunctional, the general climate and auxiliary agencies reinforced by pecuniary, cultural compulsions claim quite a few victims. As far as the Principals are concerned they serve only as "watchmen for the Managements" on the Campus. Their growth is determined by what Andreski has called "The law of Lighter Weights Rising to the Top" and "Gresham's and Parkinson's Laws Combined".[38]

If the conclusion of Suma Chitnis, that "In order that teachers function effectively it is necessary that the academic organization provide conditions that are conducive to encouraging scholarship and dynamism on their part",[39] is valid for the "norm setter" colleges, I can assert with greater justification that for the college teachers to be held responsible for what they do as teachers the crippling control of education by extra academic private interests must be curbed. The ghastly *gherao* on education has not created colleges swamped by sycophants *alone* and teachers do not act *only* as agents of mental pollution is proved by the existence of teachers who value study, teaching and research even in the worst afflicted colleges described in the foregoing pages. To know a source of the deepest degradation of the teacher, his dependence on the extra-academic control, is to take the first step towards its elimination. Happily man's practice and consciousness can never be fully determined by his circumstances.

REFERENCES

1. See, Kanpur University Executive Council Minutes 1967, p. 12, Item No. 1(a), pp. 37-38, Res. No. 17(b), pp. 49-50, Res. No. 10; 1971, p. 9, Item 33; p. 401, Item No. 3; 1972, p. 8, Item No. 35, p. 102, Item No. 13, pp. 125 and 128, and p. 480, Item No. 11 and 1974 meeting of 10.2.74.
2. R.S. Mathur, *Higher Education*. Kanpur: D.A.V. College, 1973-74, p. 19.
3. See, K.U.E.C. Minutes, 1969, p. 12 and 1970, p. 491.
4. See, Kanpur University E.C. Minutes, 1969, pp. 193-194; 1970, p. 44; 1971, p. 9, 401; 1972, pp. 102, 121, 238 and 287.
5. Prospectus for 1974-75, D.A.V. College, Kanpur, p. 15.
6. See, The *National Herald*, 13 September and 7 October, 1974.
7. See, "Principal of D.A.V. College Gheraoed", the *National Herald*, Lucknow, 14 October, 1973.
8. The Board of Management of D.A.V. College Resolution on April 5.
9. See, The *National Herald*, 24 and 25 March, 1974, 1 and 6 April, 1974, and Readers Column in the same paper, 24 April, 1974; *Ailga*, a local Hindi Weekly, 6 April 1974 and *Nav Chetna Abhiyan Memorandum* to the Chief Minister, Uttar Pradesh, dated 4 May, 1974.
10. It is ironic to observe Principal Mathur lamenting some five years later : "Generally in big educational institutions trouble starts by the unauthorized persons living in the hostel at the cost of the bona fide residents and they even keep arms. They are in fact anti-social elements." (*National Herald*, 21 September, 1973, 'People's Forum') and tragic to see him brutally assaulted by similar elements on 28 April, 1974, already referred to.
11. See, Robert T. Anderson, "From Mafia to Cosa Nostra", *American Journal of Sociology*, LXXI, 1965, pp. 302-10. The article traces how the traditional type of formal organisation once present in the Mafia has been replaced by a new bureaucratized structure both in Sicily and more so in U.S.A. The racket at D.B.S. College is in the initial stage of Mafia organization. It collects taxes to maintain order on the Campus and let some do legitimate or illegitimate business in the name of education and examinations. We may understand by Mafia organization an informal State within an ineffective formal State. Here in this college apart from the formal Management and the Principal and the Superintendent of Examinations, we have ex-student toughs, teacher accomplices, organizers

and people in office constituting the Mafia. That the development is not an isolated phenomenon in Kanpur can be seen by Calcutta facts given in the *Pioneer*, Lucknow, 3 May, 1975.

12. Incidentally the withdrawal of Rs. 21,000 was effected a day before Virendra Swarup's presentation of the same amount to the UPCC President for repairs of the Congress Committee office at the local Tilak Hall.
13. The *National Herald* dated 25, 28 and 29 January, 1975; and *Jagran* dated 28 January, 1975.
14. A.B. Shah, "Role of Private Colleges" in *Profiles of Indian Education*. Bombay: Parle Tilak Vidyalaya, 1971, p. 151.
15. The *National Herald*, 10 October, 1973.
16. Nav Chetna Abhiyan Memo of 4 May, 1974, to the Chief Minister stated : "Killer Glucose episode in the Kanpur G.S.V.M. Hospital is a shame on the whole country. The two partners of the firm were teachers at D.A.V. College and belonged to the inner circle of Sri Virendra Swarup. One of them, a former personal assistant to Sri Swarup, was granted long leave to indulge in this ill-fated business. The involvement of Mr Swarup in B. Jay Pharma and its predecessor S.P.A. Pharma have been pointed out in the Press. A close relative of Sri Swarup was a partner (*Blitz*) and Mr Swarup had, through a letter, interceded on behalf of the accused firm to get a production licence. Even Vidhan Parishad Secretariat assistance was used (*AILGA*, Kanpur).
17. The *Indian Express*, 15 January, 1976.
18. Singh and Altbach, 1974, op. cit., p. 291.
19. See, Kanpur University Executive Council Minutes, 1970, pp. 148-50, 153, 162, 345-353 and 480-482.
20. See, Kanpur University Executive Council Minutes, 1971, p. 2.
21. Ibid., pp. 118, 131-135.
22. K.U.E.C. Minutes, 1967, p. 22.
23. Refer to the Registrar's Memo on Examination, 1973.
24. See K.U.E.C. Minutes, 1973, pp. 76, 81-82, 127; and Minutes, 1974, Item 8 of 18 March and meeting of 10 August, 1974.
25. K.U.E.C. Minutes, 1967, p. 36
26. K.UE.C. Minutes, 1970, pp. 143, 151-152.
27. K.U.E.C. Minutes, 1971, p. 105.
28. K.U.E.C. Minutes, 1973, व 20.
29. See, K.U.E.C. Minutes, 1971, pp. 117, 124-126.
30. Ibid., p. 483.
31. K.U.E.C. Minutes, 1972, pp. 219-20, and 287-88.
32. Chancellor's Order No. 8546/GS dated 7 April, 1973.
33. See, for example, Minutes 1973, p. 58 and similar decision about 1974 walkouts by D.A.V. College and D.B.S. College examinees already referred to earlier.
34. K.U.E.C. Minutes, 1969, p. 333; 1970, p. 44.

35. S. Shukla, "The College as a Social System". Delhi: *New Frontiers in Education*, June 1974.
36. *Profiles of Indian Education*. Bombay : Parle Tilak Vidyalaya, 1971 p. 156.
37. B.S. Bhanage, "The Teacher and His Role" in *Profiles of Indian Education*, op. cit., 1971, p. 144.
38. Stanislav Andreski, *Social Science as Sorcery*. London : Penguin, 1974, Chapters 14 and 15.
39. Suma Chitnis, "Teachers in Higher Education" in Singh and Altbach, 1974, op. cit., p. 247.

CHAPTER EIGHT

STUDENTS UNDER CONDITIONS OF PRIVATE MANAGEMENT

"IN A well-known bit of American folklore the educational process has been pictured as a log with the instructor at one end and the student at the other. . . .It is the student who helps complete the process of preserving, transmitting and advancing knowledge."[1]

The quotation fails to do full justice to the pivotal place of students in the educational endeavour. One can assert without fear of contradiction that an educational institution has no justification, to exist or to prefer a competent claim to community's support, outside what it does to its student charges.

Earlier I have discussed the logical basis of the "self-fulfilment" norm ideally informing the adult society in arranging its educational institutions. To the extent that these institutions carry out their intended and declared functions and, by and large, in actual practice they do, the "self-fulfilment" norm provides the running thread. This is so irrespective of the larger social milieu in which the educational institutions have to function; though the deviation from the norm and the consequent malfunctioning of educational institutions is not a rare phenomenon.

The quantity and quality of this divergence and difficulties of normal functioning take on a variable character with changes in social formations and cultural compositions. This needs to be investigated in its concrete historical form to ward off the more probable dangers.

The values professed and practised by those who establish and administer an educational institution are bound to affect the actual role-definition of students. As perceptive an observer of the Indian educational scene as J. P. Naik has noted that the individualistic and competitive philosophy, on which the Indian educational system functioned before 1921, still continued to be the basic philosophy underlying the educational system.[2] In the educational institutions, under private management this philosophy is more vociferously professed but it takes on varied forms. It would be my endeavour here to bring out the variations exhibited by the different colleges with reference to their student policies and the consequences for the student role.

The purpose of this study is to attempt an evaluation of the control mechanism of the colleges under study and to develop, in howsoever a tentative way, a logical interconnection between the control mechanism and the behavioural data gathered about the various human constituents of these institutions. It may be possible, at some future date and by the efforts of more competent persons, to develop sophisticated measures of ends-means relationship, capacity, level of performance, efficiency and comprehensive evaluation—the five issues of quality enumerated by Naik[3]—and to come to more emphatic conclusions. What has been strived here is probing of some significant sectors of behaviour of managements, teachers and students to discover the relationship between control mechanism and role determination of students.

Students are the most important output of the educational system. It is easy to count their numbers or reckon the degrees they receive but an assessment of their values and character may defy objective quantification and precise measurement.[4] But mere numbers and the degrees procured are seen to great extent to be a function of many non-educational resources for the management. Therefore, a qualitative, even though imprecise, evaluation of the character of the students as output will be attempted.

Specific rhythm and style of effort

The seven colleges that I have studied, though united by a number of common parameters—private management, location in the city of Kanpur and affiliation to Kanpur University—differ in their genesis, historical growth, teacher and student policies, subjects taught, the type of students attracted, location in the city, etc. As such, with all their similarities, they are different from one another with their specific "rhythm and style of effort".[5] The way these different sub-cultures mould their students will also be analysed.

Perspective on "role" reiterated

The precarious nature of role-status has already been discussed in the preceding two Chapters on Teachers. The partial determination and its being in perpetual flux need no recapitulation here. Managers, principals, teachers, with their respective expectations, acceptance, exhortations, and extortions the University and the college rules with their corresponding constraints and loopholes, the parents and the adult society in general with their differential support, and "conventional tolerance of unconventional behaviour" of students recognizing the marginal character of the passing phase, all these contribute to the making and unmaking of the student role. Thus in the words of Engels, "There are innumerable interacting forces, an infinite series of parallelograms of forces, which give rise to one resultant—the historical event."[6] Instead of extricating the complex interactions involved in each historical event, as historical analysis is not the objective, I will try to underscore the part played by the control mechanism of the college management, to discover if there exists a pattern. To emphasize a relationship is not the same thing as denying the existence of others, nor need it result in succumbing to the temptation of accepting a master explanation for all events.

ADMISSION PROCESS

Numbers

The demand for admission, both for instruction and residence, generally far exceeds the availability of normal accommodation in colleges and their hostels. But the effective demand is uneven and irregular. There are specific courses, where the rush for admissions creates conditions of extra-academic pressures to procure a berth and the admitting authorities impose arbitrary, irregular and even criminal conditions. So also the demand on different colleges is also unequal, denying the authorities a uniform exercise of power to deal with the admission seekers. Now the demand for admissions in different courses and specific colleges also is not of uniform intensity every year. A large number of admission seekers are motivated by the cool calculation of the value of the degree in the employment market. Real or imaginary rise or fall in the demand for certain degrees in the employment market has, as its consequence, a corresponding rise or fall in the demand for admission to these courses.

A seller's market situation

The situation makes the controllers of colleges all the more prone to keep the facilities, specific to certain courses, down to the bare minimum, lest they should be burdened with dead resources if the demand falls. In spite of the uneven, irregular and varying nature of the demand for admission by and large, the admissions in the colleges, seen as a commodity following the laws of "free" market, are characterised by a seller's market situation. Now, to the extent market ethics dominate the give and take of admissions to educational courses, we are face to face with a pathological situation wherein educational considerations take a back seat.

If we have a look at the all-India figures we find continuous and increasing growth in the number of institutions imparting university education, in the percentage of students in the age group 17-23, as well as in the absolute number of students at the University stage. Comparatively speaking, if we find the increase in the absolute number of students running ahead of the increase in the corresponding percentage in the total population in the college-going age, it may be explained on the basis of absolute growth of population. But compared to the increase in the number of colleges, we find a phenomenal increase in the absolute number of college students; it is indicative of a greater rush for relatively limited resources and accommodation.

The seller's market situation not only creates greater power in the hands of the controllers of the commodity but at the same time lowers the share even for the fortunate ones who get admitted. The private control of colleges, with the major motivation being of increasing benefits to the controlling authorities, makes it difficult to plan any rational distribution of the scarce resources or their balanced development in future, as the public and private interests work at cross-purposes. Sethi, analysing the national economy, has noted that the presence of the private and the subterranean "black" sector of economy, along with the public sector, has made national planning an impossible task.[7] The situation is very similar in the case of education, with major sectors under private control, including the "black" sector, which need not be seen only in unaided and unrecognized teaching shops. Most of the latter type are flourishing by arrangement with the aided and the recognized ones.

TABLE 7.1: **Growth in the number of colleges and students in India, 1950-1972.**

	1950-51	1955-56	1960-61	1965-66	1972-73
1. Number of students at the University stage—arts, science and commerce (in lakhs)	3.6	6.3	8.0	14.9	29.3
2. Percentage of students in the population in 17-23 age group	0.8	1.4	1.8	2.7	4.0
3. Number of Arts, Science and Commerce colleges	542	772	1122	1788	2876

Note: Figures for 1972 are provisional.
Source: *India 1975*, Publication Division, Government of India, p. 48.

A picture of worsening teacher-taught ratio

Guru Nanak Girls Degree College is the youngest and the smallest amongst the seven colleges studied. Starting in 1965 with 33 students and six teachers, it had 391 students and 15 to 17 teachers in 1973-74. Thus starting with five or six students per teacher the ratio worsens to 23-26 per teacher. Similarly Halim College started with 133 students and nine teachers in 1959, the corresponding figures for 1973-74 were 933 and 20, i.e. the ratio moves from 12-13 to 46-47 per teacher. In the case of Dayanand Girls College which started with 275 students and 13 teachers in 1959 the later development shows a reverse trend. In 1973-74 the college had about 1,200 students and 70 teachers. Firstly, the college initially had a large number of D.A.V. College male teachers taking classes on a part-time basis and as such the initial teacher-student ratio presents a false front. Secondly, a number of appointments were made in D.A.V. and D.C. Colleges for "political" considerations, a point that has already been discussed in the preceding chapter on teachers. The figures for the students as well as the teachers are only rough approximations as different entries exist for different purposes. For example, for D.G. College the University had only a list of 55 teachers in the 1974-75 session whereas the College Magazine and the College Staff list had 70 names. D.B.S., Christ Church and V.S.S.D. Colleges which have now more or less an equal number of students, around 3,000 to 3,500 have 80 to 138 teachers with Christ Church on the lower side, D.B.S. in the middle and V.S.S.D. on the top, both for students and teachers. D.A.V. College has the distinction of having more than 300 teachers and above 6,000 students.

The overall picture that has emerged is that as the colleges grow to a more or less stable strength the student-teacher ratio comes to about 25:1. But the ratio is not indicative of the actual conditions of imparting of education, as subjects which involve practicals or laboratory work, as part of the curriculum, are not comparable with those where lectures may be the sole or main form of instruction.

Moreover neither the workload in terms of the periods taught nor the number of students is uniformly distributed among the teachers. Sometimes new teachers are appointed for non-academic reasons. Such teachers are not assigned adequate teaching work or students load. Thus actual teacher-taught ratio for most teachers is worse than the one shown by figures.

Within the physical limits of buildings and laboratory facilities maximized by shift working and availability of admission seekers the private managements show a tendency to take in as many students as they can. As a consequence of this policy, the facilities of teaching, equipment and other aids to education and cocurricular activities get reduced day by day.

Differential power of attraction of colleges

As has already been mentioned Christ Church College attracts the upper-class students of the City, specially those who had a tradition of higher education in their families. The management boss of V.S.S.D. College and a former Principal of D.A.V. College and the present President of the D.B.S. College Managing Committee and two sons of the Sansthan boss are former students of this college. The college has a reputation of comparative peace on the campus, manageable number of students in the class-rooms and the laboratories and a wholesome co-curricular environment and a large number of co-eds. Those who are interested in anything over and above a mere degree show a definite preference for this college. The fact is recognised by the students, parents, teachers and management people in other colleges.

So, in a way, other colleges get the left-overs from this college. But there are quite a few reasons for students to seek admission in other colleges, even if their academic record could have secured them an easy entry to Christ Church. Firstly, the college does not offer many courses available at other colleges, for example Law, Education, Statistics, Geography, Psychology, Philosophy and up to the 1974-75 session Commerce. Secondly, many parents do not want their sons and daughters to study in a co-educational college—the college climate is too mod for the tradition-bound parents. Thirdly, as the college campus is dominated by upper-class, urban-origin and cosmopolitan students, a rural-origin and meek first-generation student feels crushed under an alien culture, even though he may be a good student. To be on the bandwagon such a student may be carried off his feet due to non-support from the family background. Fourthly, D.A.V., the bigger college, may be in a better position to offer economic aid in the form of freeship, free books, free hostel accommodation and scholarship. Lastly, adherence to University stipulations of compulsory attendance and low availability of aids for passing the examinations also repels a section of the students. The paradox of the situation is that high power of attraction can lead to both improvement in educational environment and greater exploitation of the admission seekers. The decisive variable is the basic normative orientation.

D.A.V. College has its own power of attraction for the students. It is the biggest college and as such can provide more collective advantages to the students. In the variety of courses offered and in its managerial linkages with other educational institutions, it provides its students an added advantage for admission to higher courses and securing employment within the empire and its subsidiaries. Sportsmen have greater economic support from the institution, better chance of selection, in the university team, and a much wider base for team recruitment. Compared to Christ Church and in some respects V.S.S.D. College, the authorities are no sticklers for University regulations. Availability of a big and cheap hostel is another attraction for the rural entrants and the employed students. Quite a large number continue as residents without any payment or authorization. Location of D.A.V., like Christ Church, being in the centre of the City, also gives it an edge over the far-off colleges.

Its closure, year after year, due to student strikes for long periods and recurrence of violent demonstrations has had a dampening effect on many admission seekers' enthusiasm. When in the 1974-75 session there was a sudden fall in the admission seekers in the B.Sc. (Physics) course, D.A.V. College was the worst affected, rendering many teachers surplus. The teachers of the college, some former students and parents and even some persons connected with the management gave the disturbed history of the college campus as the main cause. One guardian said, "How can I send my son to a college where even the life of the college Principal is not safe ?" A student, who had switched from Christ Church to this college for his second year of B.Sc. said that at D.A.V. he had better chances of securing a University colour in the game he plays. The calculation is based on the pull that the management and as a consequence the sports authorities of the college can exercise on the University bodies. The academic intake that a student expects in this college is lower than in Christ Church and V.S.S.D but when other facilities and laxity in the application of rules outweigh the disadvantage, this college is definitely preferred. Moreover, in reputation as well as actually, working conditions in this college are better than those at D.B.S., D.G., Halim, Guru Nanak, etc. Apart from Christ Church and V.S.S.D., only P.P.N. College and A.N.D. Girls' College have a fairer academic reputation.

V.S.S.D. College has a fairly good reputation in academic input and is not plagued by prolonged student disturbances. The college and University rules are also not ordinarily waived. It is the oldest Commerce College and has hostel accommodation for about 475 students out of some 3,300 students of the college. Its location at one corner of the city called Nawabganj makes it attractive for students from the vicinity. This college like the D.A.V. attracts a large number of students from outside the city of Kanpur, especially the less affluent. Because of this and the negative attitude towards English medium and the R.S.S. dominance over the management, Christ Church people call it a "Maghaiya" (uncouth) college and they in turn get dubbed as "snobs". The two stereotypes have opposite appeals.

Halim College attracts students who reside in the vicinity, Muslims who cannot join Christ Church College and others who fail to qualify for admission in better colleges. Both Christ Church and P.P.N. College attract the better and also the affluent students.

"Bastard" institution is also functional

Now we come to D.B.S. College. Two characteristics that marked out this college at the time of its birth continue to determine the colour of its students even today. It is located in a part outside the main city that came up across the railway tracks on the city fringe as a refugee colony, mostly inhabited by Punjabis and a sprinkle of industrial employees. Secondly, the college was brought into being in the wake of still birth of a private engineering college, without even a semblance of a building. Initially, in contravention of all University rules and requirements of affiliation, the "college" had only a part-time Principal and some part-time lecturers from D.A.V. College. Like its twin creation P.P.N. College, it attracted those who could not secure admission elsewhere or were unable to attend classes for being employed or could not be in Kanpur to put in the requisite attendance. D.B.S. College provided these educational orphans a chance of having a go at the University examination and possibly winning a degree. Its power of attraction continues for those who cannot come out of that locality and also for those whose only chance, of circumventing the harsh University rules and procuring a University degree, jumping the prescribed procedures and authentic arrangements, lies in conniving controllers of the college.

"Bastard intitutions" is a bad nomenclature invented by Hughes. He wrote : "Some are the illegitimate distributors of legitimate goods and services; others satisfy wants not considered legitimate." But he rightly adds : "They are corrections of faults in institutional definitions and distribution." [8] There are quite a few, whose circumstances do not permit joining a regular course of study but are bewitched by the seductive charms of a University degree.

Some colleges owe their power of attraction to being able to provide means of satisfying a craving that is not satiable within legitimate means. Opening of correspondence courses, change of university rules to permit all male candidates also to take university examinations as self-studying students will weaken the base of the demand and when much-talked of delinking of white-collar better-paid jobs from University degrees takes place, probably the last prop of these "bastard institutions" in education will be knocked off. Presently colleges like D.B.S. are "corrections of faulty institutional definitions"; they cater to the needs of that section, which all others shun.[9]

The picture drawn in the above paragraphs is not true in the case of each student. In fact the field data support Millet's contention that "student popularity may reflect other factors besides scholarly worth. And academic value may be contributed through other forms of scholarship than that indicated by large enrolments." Moreover "a few students of great ability may be found in almost any college."[10]

Girls colleges

The competition for both Guru Nanak and Dayanand Girls College is offered by A.N.D. Girls College with better discipline, teachers, library and other facilities. Those who cannot get into A.N.D. seek the other colleges. For D.G. there is one more successful competitor in Sen Balika Degree College. Sen Balika has grown out of the oldest girls high school, has a good reputation but offers limited courses for the first degree only.

In the case of girls the physical distance between the residence and the college location plays a major role in deciding students' preference, in many cases overriding all other considerations.

Differential attraction of courses
Apart from choosing the "right" college, the students also choose the "right" courses, although often for the wrong reasons—that every one goes to them or that a specific course is believed to offer more openings in the employment market. The greatest rush is for the B.Ed. course. The prevalence of market mechanism, an alien normative pattern in the educational area, produces a pathological situation. A similar situation, though with lesser coverage and intensity, prevails in M.Sc. courses. I would be discussing this in some details in the following section.

Of late, the employment situation for engineering graduates and physics post-graduates is not as bright as it used to be.[11] As a consequence a move away from Physics-Mathematics combination and towards Commerce is discernible everywhere. It starts at the secondary stage and affects the colleges also. Two reports in the *National Herald* amply reflect the situation. On 13 September, 1974, it said in a headline, "Degree Teachers Worried Over Retrenchment Move" as a result of reported sudden slump in Arts and Science subjects, specially at D.A.V. College, Kanpur. On 7 October, 1974, one more headline said, "Science Courses Losing Glamour for Students".

Thus the perception by students and their parents, real or illusory, of the marketability of the degrees determines their course preferences. If such a free play is allowed to blind the market forces in determining educational preferences, no planning of education can be conceived. Private controllers of education are ill-suited to withstand those market "trends" for any length of time.

Christ Church College and P.P.N. College, another college with an academic reputation, have opened in 1975-76 B.Com. classes to cater to the students' preference. If we see this as a consequence of allowing market-place norms to dominate educational decisions, the day is not far when the present malady of "overproduction" of Science graduates overtakes the Commerce graduates too. The cycle of overproduction and underproduction of certain "commodities" as measured by market demands would be a recurrent phenomenon with each crisis being more intensive than the preceding one, shifting from one focal area to another.

The case of B.Ed. and M.Sc. admissions

The two day conference of the Vice-Chancellors of U.P. held in Lucknow on 19 and 20 January, 1975, decided that the universities should lay down norms for admission to the B.Ed. classes. The Government also felt that a mechanism should be evolved to ensure admission of suitable candidates to the B.Ed. classes.[12] How is it that the Vice-Chancellors and the Government woke up so late in the day to this problem, that has continued to balk solution for three decades? The story of Kanpur B.Ed. classes and admissions bring out clearly the role private managers of colleges have played in creating and sustaining the problem.

The growing gulf between the promised land of the planners and the practical possibilities for the people has created an appetite that the social system fails to satiate. While on the one hand University degrees no more work as valid passports to a high social status and professional positions, they still provide a necessary leverage to the holder over those who do not. Thus a devaluation of the degrees as compared to the past, instead of driving away the suitors has made them desperate to grab them before others do it, as the only prop to support their upward mobility or at least to secure as a lifebelt to prevent sinking.

The objective situation in the post-student adult world is well brought home in two reports in the *National Herald* of 12 November, 1974, and 16 January, 1975 from its Kanpur correspondent. The first report said :

> With the fall in average of notification of vacancies by more than 50 per cent the Regional Employment Exchange here is witnessing an unprecedented rush of job-seekers for registration. Following the belated announcement of results by Kanpur University this year, 300 to 400 educated unemployed are coming to the exchange per day. So much

so that makeshift arrangements have to be made to print registration cards to cope with the rush. . . .

The second report referred to the fact of there being 93,321 educated unemployed on the live registers of the Regional Employment Exchange, Kanpur in January 1975. The previous year the number was 1,02,798. During the year 1974, there were 87,415 fresh registrations.

It is no wonder that some private managements have exploited this situation to their advantage, as they do not subscribe to the "self-fulfilment" norm of education. They apply the market norms of exchange in an asymmetric power situation, to get the maximum price, cash or kind, for the gate ticket to university degrees, that they lawfully hold as managers of affiliated colleges of the University and unlawfully sell against the University stipulations.

A perusal of the Kanpur University Executive Council's Minutes shows a running battle fought by formal attempts by the University authorities to formulate some "Norms for Admission to M.Sc. and B.Ed" and private controllers of higher education foiling these attempts and admitting at will those who add to their private coffers, augment their political prowess or satiate their elemental appetites.

The *Pioneer*, a Lucknow daily, had reported on 22 March, 1969, gross irregularities in admissions to B.Ed. and M.Sc. courses in some college of Kanpur. The E.C. of the University decided to form a sub-committee to enquire into these allegations.[13] Earlier the E.C. had decided that norms for admission should be adopted in a meeting of the principals and the colleges should select 25 per cent from their own students and the remaining 75 per cent from other colleges and both the lists should be put up on the college notice board along with the norms and a copy should be sent to the University.[14] In a subsequent meeting the E.C. decided to seek the opinion of the Advocate General, U.P., if it would be lawful to determine norms for admission of students in its affiliated colleges in accordance with its Act and Statutes.[15] In its meeting on 2 November, 1969 the E.C. discussed its decision on setting norms for admission and also the failure of D.B.S. College, Kanpur, D.S.N. College, Unnao, and D.W.T. College, Kanpur (all

Sansthan colleges) to furnish to the University the list of admitted students and the basis even on demand by the University and the Vice-Chancellor was authorized to set up a sub-committee to consider the issue.[16] On 12 July, 1970, the E.C. accepted the recommendations of the sub-committee on norms for admission to M.Sc., B.Ed. and M.Ed. and decided to send an ordinance in this connection for the Chancellor's approval.[17] The E.C. in its meeting of 4 August, 1974, noted the information of admissions in B.Ed., M.Ed. and M.Sc. given by colleges in accordance with the norms fixed by it.[18] The information is revealing.

TABLE 7.2 : **Statement showing permitted and actual number of students in B.Ed. and M.Ed. in 1969-70 and 1970-71.**

Name of College	Degree	1969-70		1970-71	
		Sanct-ioned	Admi-tted	Sanct-ioned	Admi-tted
1. D.W.T. College	B. Ed.	140	192	140	187
	M. Ed.	48	45	48	49
2. D.B.S. College	B. Ed.	148	165	148	223
3. A.N.D.M.N. College	B. Ed.	90	93	80	116
4. D.G.[College	B. Ed.	..	..	160	163

Note: The entries for colleges outside Kanpur City have been omitted.
Source: Kanpur University Affiliation Branch Records.

We find that apart from admitting students for non-academic considerations even the limits of seats, sanctioned by the University, while granting affiliation have been violated with impunity and the University Executive Council merely notes the information. Among the members of the E.C. who attended this meeting is listed, third from the top, Virendra Swarup, the management boss of the violating colleges.

The information on M.Sc. admissions lists only D.A.V. College, Kanpur, as the major offender. In Physics it had only 24 sanctioned seats, but in both years it admitted 30 and 31 students for the previous and it is a good commentary that in the final class it could get only 20 and 15 respectively.

In Chemistry 95 and 104 were admitted against 80 sanctioned seats in the previous but could retain only 75 and 50 in the final. In Mathematics 96 and 99 were admitted against 60 sanctioned seats but only 26 and 28 could join the final. In Zoology the sanctioned seats were 60 and actually admitted in the previous for the two sessions were 120 and 127 and when for 1970-71 the college could get applicants even in the final 98 were admitted. In Botany against the sanctioned strength of 40 as many as 116 and 92 were admitted in the previous in 1969-70 and 1970-71 sessions. The sanctioned strength shows the maximum laboratory seats and equipment available at the college.

As years have gone by such violations by the colleges under the Dayanand Shiksha Sansthan have only increased, with the political pull or the paying capacity of the candidates deciding the limits on violation of University rules and academic norms.

The U.P. Government through अ० शा० १०/१२/७४/१५ dated 15 February, 1972, wanted curbs on B.Ed. education as the number of trained teachers exceeded the demand for them, and suggested that a ban should be enforced to limit the actual admissions to the sanctioned seats and to admit such candidates who had subjects for their basic degree which are taught at the secondary level. E.C. in its 22 March, 1972, meeting decided to communicate its disagreement with the Government view. No reasons were mentioned but both Virendra Swarup and Narendrajit Singh were present in the meeting and so also Devendra Swarup, the elder brother of Virendra Swarup.[19] In fact the same meeting decided that the Principals of such colleges where students had been admitted to the B.Ed. and M.Sc. courses beyond the sanctioned number should assure that in future they would admit according to the University rules. For the 1972 examinations, the candidates who were given unauthorized admission that year should be allowed to take the examinations.[20] On 2 July 1972, the E.C. accepted the recommendation of the sub-committee which had considered irregularities and illegal money collection at the time of admission and the conditions of B.Ed. affiliation and had only recommended consideration of the issue of admission through the colleges and "norms" to be considered by the Principals' Committee.[21] On 10 June, 1973, the E.C. considered the legal opinion in accordance with the 30 September, 1972, resolution to fix the date for enforcement of "norms" for admission to M.Sc. and B.Ed. accepted in 12 July, 1970, meeting and resolved to accept them as enforced from 10 June, 1973, and at the same time resolved that a sub-committee be formed to seriously reconsider the provisions of three norms to amend suitably the ordinance. What a strong will to enforce the norms![22] The E.C. decides and the E.C. undecides. The game of private gain goes on.

The reality is well brought out by the D.B.S. College B. Ed. admissions. The college has been continuously making admissions, whose number bears no relationship with the sanctioned seats. In 1974-75 the sanctioned seats were increased to 160, probably to decrease, in the only possible way, the gap between the actual and the sanctioned number a little.

The controllers of the college were in a little trouble because of the exposure in 1973 of the University examination racket, run at the college, as a consequence of infighting among the racketeers. As an eyewash the Principal and some teachers had to be formally suspended by the Management, but the profitable business of B.Ed. and M.Sc. admissions continued unabated. Though exact numbers could not be ascertained it touched 500 in 1973-74 and 560 in 1974-75, defying all governmental and university resolutions.

A former member of the Executive Council of the University said that according to the Vice-Chancellor Virendra Swarup had given an assurance to the Governor in the 1973-74 session that they would not admit students in future beyond the University sanction and only then the unauthorized admissions were allowed to stand and the Examination Admission Cards issued to them. Another member corroborated this story but quipped that D.B.S. was "five lakhs" per annum college for Virendra Swarup. This gentleman himself manages a B.Ed. College and should be knowledgeable but in his own case he cited a case of Rs. 2,000 only as capitation offer.

TABLE 7.3 : **Number of admissions in B.Ed. at D.B.S. College**

Year	Actual admissions
1961-62	112
1962-63	100
1963-64	98
1964-65	97
1965-66	105
1966-67	154
1967-68	183
1968-69	222
1969-70	167
1970-71	226
1971-72	305
1972-73	418

Source: D.B.S. College Cash Books.

Selling of seats in coveted courses at the Sansthan colleges enourages other managements also to attempt the same but the absence of supporting factors like political pull and control over University bodies to bend regulations and presence of countervailing forces like democratic pressure from the community or pretence to moral code of shunning exploitation contains these attempts.

Distasteful consequences

The policy of maximising the number of admissions and selling the coveted berths to the highest bidder has a number of distasteful consequences for the educational process. The students whose very entry into a course of study is based on unacademic considerations is well set on the way to achieve his/her objective of a University degree through similar circumventing techniques. The teachers and the Principal, who must cooperate in administering the policy, soon learn that being in the business of doing is more profitable than teaching. We have already seen that the teachers of the Sansthan colleges had secured the "fringe benefit" of getting one admission each in B.Ed. without transmitting the capitation fee to the "boss".

Student "leaders" also start sharing the profit. The Union President of D.A.V. College for 1974-75 had reportedly secured a couple of admissions to a coveted course as donation of the "boss" to his election fund. The D.B.S. case we have already discussed in the preceding chapter, wherein the former President of the Student Union had developed a minor Mafia of his own. Another unsavoury sequel is the unavoidable presence of toughs, politically dare-devils and monetarily heavy weights on the campus. Such "students" show scant respect for those who intially sold them the ticket.

They make it difficult for others who have a different view of education, be they students or teachers. In the 1974-75 session both the groups involved in the "Principal Mathur assault case" and "Mahesh Murder case" were in D.A.V. and so also some other youth "leaders" from other colleges.

In order to protect excess admissions in B.Ed. in the 1974-75 session recourse was taken to "legal" tactics of procuring a temporary injunction from the District Courts and effecting admissions overnight. A reported influence on the University standing counsel, the case being taken up in the absence of the special counsel engaged by the University and an obliging presiding officer resulted in repeating the old game of beating the University norms in new ways. The students also learn this subornation tactics and rush to the court at the slightest provocation. A former Principal of D.A.V. College and current President of the D.B.S. Managing Committee bemoaned that "the corruption rampant in teachers, management and students has made the whole thing disgusting". The admission policy of private controllers is no mean contributor to this situation.

Colleges which formally show preference for certain communities make separation a part of the hidden curriculum through admission policy. In actual practice it was only at the R.S.S.-dominated college that signs of this malady could be discerned.

Work in classroom

Colleges differ not only in their teacher recruitment-promotion policies, in their power of attraction for students with diverse motivations but also in the quality and quantity of classroom work, laboratory practice and library use. These are interrelated phenomena, each determining and in turn getting determined by the other. If they have been discussed separately, it is only a descriptive device and not an acceptance of their objective separability. Moreover the stance of this study is to see the relationship with the managerial control of the various phenomena connected with the College life.

After a student gets admitted to a college to some extent his educability depends on the assumptions, values and aims he brings with him to the campus but those personified by the teachers and embodied in the institutions organization also determine his educability.[24] The common factor in the educability of the students admitted to a college are made up of the teacher and management contributions. The movement of students from one college to another and exchange of information and experience which have to clear comparatively much lower hurdles than similar movement of teachers and management persons tend to round off the differences of the college subcultures.

The formal functioning of the colleges as enacted institutions is consciously built round university regulated courses and a minimum of working hours and days in the classrooms and laboratories governed by University Statutes. Other activities are built round and on condition that the former are put in practice, though not dispensable on that count. The humdrum practice of these basic activities makes no news but a breakdown in them or a dereliction does catch the newspapers' notice. Of the 140 and odd newspaper cuttings of the *National Herald* that I gathered for my work none has a direct bearing on this aspect.

Differential in classroom work—A function of management

The greater attraction power of Christ Church and then of V.S.S.D. for sober sections of students is to a great extent determined by the reputation of the classroom work done in these colleges. The continuing tradition is helped by a comparative peace on the campus, the quality of teachers recruited and students attracted with mutual reinforcement.

That the consensus about the differential placement of the colleges in this regard is not just a mythical tradition, though that too has a reality effect, could be instantiated by the fact of different dates of starting the academic session 1974-75, all colleges having closed the last session on the same day. The Admission Committee of the University met on 21 July, 1974, and decided that (i) admissions should start by 26 July, in colleges where they had not started, (ii) teaching should start fully by 2 September, 1974, (iii) last date of admission be fixed as 30 September, and (iv) in B.Ed. no section should exceed 40 and teacher-taught ratio should be 1:14.[25]

When this meeting was held, for a number of classes, where the results of the qualifying examination had been declared, the admissions were already complete and regular classes were being held for a fortnight at Christ Church and a week at V.S.S.D. College. For the Sansthan colleges the notification for the holding of classes was issued after this meeting of the Executive Council and the date was the last date given by the Admission Committee. One reason for the unusual delay even for a formal announcement was that examinations of the University were held from 1 July and this year there was a slump in the admissions. But the Intermediate results were out in time and B.A., B.Sc. and B.Com. Part I could easily start.

Earlier I have reported that a lecturer in Hindi at D.A.V. College had felt self-satisfaction in the fact of his having met the classes assigned to him for 22 days only in the 1973-74 session. Similar was the fate of other classes with some a couple of days more or less. What happens is that the process of admissions continues till admission seekers continue to trickle in. Then before the classroom work starts in full swing the Union and Association elections make regular classes difficult. Only the "crazy" ones continue their classes with doors closed undaunted by the slogan-shouting, flourish of trumpets, occasional fracas or loudspeakers blasting music and abuses alternatively. As soon as the Union elections are over the preparations for seasonal strikes start and soon the college is "politicalized" with the law and order machinery of the District being brought in.

Of course, the religious holidays of all sorts, periodic vacations and timely closure for preparatory work for University examinations provide standardization to the academic schedule of the college. Only 15 November to 15 December, and the month of January are classroom periods, with the former occasionally taken over by students' strikes. In February the laboratory work is suspended to accommodate University practical examinations.

This "indulgency" pattern suits the teachers whose only interest is the salary every month, the students who join the college to be entitled to have a go at the University examinations and the management which gets all the resources under its control saves a lot of recurring expenses specially on the laboratory equipment. The only unhappy people are those who enjoy teaching, acquiring knowledge from those who possess it and managing educational endeavour.

The report of the University Executive Council Sub-committee, which considered the representation of the examinees of M.Sc. (Final) Zoology and M.Sc. (Prev.) Statistics, who had walked out of the examination hall in two papers, amply illustrates the state of affairs as far as classroom work is concerned. The Head of the Zoology Department complained that earlier papers were set by internal examiners and that year the trend was changed because the papers were set by externals only. Another senior teacher admitted that some questions asked in the examination had not been done. Students' evidence said, "The complete course was not taught and no regular classes were held. There was no journal in the library and books were not available to most of the students. Ecology was taught for one day and that too in an extra class." The Committee of the University Executive Council to look into the problem concluded : "On the whole it was gathered that the teachers used to give lectures on only some important topics, and the whole course was never taught. The laboratory and the library are ill-equipped, so much so that the students could hardly be benefited by their being in the college. Most of the prescribed practicals were not undertaken by the teachers."[26]

Now, not in all papers examinees walk out nor is a Committee of the E.C. appointed to look into the quantity and quality of classwork done. Let it be noted that the college had admitted the previous and the following year more than double the sanctioned strength of 60 to M.Sc. (Previous). The management, obviously, continued on its charted course of managing the college by securing University sanction for more subjects, more students and more teachers, getting more grants from the authorities and selling more tickets to the University examinations and for more money.

Differential diffusion of subculture traits

What happens at D.A.V. College, sooner or later, brings pressure in other colleges to follow the path of least effort and maximum benefit. A score of teachers, who are not recognized even by their own colleagues as they seldom put in an appearance at the college, surely practise classroom teaching with the help of Extra Sensory Perception. When the Christ Church College staff discussed the desirability of working for "Autonomous College" status, the dissenting voices quoted the easy life at D.A.V. both for the students and the teachers with equal or better emoluments for the teachers and marks for the students as a practical ideal.

When M.Sc. classes outside the normal working hours were started in D.A.V. degrees, even first class, could be purchased by giving capitation fee or political promise with little laboratory training or acquaintance with theoretical work. Quite a few of the beneficiaries of the scheme have grabbed teaching posts in other colleges. V.S.S.D. College has a subculture of regular class and laboratory work. There, the marked difference between the effort put in Physics and Mathematics on the one hand and Chemistry on the other can be explained on the basis of the "night-class" training of D.A.V. in the case of the Chemistry Head. So also a section of the Hindi Department carries the D.A.V. culture into their teaching career. At Christ Church College I found a marked difference in the attitude towards classroom work among those who had the "D.A.V." training and others. But neither at Christ Church nor at V.S.S.D. the neglect of classroom work gets encouraged by the controllers, except that it gets tolerated at V.S.S.D. if the defaulter is ideologically or socially near the boss.

When some young lecturers approached the D.G. College authorities that the laboratories should be kept working for some more days as some equipment was not available earlier and a dislocation of work had taken place due to teachers strike at the fag-end of the working session, the request was turned down. The story is told to bring home the socialization proccss by which some subcultures and some control mechanisms encourage commitment to intensive work whereas others throw cold water even on voluntary effort. The saving on chemicals and other consumable material is considered more important than training imparted to students by the private managements who can delink University results from classroom work and laboratory practice.

D.A.V. as a reference group

For Halim and Guru Nanak the D.A.V. College serves as a reference group. The managers, the teachers and the students try to find out how things are done at D.A.V. and if conditions permit they reproduce them in their own college. Within the limits of inexperienced management, mediocre teachers and left-over students they carry on average classroom work, as managing University authorities or granting bodies is not easy for them.

Once when I visited the Christ Church College staff room, a heated discussion was on amongst members present about the utility of half-yearly home exminations announced by the Principal. The argument was advanced that the college could save paper in these days of scarcity as the students no more took home examinations seriously. My inquiries at other colleges revealed that V.S.S.D. College and Guru Nanak Girls College were the only other institutions which have attempted home examinations for the past five years. At the Sansthan Colleges such "farces" were never heard of. Four rupees was charged as the Examination fee from each student per annum only to remind us of the resilience of old institutions.

The classroom work is impaired for a number of other reasons also. If there is no seat in the class or the laboratory for the large number admitted much beyond the strength that can be accommodated, nothing can be done by the teacher. It is not only the excess number that suffers but even the sanctioned strength has to go without teaching. In the B.Ed., the teacher-taught-ratio at the D.B.S. was 1:74. One can only imagine what type of classroom work or guidance of practical work in this professional course can be done in such a situation. Moreover for each one of the 500 and odd pupil-teachers, where would they get school classes for practical training?

D.A.V. College has a number of stories passed on from year to year for the guidance of students and teachers alike. A former Principal of the college who rose to become the Vice-Chancellor of Agra University was famous for marking attendance only once a week when he used to lecture huge classes and the class used to be replenished every five minutes of the roll call with those, whose names had already been called, making room for others. No classroom could accommodate all of them. Now even this weekly ritual has been dispensed with in many cases. He was also famous for teaching only those 10 questions in a session that appeared in the examination paper. Once it so happened that due to memory mix-up he taught questions set in a different University. When the students threatened to walk out from the examination hall, he personally persuaded them to refrain from this act of indiscipline (indiscretion in fact) as after all he would evaluate the scripts; the examinees were amicably won over to the side of "discipline" without police or danda. It is not the exact veracity of the story that is important but that such stories are continuously being used to socialize the students and practice reinforces the moral.

Manipulation for money

Many teachers especially in Science and Commerce faculties make substantial earnings through private tuitions The need, for seeking this paid tuition, arises because the class work is deficient and these teachers have a leverage being connected with the evaluation process. Some other students depend upon aidbooks and other coaching institutes but these instruments do not have live contacts with the evaluation system.

I will close this section by citing a few examples from D.B.S. College to show that even the specific grants, aids and other instruments of improving classroom and laboratory work remain under utilized due to the contrary interest of the management. Vide U.G.C. letter No. F/20-6/60 (Sc. I) dated 2 August 1968 a grant of Rs. 5,000 was received for the purpose of purchase of semi-micro analysis equipment, but no such equipment was ever added to the college, according to Chemistry teachers. Vide letter No. F. 20-16/67 (Sc. (I) dated 1 March, 1968,

Rs. 35,000 was received for development of post-graduate studies in Chemistry. What happened to this grant the teachers do not know. Vide F. 20-16/67 (Sc. II) of 29 January, 1967, Rs. 11,250 was received for the development of science (Chemistry) subjects. The fate of this is also unknown. Due to infighting the Head of the Botany Department was suspended and the laboratory sealed a day before the University practical examinations in the subject were due. A petrol gas plant worth Rs. 4,000 was lying idle in a verandah for so many years. In 1973-74 the U.G.C. grant of Rs. 30,000 remained unutilized when the Science Department was starving for funds. The college did not have a qualified librarian before the 1972-73 session. In the college library before the 1973-74 session no papers or journals were received and a very small number of books are bought every third or fourth year though the fee from students and grants are on an annual basis. In the purchase of books for the library and equipment for the laboratories the subject-teachers are not involved.[27]

About the situation in other colleges, nobody suspects it to be as bad as at this college. But these facts would have never come to light even in the case of this college but for "the infighting between the management, the staff and some student leaders" (*National Herald*, 23 August, 1974 and 30 August, 1974).

If all the principal parties are charged with running a college combine to cover malfunctioning or non-functioning, no ripples would be heard outside. The case illustrates the sociological truth that not all infighting is harmful. Institutional arrangements which would make it possible to detect the disease before it erupts into the open are resisted tooth and nail by all private managements, but with varied degrees of resistance.

Christ Church College was running college education improvement programmes of the U.G.C. both in Science and Social Science and Humanities (C.O.S.I.P. and C.O.H.I.P.). Its staff's movement for acquiring an "Autonomous College" status also indicates that emphasis on improvement in education and guarding the private interests of the managers do not go together. More the emphasis is on equipping the students with substantial knowledge the more would be the requirement to seek conscious involvement of the teachers, the students and their guardians. If these elements cooperatively run an educational institution, private managers become redundant. The educational interests of the teachers and the students and the non-educational interests of the private controllers of educational resources exist side by side in a perpetual duel in all these colleges, but the relative strength at the moment decides the actual behaviour.

Students' activities outside classrooms

Apart from the formal education imparted in the classroom and laboratory with the complementary help of the library to fulfil the requirements of the University prescribed syllabi, colleges provide opportunities to the students to participate voluntarily in some other activities which help in the wholesome growth of their personalities. Whereas the stay of the students in the colleges is regulated and graded through the University examination for their achievements in the structured teaching of formalized skills and knowledge, their participation in the cocurricular activities is not only voluntary, comparatively free from being structured from the top, but it demands greater initiative on the part of students and allows a freer play to their talents. Even though these activities are voluntary certain types of activities are more likely to be taken up in one college than in the other.

Sports : Struggle for control of resources

Each college is statutorily required to provide playground facilities and help organize games and sports for its students. For this purpose they charge Re 1 p.m. per student and employ Physical Directors, like other teachers. Moreover, each game and sports are run under the general guidance of people appointed from amongst the teaching staff. These functionaries appointed by the controllers of the college also control the purse-strings. The bigger the college the more the fee collected, but the number of student participants in these activities remains limited, slightly above two teams' size. Each student pays the game fee but no college arranges for games and sports for a number more than two teams in each major game. Thus the bigger the college the more the funds available for the controllers and for important sportsmen or their leaders. Thus sports politics in major colleges is money manipulation as well as muscle management. Those who manage the sports and sportsmen for the college are also associated with general discipline management on the campus. Team games are apparently played to foster team spirit and cooperation and cooperative leadership among students.

It was found in Christ Church, D.A.V. as well as V.S.S.D. Colleges that sportsmen were not all imbued with the sportsman's spirit. The struggle for captaincy and inclusion in the college team had all the attributes connected with group ganging on all imaginable bases and individual cut-throat competition. The struggle was for the control of the resources and power positions rather than for the chance to play the game. Generally the bigger colleges have better teams for they have a bigger recruitment base and also the monetary capacity to entice away well-trained sportsmen from Intermediate Colleges as well as rival degree colleges and to retain their own. In certain fields Christ Church is able to compete well or even beat the D.A.V. This is so because the college had a tradition of encouraging sportsmen even at the expense of classroom studies. The tradition was built by a sportsman Vice-Principal of the college but the tradition is on the decline.

D.B.S. College does not come anywhere near its numerical equals—Christ Church and V.S.S.D.—in spite of the fact that the Principal had sports background. The game of managerial manipulation of men, money and material seems to have taken a heavy toll. Halim College with less than one-third strength of students of the D.B.S. is able to organize sports in a much more demonstratively impressive way.

In the case of girls colleges, probably the absence of the resident students and social inhibitions preventing off-time participation in activities outside their families keeps the students away from any regular sports activities. The efforts of the managements to procure playgrounds were on. Except for the fact that large-scale manipulation of sports funds at the D.A.V. had created a racket of controlling college sports no other outstanding characteristic of this activity could be discerned. Moreover less than 50 students could be involved in this activity even at the D.A.V. on any single day and the total number did not exceed 250, i.e. less than 5 per cent.

Debating clubs, public speaking, hobby house, etc.
Though there were some individual debaters, in none of the colleges could I discover any functioning of a debating or public speaking club. Hobby workshops were formally announced at D.A.V. College for photography, electronic and electric appliances and clay modelling. As funds are available from granting authorities for buildings and equipment certain activities are formally shown to exist. Their empirical reality depends on the unreliable whims of the incharges. There are subject associations in all colleges for almost all subjects but they have an inaugral party, a closing party, a group photograph and in some cases a farewell party. Regular annual magazines are brought out in all the colleges except the D.B.S. under the direct control of the Principals but voluntary initiative on the part of students could be found only in the case of D.A.V. students who occasionally brought out badly written anti-management leaflets. Even the union election literature did not show any issues being debated. Similarly I learnt that Christ Church and D.A.V. colleges used to have productive dramatic clubs but I did not come across any sign of such activities during February 1974 to July 1975.

N.C.C. and N.S.S. are two other activities. The former is more organized and regular in all colleges. The control of the private management over N.C.C. is minimal but allegations of converting student amenities in to private advantage were not wanting. I learnt of a good N.S.S. camp of students in a village doing Shramdan under the guidance of teachers. An interesting point was that the management's patronage was to a parallel camp run by the R.S.S. in another district.

Student unions : Elections, division of spoils
Student unions existed at the D.A.V., Christ Church, V.S.S.D., D.B.S. and Halim Colleges. All students become members of those unions at the time of admission by paying a levy of Rs. 3 each. Compulsory membership and democratic constitution of the student unions were important planks

for organising student movements, as an adjunct to the national movement against the British. As the country became free, under the changed political climate the demand (for compulsory membership and democratic constitution of union) could no more be resisted by the college authorities. Students' Federation and Students' Congress which originally heralded the demand did not retain strong support for long. In the changed political culture, the emerging student leadership had no unifying ideology like nationalism.

V.S.S.D. College had a union even before Independence but D.A.V. and Christ Church Colleges agreed to have a compulsory democratically elected students' union after adult franchise was accepted on the national plane. Everywhere the Union was used as a training ground for political roles and for presenting students' demands against College Management, Principal and teachers. For the first function only students moved by the left opposition were generally available and those who came in provided the new cadre for the C.P.I. and the Socialist Party. Soon the R.S.S. oriented students joined in.

The second function resulted in an importation of an alien factory model of collective bargaining into the educational arena. The antipathy of the private managements towards the Unions was too apparent and the absence of a "self-fulfilment" element in the control of education strengthened the alien model among the students. Moreover the earlier toady role of D.A.V. and V.S.S.D. managements had identified them in the eyes of the students, as exploiters. The picture continued to be strengthened. As opportunities for professional education, and occupational mobility grew after Independence the tendency of academically brighter students to steer clear of union involvement left the field wide open to the less talented.

Controlling a union of 6,000 students meant control over Rs. 18,000 annually and a chance to share in the spoils system of the management. For more than two decades the union at the D.A.V. has been controlled by Raj Narain socialists, with no pretension to academic excellence or ideological sophistication, with an occasional interlude by R.S.S. or Congress or the C.P.I.-oriented boys. Four such former

Presidents have secured teaching jobs through the "benevolence" of the management boss. One found a place in the State Legislative Assembly.

The training that the students get through union functioning is through electioneering with caste and regional appeals, use of tough tactics and abusing the management to win public applause. After the elections the losing faction with the management's connivance obstructs passage of the budget or uses a court injunction to freeze the funds. The winners overcome the opposition tactics by managing official support, by working out a sharing formula both for money and power. Students come to know of the underhand dealings and internalize "politicking" as the universal moral orientation from student leaders, teachers in charge of union affairs, the Principal and the Management. The Union or the defeated faction or both together must organize a strike on some demands to show that they are fighters and secure better settlement terms from the management. The management is a little unhappy because of the abuses on the public adress system but is sure of the result generally and is happy to save some money on recurring expenditure and a valid excuse for a defunct library, laboratories, etc.

Management orientation determines student make-up

Christ Church College, because of the class composition of the students, large number of coeds and their friends, absence of naked control by management, the Principal being the only visible boss and the comparatively low total budget, had had relatively better students, higher class students and docile students as Union leaders. Even when they had S.S.P. or R.S.S. orientation, they presented this social profile.

Orderly inauguration and a couple of other functions, then most of the budget is spent during the college week functions. Once an S.S.P. boy who had migrated from the D.A.V. got elected and tried to disrupt a dramatic show. That proved to be his last year at the college. Once more, after a lapse of eight years, Union leaders attempted to paralyse the college functioning. They failed and were expelled without arousing any protest from other students nor from the staff which in fact fully supported the action. However, here the Union helps the students a little in training in public speaking and organising socials. Strikes, gheraos and street demonstrations have low appeal.

The Union at V.S.S.D. College has been generally controlled by R.S.S. boys, with the active help of the Management boss and R.S.S. teachers recruited by him. In this process of ensuring this control they expose themselves as partisans in student politics and sometimes in desperation the non-R.S.S. toughs resolve to meet R.S.S. muscle and management-backed power with violent demonstrations. I have already referred to the shooting incident on the campus at the end of 1973-74 session and the violent disturbances in the wake of Union elections in 1974-75. The managerial policy of partisan politicking has an adverse effect on the functioning of the Union. The students are in love with the Union and they would not like it to be wound up even though they are not much bothered about its actual functioning much of which is ritualistic.

The Union at Halim College with its 60:40 ratio of Hindus and Muslims has not posed any problem on that count. In fact every year they have been able to bring forth a joint team. Only when the Principal and the Management fell out, the students struck work against the then Management, allegedly instigated by some important citizens who had an eye on the control of the college.

Student power

It is only at the D.B.S. that the student power has been used successfully to get U.G.C. grades for the teachers implemented, for organizing use of unfair means in the University examinations in the form of racket and snatching a share from the unwilling hands of the private management in the huge capitation fee, by clever manipulation by the teacher in charge of union affairs. Thus we see that student power does not have *uniform* function in all the colleges.

One conclusion is that private control of college affairs and the desire to strengthen it has by and large resulted in reducing the Union activities to strengthening the alien "collective bargaining model" of industrial factories in the educational arena and orienting the general students to develop the root metaphor of manipulation as the overarching moral code.

University examinations

Amrik Singh in "Examinations : The Strategy of Change" has rightly emphasized that the real issue in higher education is the poverty and ineffectiveness of teaching and bad and unrealistic examinations are only one aspect of it. Therefore to regard examinations as the central issue in higher education is to start with the wrong premises, according to him. The essential unity and indeed interdependence of instructions and assessment must be kept in view if improvement is to be attempted.[28] It is strongly suggested by my study that this unity and interdependence provide a proper basis for the understanding not only of efforts at improvement but also of the present malady. The poverty and ineffectiveness of teaching leads to bad and unreliable examinations but bad and unreliable examinations call forth poor and ineffective teaching.

In a situation where adult adjustment in the occupational structure is determined, to a large extent, by the quality of the degree one holds, i.e. examination result, if the examination process and results can be manipulated the instruction becomes redundant. The private control system of educational institutions, with degree spinning as the central productive process, encourages students to concentrate on the end-point both as customer and as end-product. The teachers being assessed on the basis of this production have to gear their talents and effort to the same end and the management does its job by making the machine work. The degree orientation that already exists among students when they enter the college is reinforced by the managements' willingness and capacity to short-circuit the normal process of acquiring the degree. As most of the things in connection with the making and unmaking of the teacher have already been discussed, here they would only be recapitulated for their contribution to the "student's" make-up.

(i) The managers through their hold on the Executive Council of the University get themselves and their proteges appointed to the committee that selects paper-setters and examiners.[29] The committee disregards academic considerations in the appointment of examiners and deletes names recommended by Boards of Studies for different subjects, if they feel that they are not amenable.[30] Not only the actual favour that they secure in contravention of the rules of fair play in the examination but the knowledge that they are in a position to choose examiners makes certain colleges preferable for students, who want their examination results to be fixed. The presence of such students on the campus adds an element in the subculture to denigrade classroom teaching, library and laboratory work.

(ii) In practical examinations, different students are allotted batches according to the favours that important examinees may be able to secure from specific examiners, both internal and external.[31] The malpractice gives rise to heart-burning among students and at the same time tells them to be on the right side of the College authorities if they want good results. When the University E.C. decided that in future batches once allotted will not be changed and warned the deviant teachers, it had no practical consequence except that the management would attempt to contain the complaints by being more subtle or distributive in administering favours.

(iii) The deviant teachers were not disciplined by the management. So also two others found guilty of malpractice in the Pre-Medical Test did not invite punishment from the management.[32] Even when the Principal reports a "very hardened case indeed needing deterrent punishment" no action is taken.[33] Teachers involved in the criminal subversion of University examinations of 1973 at D.B.S. College could get exhonerated.[34] The lessons for the students are plain that "unfair means" is an unfair phrase as far as the *Sansthan* college centres are concerned.

(iv) When the examination held at D.B.S. College along with at three other centres was cancelled and a special examination ordered by the E.C. highest political strings were pulled and lowest tactics of "mass" demonstrations were managed to get the results declared on the basis of the old vitiated examination.[35]

(v) The University examinations conducted at D.B.S.

College, Kanpur, and another Sansthan College year after year are only an excuse to auction university degrees to the highest bidder.[36]

(vi) Information secured through official positions connected with the University examinations is leaked out to specific candidates and when under advice the students make representation to secure better marks, position on University authorities is used to help them.[37]

(vii) When management of appointment of amenable examiners is not possible and papers are set according to the prescribed syllabus rather than prepare the examinees, walk-outs by students are winked at. The proof of the encouragement lies in the decisions that follow, of declaring the results on awarding the average of the remaining papers in the skipped paper.[38] Sometimes complaints to University authorities result in general increase of marks.[39]

(viii) The scheme for central evaluation of scripts of B.Ed. and post-graduate examinees was thwarted by using legal, political, tactical, subversive mechanism and finally the Chancellor's letter No. 616/G.S. quashing the E.C. resolution of 14 November, 1971.[40]

(ix) Postponement of examinations is secured either through persuading the University authorities or by organising student demonstrations.

The 1974 examinations were due to start on 12 April. They were postponed to 2 May by the University, without assigning any reasons. Elections to the U.P. Legislature Council from the Graduates Constituency was due at the end of April. Almost all the employees of the Sansthan Colleges were busy in electioneering for Virendra Swarup, who was seeking re-election. This first postponement of the examinations was allegedly managed to help Virendra Swarup. A second postponement of the examinations to July was forced through students demonstration at the Vice-Chancellor's residence. On 4 April, the Vice-Chancellor had announced the first postponement.

From this day to April 24 the news about the postponement, demand for further postponement, about demonstrations for and against the postponement had appeared on 12 days consuming a total space of 64 inches of the *National*

Herald. Thus the control system of education had resulted in orienting students to street demonstrations, mutual bickerings and political grouping exactly in the period when they should have been busy only with preparing for their examinations. The whole episode ended in the University examinations being held in July which were termed as "Varsity's Most Policed Examinations".[41]

The summing up of all this is that the Management bosses subvert the assessment system of the University to procure "good" results for their "clients". They protect examinees and examiners who normatively ought to be hunted out of the system. They present examples before the students to follow the "short-circuit" tactics to secure degrees. This, in turn, reduces the incentive for richer and more effective instruction. The differential in the behaviour of various elements of private managements is due to the differential degree of "fit" in the "pure" type of private control.

In conflict and cooperation

The students are caught between the opposing pulls of growing devaluation of the University degrees and increasing hiatus between the life chances of those who dangle on degrees and those who cannot. The more they join the rat-race, the more they have to surrender themselves to the process, which is recognized only as a means to an end. As the movement towards degrees, without the requisite educational content, is helped by the private controllers of higher education the need to cooperate with the teachers, libraries and laboratories diminishes. Students develop an ambivalence even towards these managers who are seen to have made a fortune while the students as students get morally and intellectually degraded. The situation leads to a state of mind where conflict erupts on all conceivable and inconceivable counts, without contributing to a movement for transcendence of the situation. Here the choice is between no degrees and the fake ones. The students feel thoroughly lost.

D.A.V. College has witnessed a conflict between the students and the management erupting on to the streets, necessitating prolonged closures of the college almost every year. So much so that if a strike does not materialize in time, the atmosphere is charged with a suspended expectation, causing tension like the delayed monsoon. As no fundamental issues of control system are seriously raised, the parties in conflict have a fair anticipation of the end. The management keeps itself waiting to "concede" some demands of the "students" like admitting some more deserving and undeserving cases, partially accepting advice of the Union leaders about freeships to be granted and a greater control over Union funds only as a settlement of the strike. And the student leaders secure cooptation into the ruling clique on a temporary basis, in return for public applause for the boss.

"Struggle-Compromise" model not universal

The D.A.V. model is sometimes sought to be duplicated by student leaders in other colleges also with much less success because of the difference in the control mechanism and the student policies pursued. In the 1963-64 session the "struggle-compromise" model, sought to be attempted at Christ Church College, was foiled by a determined bid by a majority of teachers not to allow pampering of the Union President by the Principal, who was also the Secretary of the Managing Committee. Students too showed apathy towards their leaders' tactics of disrupting normal working of the college. Once again, in 1973, Union leaders tried to fan communal feelings against the management by demanding installation of a statue of Goddess Saraswati on the Campus. They were rebuffed by the students and were unitedly faced by the Principal and the teachers.[43] This was made possible because of the objective absence of favouritism as a policy of the controllers.

At V.S.S.D. College the model does not work because of R.S.S. ideology informing the Union leaders and the management alike. It is only the anti-R.S.S. student leaders who attempt it. The conflict that arose after the Union elections in the 1974-75 session is one example. At Halim College the conflict between the Principal and the Management had resulted in a strike but the Managing Committee's readiness to hand over the control of the college temporarily to the Government diffused the situation and demonstrated that it had not as yet developed into a "pure" type private management.[43] But the conflict was egged on by an industrialist aspirant to control the management. There was no major incident of conflict between the students and the management at the girls' colleges.

D.B.S. College is a more developed version of the parent institution, D.A.V. College. Here the conflict of the students with the management had resulted in a strike, hirelings trying to break the strike, a shooting incident and police intervention. The resulting compromise was the birth of a Mafia with the Principal, some teachers and some Union leaders and former students which underwrote the admission-cum-examination racket at the college. The fission in the combine came into the open in the 1973 University examination and the exposure that followed, which again resulted in a hush-up compromise. The stakes here were "Rupees Five Lakhs" annually on a single item—admissions to B.Ed.

Private managements instigate student-public authority conflict for private gain

The strategists of the private management know that a conflict can be managed by diverting it to 'desirable' channels. Even as early as early fifties the then management had openly instigated students of the D.A.V. to occupy the adjoining Green Park, which was a public sports stadium. The strategy of winking at the conflict with the public authorities continues provided the involvement can be successfully concealed. In such an eventuality the college authorities and the public authorities come nearer and useful contacts are established. Kanpur students' violent demonstrations, setting many vehicles on fire and destroying property worth Rs. 10 lakhs in November 1973[44] and widespread disturbances on 24 and 25 January, 1975, involving the hostel residents of V.S.S.D. and D.A.V. Colleges resulting in clamping of curfew are two recent dramatic examples in view.[45]

Substitution of targets of aggression is also effected by making sections of students fight other sections or directing the students against the Principals or teachers, as *apparently* they control the college affairs. As all the actors in the drama are human beings with varied consciousness of their selfish and narrow group interest, the stratagem of putting the other parties against each other is sometimes attempted by students and teachers also. If the managers succeed more, it is so because of their being at the top of the power hierarchy.

At D.A.V. College, the management regularly pays money to the Samyukta Socialist and R.S.S. leaders on the campus. The murder of Mahesh on 23 March, 1974, was the extreme expression of this policy, sacrificing Principal Mathur as a scapegoat.[46] Shooting of Santosh Chand, a student of D.A.V. College, the fifth victim of assault and consequent students' strike[47] is another example of group fighting of students encouraged by management tactics.

The assault on the Superintendent of D.A.V. Hostel, later on the Principal of the college, misbehaviour of the Christ Church Union President towards the Proctor and a host of other teachers in 1963, the assault on the Head of the Department of Hindi and a Chemistry lecturer at the D.B.S. are some examples of the managements' effort to provide visible targets to student pugnacity, heightened by the hollowness of the educational endeavour.

When two teacher-leaders were suspended by the Management at Christ Church College the students were instigated by the teachers to intimidate the management to withdraw the punitive action. Similarly they were successfully made to fight the Principal and the management at the D.B.S. to wrench U.G.C. grades from the unwilling hands. The Sansthan management in April 1975 tried to break the teachers' strike with the help of blacklegs' procession marching into the college in April 1975. The striking teachers used the hostel students to humiliate the blacklegs by physical assault and hurling choicest North Indian abuses.

In short, private control of colleges leads to a situation where the motive of maximising personal benefit ideally informs the behaviour of all the constituents of the system. The actual permutation and combination of cooperating with or fighting against is a function of contending manipulations for non-academic ends. The probability of the managers, the teachers and the students succeeding is in that order because of the control structure. The loci on which the conflict and cooperation move are determined by the individual's prowess of manipulation also, apart from these widely recognized role structures. Moreover today's students sprout into tomorrow's teachers and managers. Today's managers and teachers have also passed through similar socialization as students of yesterday.

Private control of colleges has tended to mould the student role away from learning and acquiring knowledge. The system accentuates the degree orientation of students, that is fostered by the wider societal organization. Attempts to convert all resources of men, money and material belonging to the colleges into private assets independent of the educational process result in substitution of teachers' libraries and laboratories by the art of manipulation. Thus a very different role-set defines the students role. Psychological and organizational tricks to divert the attention from the control system as the cause of student detraction results in further disjunctions in the role. The degree of purity of private control is found to be different in different colleges even in relation to the making or unmaking of the student role.

REFERENCES

1. John B. Millet, *The Academic Community : An Essay in Organization.* New York : McGraw-Hill, 1962, p. 106.
2. J.P. Naik, *Equality, Quality and Quantity : The Elusive Triangle in Indian Education.* New Delhi : Allied, 1975, p. 55.
3. Ibid, pp. 40-41.
4. Ibid, p. 71.
5. For an interesting discussion of differentiation and standardization to a common model of different colleges in an American setting, see E.C. Hughes, "How Colleges Differ" and "Quality and Inequality : American Educational Enterprise" in his *The Sociological Eye : Selected Papers.* Chicago : Aldine-Atherton, 1971, pp. 29-37 and 38-51.
6. K. Marx and F. Engels, *Selected Works.* Moscow : 1962, Vol. II, p. 489.
7. J.D. Sethi, *India in Crisis.* Delhi : Vikas, 1975, p. 4.
8. Everett C. Hughes, *The Sociological Eye : Selected Papers.* Chicago : Aldine-Atherton, 1971, pp. 98-105.
9. Ibid, p. 32.
10. Millet, 1962, op. cit., pp. 120, 129.
11. H. Cornack, "Indian Higher Education in 1960s : Hope in the

Midst of Despair" in Philip G. Altbach (ed.) *Turmoil and Transition in Higher Education and Student Politics in India*. Bombay : Lalvani, 1968.

12. The *National Herald*, 21 January, 1975, "Consensus on Involvement of Universities."
13. K.U.E.C., 1969, p. 228.
14. Ibid, p. 227.
15. Ibid, p. 233.
16. Ibid, p. 262.
17. KUEC, 1970, p. 154.
18. KUEC, 1971, pp. 157, 242-43.
19. K.U.E.C., 1972, pp. 129 and 139.
20. Ibid, p. 136.
21. Ibid, pp. 287 and 316.
22. KUEC, 1973, p. व 57.
23. Report on "B.Ed. Admission on Merit Demanded", *National Herald*, 13 September, 1974.
24. J. Ploud, "The Sociology of Education" in A.T. Welford (ed.) et al, *Society*. London : Routledge and Kegan Paul, 1962.
25. K.U.E.C. Meeting, 10 August, 1974.
26. K.U.E.C., 1971, pp. 103-105.
27. These alleged facts are from the evidence produced before the Pande Commission of Inquiry in the affairs of the college already referred to. Credence to the statements is given because the Commission had found a large number of charges against the controllers of the affairs of the college as established and some others as tenable.
28. Amrik Singh and Philip G. Altbach, 1974, op. cit., pp. 291-311.
29. See, K.U.E.C. 1967, p. 36.
30. See, K.U.E.C. 1971, p. 352.
31. See, K.U.E.C. 1972, p. 109.
32. K.U.E.C. 1973, p. 20.
33. K.U.E.C. 1971, p. 120.
34. Registrar's Memorandum regarding 1974 exams.
35. K.U.E.C. 1970, pp. 130, 153, 162, 345-53.
36. See, various Registrar's Memos on University Examination and also Evidence before the Pande Commission of Inquiry in D.B.S. affairs.
37. K.U.E.C. 1971, p. 145.
38. The *National Herald*, 31 August, 1974 and 8 September, 1974.
39. K.U.E.C. of 10 February, 1974.
40. K.U.E.C. of 1972, pp. 219-222.
41. The *National Herald*, 31 August, 1976.
42. The *National Herald*, 10 October, 1973.
43. The *National Herald*, 1 January, 1973.
44. The *National Herald*, 24-25 November, 1973.
45. The *National Herald*, 23 January, 1975 and *Jagran*, 28 January, 1975.
46. The *National Herald*, 3 and 4 April, 1974.
47. The *National Herald*, 10 and 11 January, 1975.

CHAPTER NINE

IMPLICATIONS OF THE EMPIRICAL FINDINGS

PERSPECTIVE ON EDUCATION AND SOCIETY

I BEGAN by briefly sketching a perspective on the educational sub-system and its relationship with the State and Society in post-Independence India. Later on a historical review, of the growth of education in India in general and private enterprise in particular, was attempted. Concrete data was gathered on the historical make-up and present-day working of the control mechanism of seven colleges of Kanpur, under private management. I have also presented findings on the way teachers' role and students' role were determined directly or indirectly by the decisions and practices of these managements.

It was stated in Chapter 1 that the ruling classes would expect the educational set-up to ensure four things:

(a) a perpetuation of the existing privileged position of the ruling class;

(b) a minimum supply of scientists, technologists, managers of public and private industrial and business establishments, competent professionals and civil servants, mainly recruited from the upper middle class;

(c) a wider supply of personnel recruited from the lower middle class and the new entrants to the ranks of the class to fill the lower rung of the supervisory staff, with only a semblance of general education, which marks them off from those who work with their hands, holding a theoretical hope for the "really talened" to pass into the top elite by individual achievemnet; and

(d) a general belief in the legitimacy of the regime managing an open society, maintaining and extending an open-door educational set-up for the masses, keeping the dissatisfaction with the existing socio-economic arrangement channelized into an open race where the handicaps remain hidden.

As part of the grand design, a dual system of education—with two sets of institutions at all levels, two sets of class clientele, two principles for admission criterion, two bases for financing and two control mechanisms—was forged. It worked more or less satisfactorily to meet the expectations of the ruling class.

It was further put, in the scheme showing association of type of control, level of education, class clientele, quality of education and students' share of cost of their education, that higher education under private control caters to the middle-class clientele, is characterized by low educational standards and allows students to bear a low share in the total cost of their education.

In order to test the broad perspective on education and society in India, a much more comprehensive study on a national plane was called for. The design of the present field study and the limited range of the sample did not, on its own, permit any incontrovertible strong assertions about the national scene. The field data was not logically expected to provide adequate justification for the general perspective. On the other hand, negating reality of the seven colleges studied could have compelled a rethinking on it. The facts discovered in the course of the investigation and reported in the earlier chapters do not demand any basic recasting of the general postulates about the educational sub-system and its relationship with polity, economy and society in the post-Independence period.

Mealy-mouthed apologetics and perfidious performance

The private control of a part of education, as concretely manifested in the seven colleges of Kanpur, however, has provided many moments of embarrassment for the controllers of the State. Actual working of the control mechanism did bring into open a number of contradictions inherent in the arrangement.

The policy of the Government to encourage the growth of private institutions has been publicly pegged on (i) healthy growth of democratic traditions in education, (ii) preservation of academic freedom and (iii) promotion of educational progress and experimentation through this arrangement.[1] The overall picture that emerges out of the mass of data on management structure, actual practices, its contribution to the definition of teachers' and students' roles, almost totally belies these publicly pronounced hopes of the policy framers. A number of dramatic events discussed in the earlier chapters were too noisy to be passed over by the political leadership. A convenient excuse to avoid the responsibility of unsavoury consequences, flowing from their own policy of encouraging private control of one part of education, is to take shelter behind the principle of autonomy of education—misconstrued as autonomy of the controllers rather than of the academics and the scholars.

The general response of the political leadership has been of allowing a free hand to the private managers, unless the consequences acquired the form of public scandals or created law and order problems. Normally the private managements get full backing of the dominant political leadership. When these managements get morally and legally cornered and find themselves arrayed against mounting adverse public pressure, the political leadership bails them out by securing a compromise with minor concessions on the part of the erring managements, short of changing the basic control mechanism or imposing normal legal punishment. The proposition that the dual system of control of education is functional to the prevailing socio-economic structure emerges as highly plausible.

When elections to the U.P. Legislative Council from the Kanpur-Jhansi Graduates' Constituency were held in 1974, the management boss got the joint support of H.N. Bahuguna, the Chief Minister, and Charan Singh, the Leader of the opposition, against the Teachers' Association nominee. Since the very inception of Kanpur University private managers of colleges were continuously nominated by the State Government on the Executive Council and even on the Academic Council and Examination Committee, etc. In the University bodies,

M.L.Cs, M.Ps and even the Chancellor supported these management representatives on a number of disputes on academic matters. The management boss was honoured by the Prime Minister herself by publicly accepting him and his 400 and odd employees into the ruling party despite his dubious and unreliable political past. This was done in November 1973 in a public function at I.I.T., Kanpur with fanfare. These are only a few of the instances establishing open support of Government leaders to the private managements.

The academicians attempted to reform the University examination system, to check outright cheating by proposing Special Examination and Central Evaluation. The management boss was successful in foiling these efforts with the help of political support at the highest level in the State and at the Centre (discussed in detail in Chapter 6).

In utter disregard for the legal provisions underpayments to teachers, embezzlement of provident fund and misuse of Government grants were practised by three colleges. When these facts were brought to the notice of the government no action was taken. The teachers of Sansthan colleges went on a strike to force the management to withdraw illegal demotions and dismissals at the end of the 1974-75 session. The action brought teachers of other colleges also on to the streets. The State government leadership intervened to secure a withdrawal of the illegal order, without providing any deterrent punishment to prevent such occurrences in future. Without the strict pressures of strikes and demonstrations all representations to the State and Central Government leaders about the criminal and near criminal debasements of the educational process by the private managements went unheeded.

When the public scandal of D.B.S. College became too big to be veiled a commission of inquiry was set up. The findings of the inquiry condemned the controllers of the college in no uncertain terms on various counts and yet the same old private control continued with impunity. The murder of a student leader and a host of other violent incidents, implicating the control mechanism of the colleges, were treated by the Government as issues deserving no special investigation. The Government had recognized the existence of sick colleges under private managements but took over the management of only one college, for about a year or so on the request of the management itself and this was not a case of chronic or critical illness in comparison with other colleges of the city.

When the U.P. Government decided in December 1974 to grant new U.G.C. grades for college teachers a dent was made into the private control of colleges by the Bahuguna Government's decision to simultaneously bring disbursement of teachers' salaries under State control. This partial curb, on public resource put under private control, was also accepted by the dominant political leadership under extreme political exigency for extending the electoral base, in order to salvage the sinking ship of the ruling Congress Party by mobilising organized middle-class opinion-builders.

Private control of colleges and national values[2]

Out of the seven colleges studied three belonged to the Arya Samaj denomination, three to Christian, Muslim and Sikh minorities and one to Sanatan Dharma, controlled by the Rashtriya Swayam Sewak Sangh boss. The very names of the colleges called forth opposing attitudinal responses to divide the teachers and the students on communal lines. The constitutions of the managing bodies showed narrow preferences in teacher and student policies, where all teachers and students could not be treated on a par irrespective of religious beliefs and practices.

In one of the colleges the aims proclaimed by the management not only talked of Hindu shrines and cow but unabashedly included "to preserve the caste system among the Hindus as enjoined by the Shastras" and all the resident students were compelled to participate in Hindu religious festivals. An incident of communal violence emanating from the hostel of the college had plunged the whole city in a total breakdown of normal life for a week. In other cases, no such dramatic display of communal frenzy was noted but pressure to participate in daily religious prayers and other communally organized activities for teachers and students noted in the Sikh college had generated anti-secular values, defeating the objective of national integration. Not all the private managements displayed this anti-secular stance to the same extent but potential mischief exists in the control mechanism itself.[3]

The organization of private control of these colleges was found to display a tendency towards a monopolization by a family or a small clique as the institution under its control grew in size and became otherwise viable. Moreover the growth of "pure" management divorced from the educational process, with specialization in manipulating favourable University decisions, funds from Government agencies and escape from normal rules and regulations, demanded continuous manoeuvres to play various interests against one another. Such a control mechanism presents a model for imitation and often compels similar manipulative "politics" played by teachers and students. Thus democratic values were given a distorted definition. It created divisive tendencies. The private control of these colleges was also found to clash with the working of internal democracy of the colleges. The mangers doggedly opposed teachers and students' share in decision-making. We have noted instances of the strong managements denying to its teachers even a limited role in management, envisaged in University rules. Appointments of teachers were made, in four colleges, in clear defiance of existing University rules without allowing University appointed subject experts to participate in the selection process. Hurdles were put in the democratic functioning of Student Unions and Teacher Associations by private managements of five bigger colleges.

Thus the formal structures, everyday functioning, teacher policies and student policies of the private managements with varying degrees of intensity, tend to foist anti-democratic values[4]. The only value propagated by "pure" management through precept and performance was revealed to be manipulative competition with no holds barred. Could this be termed modern and national outlook ?

If the political leadership has winked at all the subversion of professed national value, one can legitimately surmise that controllers of the state find the values generated by the private control of general education, low standard, highly subsidized, middle-class colleges as not too disturbing, while they swear by Secularism, National Integration, Democracy and even Socialism.

Diversities and convergence of private managements

Private managements in Kanpur differ in their historical growth, have followed different adjustment processes to the wider political context and display dissimilarities in the ideology of the parent-body founding the institution and the personality of the key person(s) constituting the managing bodies. The Principal and to a lesser extent other members of the teaching staff and the student clientele made a college what it was. These differences in the make up of various managements bring out the basic sociological theorem that social institutions can never be *fully* determined by the wider context, historical compulsions or participating personalities taken singly. Society has been erroneoulsy conceived both as a prison and a puppet theatre.[5]

With all these differences and divergencies these managements have displayed a number of points of convergence and growing similarities. A comparative study of these managements reveals not only the emergence of a common type termed as specialized "pure" type but also the facilitating and hampering conditions, which have a sociological significance much beyond the seven colleges of Kanpur.

Dayanand Shiksha Sansthan has served as the prototype for the idealised and stylized presentation of the logical built-specialised "pure" management. Other managements served as control groups for different variables to cull out the supportive and inhibitive variables. The details discussed in Chapter 5 about the various managements provide partial illustrations.

Typical characteristics of specialized "pure" management

The specialized "pure" management is marked by six characteristics which serve as mutual support for strengthening one another. The first three refer to developing a specialized know-how: (i) a mastery over legal and extra-legal mechanisms of securing grants from various governmental agencies, (ii) expertise in obtaining University affiliation in coveted courses of study, circumventing formal conditions and requirements and obstructing similar efforts on the part of rivals, and (iii) skilful use of one authority against another, or forging appropriate coalitions of diverse interests like groups of students, teachers, state and Central Governments, their agencies and political personalities. The other three pertain to the "purity" of management : (i) the managers take to management of educational resources as the main occupation, keeping the interests in business, legal or medical practice, missionary activity, ideological or party politics as subsidiary to the main occupation, (ii) the managers break free from the fetters of value commitments of the founding fathers like sacrifice, self-help, economy or sectional dogmas and (iii) they divest the management of encumbrances due to commitment to internal norms of educational process, like autonomy of the Principal and other academic staff regarding hiring or firing of staff, course content, classroom work, admission criterion for students and creating congenial conditions of work for teachers and students.

Conditions facilitating or hampering growth of specialized "pure" type

Institutions are enacted or they grow as established and recognized ways of responding to certain external environmental stimuli, but once established they develop their own autodynamism—autonomous existence relatively independent of the specific social or historical context that initially gave rise to them, with persistent structures and repeated subcultures. It is the distinctive autodynamism of the various managing bodies of colleges which made some managements gravitate towards the specialized "pure" type and others show signs of resilience or incipient resistance to new societal pressures.

1. A powerful block against the onward march of the "pure" is provided by a tradition of actual participation by the founding managers in classroom teaching, sharing residential accommodation with students and teachers and joining on the playground or on the stage. This active sharing of leadership with students and teaching staff prevents the business of management being free from the encumbrances of internal norms of academic activity. We could see this exemplified in Christ Church College where the founders established the participatory tradition. Even the Sanatan Dharma management provided this check partially in the concern shown by the ideologically oriented management boss for such norms.

2. Certain commitment to broader values of human existence like discent and tolerance of other views and 'even scriptures to be read with a critical mind', service to the suffering, say, in times or epidemics or communal riots, sympathy with political movements for national and human emancipation, prevents the growth of all three characteristics of "purity", enumerated earlier especially the second. It does not allow the growth of single-mindedness required for developing the specialist's expertise. Moreover, the consequent make-up of teachers and students offers resistance against reversal trends. The case of the Christ Church management's failure to switch over was a clear example. In the case of S.D. and Guru Nanak Colleges, the commitment of the managements central figures to some of these values, however distorted in terms of religious world-view, has hampered degeneration to "purity".

3. Democratic control of management by the wider community in whose name an institution is established also helped in preventing the growth of specialized "pure" management. It prevents the separation of management from the values of the founding bodies, or bifurcation of donors and managers and concentration of power in a single individual family, or clique. Both the cases of Halim Muslim and Guru Nanak Colleges were marked by these hurdles in the path of "pure" management's ascendance.

4. The freedom granted to or wrested by the Principal as the first among the academics, to run the college, and continuity of the same person in this office for a long time, both factors being mutually supportive, has served as an important impediment to the emergence of "pure" management. Conversely, the denigration of this office, or frequent turn-over, was found to be an equally important asset for management going "pure". Contrast of Christ Church and V.S.S.D., D.A.V. College's two periods, and so also the examples of Halim and Guru Nanak Colleges amply bring out the strength of this proposition. Dayanand Girls and D.B.S. Colleges being the children of the D.A.V. College management, they carry the genetic code from parental heredity. Moreover, in these cases, the tenure has been successfully separated from the quantum of managerial independence vested in the office of the Principal.

5. The "pure" specialized management makes the institutions under its control viable, if not exactly profitable. On the other hand a newly established educational institution, if not brought into being by an established "pure" management, needs donations and resource mobilization. After the initial gestation period, the institution can stand on its own without further investment. Quantitative growth enters here as a contributing factor. This stage of growth of an educational institution has been found to be the opportune time for the "pure" management to bid for power. Both Halim Muslim and Guru Nanak managements were found to be on the threshold.

6. The existence of a fully developed specialized "pure" management serves as a reference point for others to go "pure", but it actually prevents such a growth by using its own power and expertise to put down the growth of rivals. Others could be allowed growth only as its subsidiaries, with perpetual dependence and consequently underdevelopment written in their fate. Sometimes other managements may overly declare their abhorence of "pure" management as it happened to be their rival's characteristic, denied to them. Christ Church and V.S.S.D. managements fall in this category and Halim and Guru Nanak in the category of perpetual underdevelopment in their relationship to Sansthan.

7. Quantitative growth has been found to be both the cause and the effect of the growth of specialized "pure" management. This may be achieved through expansion of the existing institutions under control, fission, grafting or takeover of institutions under other's control. All these processes of growth were found to have aided the growth of specialized "pure" character at D.A.V. College, which could boast of being the biggest college of the biggest University of the biggest State".

8. Probably, the transmission of controlling interests in management to the next generation in the family line is greatly helpful in the growth of "pure" management. Being not a party to the toil and turmoil of initial setting up of an institution, and the viability stage having already been crossed, the donors and controllers being in two generations, it is easier for the second-generation managers to break free from

pre-occupation with other occupations, founding bodies' ideological nuances and commitment to autonomy of academics and such other internal norms. Part of the expertise has already been acquired which has now to be perfected through practice in "purity". Both D.A.V. and V.S.S.D. turned out to be good evidence to support the conjecture.

9. Apart from the above accounted factors relevant to the growth of "pure" management, which are all orthogenetic in nature, only a congenial contextual climate could contribute to the flowering of full potentialities. It goes without saying that a favourable socio-economic set-up is a crucial condition for the growth of "pure" management. This being a constant for all the private managements it need not be gone into here. If some specific management has important functionaries in the University, State Government, political leadership at the local, State or Central level organically linked to it, its specialized expertise can work with ease. No amount of expertise can bear fruit without colluting authorities. The appointment of two former principals of D.A.V. College as Vice-Chancellors of Agra University proved a significant historical "accident" that made the growth of "pure" management a reality.

10. Building of "management resource bank", where unorganized people pool their resources so that the same, converted into capital, can be profitably invested in productive industry for multiplication, is a stage in the development of "pure" management, as well as a condition for its further growth in power. Sansthan illustrates this.

11. Similarly converting educational resources under the control of a "pure" management into economic assets, into political power positions and social prestige and vice versa is the highest stage of a "pure" management's existence. In the absence of this it could be trounced by its rivals or adversaries in the form of other managements, dissatisfied politicians, teachers' movement for democratic control or student power. This interconvertibility of educational control, economic control, political control and social control becomes a condition of continuance and further growth of "pure" management. The position of Kuladhipati, of Dayanand Shiksha Sansthan economic assets amassed through capitation fee

collections, chairmanship of the U.P. Legislative Council, controlling shares in a number of universities and Boards of High School and Intermediate Examination and simultaneous investment in a number of political parties and business houses, linked through a single individual, gives substance to the above formulation.

What has been noted above is only a tendency with many discontinuities as different variables helping or hampering the process appear in innumerable permutations and combinations, in actual reality. Many more possibilities not suggested by my limited area of study may also exist.

An important characteristic present in all private managements studied by me is a lurking fear that the Government may under compulsions of democratic pressure decide for a takeover of private colleges. Hence all of them have adopted the same technique of vesting the legal title to ownership of land, building and such other properties in wider bodies away from the managing committees of the colleges. In the case of any takeover only staff and students would be there and properties would fall out of such a move's mischief.

Conditioning of teachers' role by college managements

In the definition of real-life teachers' role an important part was found to have been played by the prescriptions and expectations emanating from the managements of the colleges, the positions their representatives took in various University bodies and the student policies pursued by them. These prescriptions and expectations along with the attendant exhortations and attempted extortions were not always consistent with the idealised version of teachers' role or with those called forth by the University, the Government, the parents of the students or the students. Therefore, the actual acceptance and enactment, by the teachers, of their role could not be wholly determined. Moreover the managements were not identical in make-up, historical conditioning, rhythm and style of effort of the colleges under them or in relationship with the outer community. So the pressures exerted by them on the teachers' role were also not found to be identical. Push-button automation image of teachers as predictable outputs of management's policy inputs is not sustained by facts.

Any generalization will have to be somewhat sweeping. The unique points are glossed over, angularities smoothed and gaps in empirical observations filled in by imaginative interpolations. Minimum educational qualifications, requirements of practical experience and a judicious mode of recruitment and promotion are well-recognized ingredients of a professional role. On a number of occasions the managements were found pitted against the University regulations, U.G.C. guidelines and even the legislation in this connection. The managements, with varying degrees of intensity, considered these regulations and stipulations as too harsh and suffocating, abridging their right to administer their colleges. The strategy adopted by the managements was multipronged and flexible—legal resistance, circumvention, subversion, compromise, false promises and even confrontation—to have it all their own way, every time to lower the norms. The idealized conceptualization of a "scholar who acquires knowledge as a life-long learner, transmitter of a body of knowledge, skills and values and the researcher who extends the frontiers of knowledge" found little in support in the private managements.

In the case of the biggest and the most powerful management, in the policy for recruitment and promotion of teachers, the requirements of educational qualifications and teaching capabilities were given a low weightage. These considerations could enter only after calculating the contribution a candidate could make in winning Legislative Council elections, extending control over other educational institutions, securing patronage of political or administrative bosses, bending teachers associations or student unions to managements' will or agreeing to work without complaint on less than statutorily provided emoluments.

The over-arching norm informing the policies of the controllers of these colleges did not conform to the educational norm of "self-fulfilment" (discussed in Chapter 3). We saw the emergence of three types of relationships between the managers (=employers) and the teachers (=employees). The three types are analytical categories which were found to exist in various combinations in the colleges studied.

The first could be termed as "exploitative" in which the

teachers finding themselves in a market situation, totally favourable to the buyer, undersell themselves.[6] It is an adjustment with a power position that is not considered just by the teachers. Such a relationship existed in Dayanand Girls and Dayanand Brijendra Swarup Colleges and was reported to have prevailed in earlier times in D.A.V. College also.

The second could be termed as "indulgency" relationship, in which the employers (managers) do not demand of the employees (teachers) adherence to University stipulations of a minimum of class-room/laboratory work, qualification consideration, or insist on teaching in the college being the sole occupation, honest invigilation and evaluation work, etc. This "indulgency" relationship was practised in exchange for actual or anticipated non-academic services the teachers rendered on demand by the management and also for collusion with the management in circumvention of Government rules, University regulations and students' legitimate rights. The "indulgency" relationship was the dominant relationship at D.A.V. College and was also pronounced at D.B.S. College. It showed a weak presence in other colleges.

The third relationship could be termed as "manipulative", which is logically and chronologically a later development. In a situation of unambiguous relative power positions of the contracting parties, an "exploitative" relationship is freely entered into. The moment an escape route is visible, the weaker party, and hence the exploited one, would like to get even unless a "permanent infirmity is internalised in the form of dependency depression and neurotic fear of using one's brain". The actual working of an "indulgency" pattern sooner or later passed on to the teachers a knowledge of extra-legal, extra-moral and extra-educational manoeuvring on the part of the managers, in which the teachers were often involved as active instruments. The knowledge removes the veil over the inherent weakness of the power of the "pure" management.

The teachers in an "exploitative" relationship strived to abrogate the existing contractual relationship entered into in a different situation and demanded a new one with retrospective effect. Others in an "indulgency" situation ventured to augment pecuniary and political profits to themselves as individuals or as a group at the expense of management's profits. Thus the teachers too started an independent manipulative game of using students, University authorities, political leadership, Press and street pressures in all possible combinations to their advantage; they knew that all the resources that the management dispensed were not its property legally or morally. The dramatic unmasking of a Mafia like organization called D.B.S. College in the Pande Commission Report (discussed in Chapter 7) and the breakdown of normal working of all Sansthan colleges in April 1975 were the culmination of the processes of auto-dynamism of "exploitative" and "indulgency" relationships unfolding themselves into the "manipulative" model.

As and when a legal and open course is anticipated to be unrewarding, extra-legal and subterranean stratagems have been resorted to meet to the disagreeable counter-prescription of the teachers' role by cunning and substerfuges. The early behind-the-scene preparations of teachers' struggle against the management, both in D.G. and D.B.S. Colleges, are testimony to it.

In another college, bias in favour of obsequious flattery and partiality in favour of R.S.S. oriented teachers had partially superseded academic considerations. This had resulted in a growing but as yet weak "indulgency" relationship as far as these favoured few were concerned. As if in retaliation but, also learning from the outer milieu, the teachers who are out of favour for ideological or other reasons have attempted to build up a "manipulative" relationship as a counter-strategy. In two colleges built on secondary school foundations, the "indulgency" pattern of relationship was present in the form of genetic imprint, as Principals and some underqualified staff formed the original nuclei of the colleges. Moreover, the dependency relationship that the managements were forced to accept and the "left-over" character of the students reinforced the slowed down growth of any development. Symptoms of the infection of non-academic norms spreading to the seventh college were also detected but the specific rhythm and style of effort of the college had shown sufficient internal resistance to withstand the invasion.

This study has shown that the recruitment and promotion policies followed by the private managements keep out precisely those very qualities that should ideally constitute the academic role. Such individuals as were able to filter through with such qualities in the first instance, found the going tough as these very management representatives with their allies controlled the University and used this control point to reward their teacher partners in the "indulgency" relationship. The student policies, followed by the managements to maximise the political, personal and economic advantages to the management bosses, pushed as feedback into the college system demands on the teachers that further left the role badly mauled and maimed. The examination system was systematically subjected to subornation by the "pure" management so that any academic spirit that may have survived earlier assaults is duly subdued. Pecuniary cultural compulsions and private publishers have lent a helping hand to the private management of colleges to further allienate the teacher from studies and students.

The existence of teachers, who value study, teaching and research, even in colleges mostly prone to pollution by private profit motives, epitomizes hope in a hopeless situation.

Private managements' student policy and its consequences

The demand for admissions, both for instruction and residence, generally far exceeded the availability of normal accommodation. The effective demand was uneven and irregular over colleges, courses and times. The rush for admissions created conditions of a "seller's" market.[7] The admitting authorities could use this to impose higher academic standards for granting admissions but, by and large, they opted for imposing arbitrary, irregular and even criminal conditions, yielding non-educational advantages to the controllers of the colleges. The "seller's market" situation permitted the managers to further lower the educational facilities available to those who were admitted. The uneven and irregular nature of the demand further helped the controllers to lowers the quality of education. The mad rush for courses which for the time being seemed to produce saleable degrees and private managements' almost unlimited extension of admissions purely for monetary, political or other non-academic considerations made the chaotic market conditions even more critical. At the same time some colleges and some courses were almost starved into a competitive contest for lowering academic norms.

The average teacher-taught ratio, which is only a rough indicator of the educational facilities, was found to have steadily deteriorated in all the colleges to about 1:25. An exceptional case was found to have occurred because the exigencies of Legislative Council elections had caused a temporary increase in the number of teachers employed. It was observed that the facilities of teaching, equipment and other aids to education and co-curricular activities shrank day by day.

The differential power of attraction of the different colleges resulted in strengthening the existing class differentiation of the student clientele in college preference. The lower class having already been kept out at the school stage and the upper class with better educational and cultural family backing having found entrance to elite institutions from among the remaining chunk of the middle class the upper minority was attracted to Christ Church and partially to V.S.S.D. Colleges and the lower majority went to the worst colleges as far as academic norms were concerned. Thus even within the middle class that went for general education, the private control accentuated and perpetuated the educational handicap of the lower middle class.

The case of education of the B.Ed. and M.Sc. courses has been probed in detail (Chapter 8) to show how the dominant private management applied the market norms of exchange in an asymmetric power situation to get the maximum price. In cash or kind, for the gate tickets to the coveted university degrees, that they hold as managers of the affiliated colleges and unlawfully sell against the University stipulations. The private controllers of these colleges admitted at will those who added to their private coffers or augmented their political prowess or satiated their elemental appetite. The controllers of the state and the University were duly tamed, formal protestations notwithstanding.

An investigation of work in the classroom, laboratories and libraries showed that comparatively better conditions and actual performance were available in different colleges in an inverse ratio to the "purity" of the private managements control, with the Christ Church at the top, followed by V.S.S.D. College and the lowest position being occupied by D.B.S. College. At the Sansthan colleges, deadlock situations were found to have been manipulated by the management to cut the recurring expenditure and provide rest to their "indulgency" pattern staff, so that they stay fresh for other services. Prolonged closures due to student strikes were a regular feature, as if written into the calendar officially. It was discovered that even the specific grants, aids and other instruments for improving classroom and laboratory work were misappropriated or remained underutilized due to the contrary interests of the management.

The Union and Games and Sports were formally organized by the college authorities. In all these activities, it were not the activities per se which interested the controllers of the colleges but the control of monetary and human resources. In attempts to control these resources the college managements were found to have played all sorts of dirty tricks—employing some teachers mainly for this work, bribing student managers and activists, recruiting agent provocateurs playing one group against another. In fact, successfully managing these resources for the managers was found to be an important ladder to acquire power positions by ambitious "teachers". Racketeering was discovered to have grown round three activities : (i) admission in B.Ed. and M.Sc. courses, (ii) examination admisions contravening University rules and organized cheating in writing examinations and (iii) managing material and money belonging to student unions and games and sports. Teachers and student leaders trained and used by the management soon developed independent ambitions and clashed with rivals as well as their masters. D.A.V. College, D.B.S. College and V.S.S.D. College have all provided supportive evidence for the above formulation, with the difference that at the V.S.S.D. the motive for control by the management was not money for the managers but resources for the R.S.S. In the case the co-curricular activities also, the distortion of the students' role by the management policies was found to be positively associated with the open market norms of a free economic competition and manipulative norms of politics adopted by "pure" managements.

In the case of University examinations, we have seen earlier how the attempts to plug obvious loopholes were foiled by the management representatives. This situation disorients even the honest student who too seeks short-cuts to a good degree. In relation to examinees also the managements were found to aide the law-breakers, rather than encourage academic norms of evaluation.

Concept of "Bastard" College

My investigations have brought me again and again face to face with a situation which needs special mention. The growing gulf between the promised land of the planner and the practical possibilities for the people has created appetites the social system fails to satiate. While the University degrees no more worked as valid passports to a high social status and professional positions, they still provided a necessary leverage to the holders over those who do not hold them.[9]

The craving for a University degree exists also among those who have recently entered the middle class or even among those whose parents have had no education and likewise among those who cannot secure admission in a regular course in established institutions. I have found that in many cases the only chance of circumventing harsh University rules and procuring a University degree, jumping the prescribed procedures and authentic arrangements lay in conniving controllers of the college. The managers of the affiliated colleges were the authorized booking agencies on behalf of the University and they unauthorizedly sold the entry tickets for a consideration. "Bastard" colleges are the ones that help open the guarded gates for those whom the University debars on academic or extra academic criteria.

The "Bastard" colleges run by private managers do lower the standards of University education, indulge in illegitimate distribution of tickets to University examinations. They may also have organized outright cheating in these examinations but they have also corrected some of the faults of the bureaucratic conservatism of the University's academically indefensible dogmas.

Issues clinched

In the end, on the basis of the evidence collected about the seven colleges of Kanpur and weighed in the light of the theoretical perspective on education and society in India, some definitive conclusions can be drawn regarding managements of these colleges with plausible answers to the issues framed at the start of this study.

1. Private control of higher education has contributed to a weakening of commitment to knowledge both on the part of the teachers and students by negatively rewarding this commitment and positively rewarding commitment to private management's non-academic interests.

2. Private control has not served as a shield of academic independence and autonomy of the institutions. It has served as conduit for external non-academic assaults on the internal democratic functioning of teachers, associations and student unions. Private controllers have opposed teachers or students participation in decision-making. Even functions statutorily withheld from the managements regarding admission of students administration of boys funds and day-to-day discipline the colleges were found to have been usurped by the managers.

3. The managements initiated no educational innovation or experimentations. In relation to University examinations efforts to improve the system were doggedly opposed by the most powerful management and others acquiesed in.

4. (a) A trend towards convergence seemed to be quite strong. But it cannot be said that the difference of the founding bodies, historical make-up, student clientele, relationship with the broader community determining the specific rhythm and style of effort have been obliterated. (b) The role of the control mechanism has not been found unilinearly to support convergence or divergence. The support to divergence was in the form of a maintenance of specific informal subcultures of the colleges rather than in the form of innovation or experimentation in formal education.

5. In the past some endowments and donations were available from private munificence. Even then a good part of the finance and land grants came from the Government and Municipal Boards. Since the dawn of Independence, the total dependence of the colleges for financial support was on

Government grants and students' fees. Management contribution was discovered to be a mere paper adjustment. Moreover all the managements had taken steps to make the immovable properties of the colleges—even the ones acquired with grants from public sources—as private property of wider trusts, over which the colleges had no legal rights. A number of controllers of colleges were found pocketing part of the capitation fee collections and taking benefit otherwise from their control over the educational resources.

6. The policies and practices of the private managements definitely distorted the teachers and students' role, put them against each other and against education itself. There was an overwhelming evidence to support this proposition.

7. The growth of specialized "pure" management was a discernible trend. This type rested on an "indulgency pattern" of institutional arrangement.

Ideally, in the "indulgency pattern" the teachers did not teach, the students did not study and the managers had no education to manage. The college was a degree spinning factory with Government grants, guardians money and peoples good faith turned into private gain for those who had appropriated the statuses of Management, Principal, Teacher and Student. "Bastard" colleges distributing legitimate degrees illegitimately or illegitimate degrees legitimately are the private managements' answer to the massive middle-class clamour for degrees.

The busting of "indulgency pattern" and "Bastard" colleges into a free-for-all is a natural growth.

8. The conclusion that private control of higher education subverts the professed national values of socialism, democracy, national integration, egalitarianism and scientific and modern outlook is compelled by empirical evidence.

9. Deliberate discouragement of educational norms and scholarly aspirations by specialized "pure" management by private controllers of colleges had many failures. There are no "inviolable institutions" and private control of higher education is certainly not the one. The institution carries within its womb seeds of self-destruction. It produces its own "Prahlads".

REFERENCES

1. Address by Dr. K.L. Shrimali, Union Education Minister, to the twenty-seventh meeting of the Central Advisory Board of Education on 6 February, 1960. See, Arabinda Biswas and Suran Agrawal (eds.) *Indian Educational Documents since Independence: Committees, Commissions, Conferences*. New Delhi : Academic Publishers, 1971, p. 51.
2. M.C. Chagla had enumerated five aims of education in his inaugural address to the Education Commission on 2 October, 1964 as : (i) democracy, (ii) secularism, (iii) unity of country, (iv) socialism, and (v) modern and rational outlook. There seems to be near unanimity on these being accepted as national values. See, M. C. Chagla, *Education and the Nation*. New Delhi : Allied, 1966, pp. 6-13.
3. Durkheim had seen this potential mischief in a different context when he wrote that if there is no public control "education would necessarily be put to the service of private beliefs, and the whole nation would be divided and would breakdown into incoherent multitude of little fragments in conflict with one another." See, Emile Durkheim, *Education and Society*. Glencoe, Illinois : The Free Press, 1956, p. 79.
4. See, Yogendra K. Malik and Jerse Marquette, "Democracy and Alienation in North India", *The Journal of Politics*, Florida, Vol. 37, No. 1, Feb. 1975. Their findings are similar to those of the present study, with the difference that they report the end result and I have tried to unravel the process. They present data from two state colleges and two women's colleges (one private and one State) of Ludhiana, Jullundur and Malerkotla studied in 1971. They report that 81 per cent of the students expressing support for democracy came from Government colleges. On the other hand the strongest support for dictatorship came from students who attended the Sikh dominated colleges—31 could be clearly classified as anti-democratic.
5. See, Peter L. Berger, *Invitation to Sociology*. London: Penguin, 1966.
6. See, Manoranjan Jha, "Relations with and Management of Colleges: A Note" in S.C. Malik (ed.), *Management and Organization of Indian Universities*. Simla: Indian Institute of Advanced Study, 1971, p. 184.
7. See, Amritya Sen, "The Crisis in Indian Education" in S.C. Malik (ed.), 1971, op. cit., pp. 251-252.
8. See, (i) A.R. Kamat, *Education After Independence—A Social Analysis*. Bombay: Lala Lajpat Rai Institute 1973-74, pp. 18-23; (ii) Peter Worsely, *Introducing Sociology*. Middlesex : Penguin Book, 1970, p. 194. A similar situation is supposed to exist in most developing countries, according to Worsely; (iii) Robert L. Gaudino, *The Indian University*. Bombay : Popular Prakashan, 1965, p. 199; (iv) S.P. Aiyar, "Education and National Development" in *Profiles of Indian Education*. Bombay, Parle Tilak Vidyalaya, 1971, p. 6. These are only assorted selections to show the unanimous assessment of this situation in India among competent authorities.

SLECTED BIBLIOGRAPHY

AIACHE, *Draft Statement of the Consultation of College Autonomy.* New Delhi (unpublished), March 1974.

Adiseshiah, Malcolm S., 'Why Private Colleges?' *New Frontiers in Education.* Vol. 2, No. 3, Dec. 1972.

Aiyar, S.P., Education and National Development, In (Parle Tilak Vidyalaya (ed.) 1971).

Altbach, P.C. (ed.), *Turmoil and Transition : Higher Education and Student Politics in India.* Bombay : Lalvani, 1968.

Anderson, Robert T., 'From Mafia to Cosa Nostra' *American Journal of Sociology,* LXXXI, 1965.

Andreski, Stanislav, *Elements of Comparative Sociology.* London : Penguin, 1964.

Andreski, Stanislav, *Social Science as Sorcery.* London : Penguin, 1974.

Ashby, E., *University : British, Indian, African.* Harvard, 1966.

Azad, J.L., 'The Financing of Higher Education in India' in (Singh, Amrik and Altbach, Philip G. (eds.), 1974).

Bachrach, Peter and Baratz, Morton S., 'Two Faces of Power' *American Political Science Review,* 56, December 1962.

Bachrach, Peter and Baratz, Morton S., Decisions and Non-Decisions : An Analytical Framework, *American Political Science Review,* 57, Sept. 1963.

Basu, A.N., *Education in Modern India.* Calcutta : Orient Book, 1947.

Basu, Aparna, *The Growth of Education and Political Development in India 1898-1920* Delhi : Oxford University Press, 1974.

Beetham, David, *Max Weber and the Theory of Modern Politics.* London : George Allen and Unwin, 1974.

Berger, Peter L., *Invitation to Sociology.* London : Penguin, 1966.

Berger, Peter L. and Luckmann, Thomas, *The Social Construction of Reality.* London : Allen Lane, Penguin, 1967.

Bettleheim, C., *India Independent*. London : Haggikon and Kee, 1968.

Bhanage, B.S., 'The Teacher and His Role' in Parle Tilak Vidyalaya (ed.) 1971.

Bhatt, B.D. and Aggarwal, J.C. (ed.), *Educational Documents in India (1831-1968)*. New Delhi : Arya Book Depot, 1969.

Bierstedt, Robert, 'Sociology and Human Learning' in Bowman, Claude C. (ed.), 1973.

Birnbaum, Norman, The Crises in Marxist Sociology in Colfax J. David and Roach, Jack L. (eds.), 1971.

Biswas, A. and Agrawal, S. (eds.), *Indian Educational Documents : Committees, Commissions, Conferences*. New Delhi : Academic, 1971.

Bowman, Claude C. (ed.), *Humanistic Sociology*. New York : Appleton-Century-Crofts, 1973.

Bottomore, T.B., Modern Elites in India, in Unnithan, T.K.N., et al (eds.), 1965.

Brahmavrata Sanatan Dharma Mandal, Kanpur (year not known). *The Memorandum of Association*.

Branscomb, L.M. and Gilmore, P.C., 'Education in Private Industry : Modern Corporations need Trained Management Personnel', *Daedalus*, Vol. II, Winter 1975.

Brittan, Arthur, *Meanings and Situation*. London : Routledge & Kegan Paul, 1973.

Chagla, M.C., *Education and the Nation*. New Delhi : Allied, 1966.

Chinoy, Ely, Popular Sociology, in Page, C.H. (ed.), 1963.

Chitnis, Suma, (a) Sociology of Education—A Trend Report, in (ICSSR (ed.) 1974).

Chitnis, Suma, (b). The Teachers in Higher Education, in (Singh, Amrik and Altbach, Phillip G. (eds.), 1974).

Chitnis, Suma, (c). *The College Teacher and the College System*. Bombay : T.I.S.S. (unpublished Ph.D. thesis).

Christ Church College, Kanpur, *Diamond Jubilee Magazine*, 1952.

Christ Church College Society, Kanpur, *Memorandum and Rules and Regulations*, 1956.

Cicourel, Aron V., *Methods and Measurement in Sociology*. New York : Free Press, 1964.

Cicourel, Aron V., Basic and Normative Rules in the

Negotiation of Status and Role in (Drietzel, Hans Peter (ed.), 1970).

Colfax, J. David and Roach, Jack L. (eds.), *Radical Sociology : Readings.* New York : Basic Books, 1971.

Cormack, M., *She Who Rides a Peacock : Indian Students and Social Change.* Bombay : Asia, 1961.

Cormack, M., 'Indian Higher Education in 1960s : Hope in the Midst of Despair' in Altbach, Philip G. (ed.), 1968.

D.A.V. College Trust and Management Society, U.P., Kanpur, *Rules and Regulations* (publication year not known).

D.A.V. College, Kanpur, *Swarna Jayanti Smarika,* 1969.

Daedalus, Vol. I, Fall 1974.

Daedalus, Vol. II, Winter 1975.

Damle, Y.B., 'The School and College as a Social System' in (Gore, M.S. et al (eds.), 1967).

Damle, Y.B., 'Role of Teachers in a Developing Society' in (Ruhela, S.P. (ed.), 1970).

Dawe, Allen, 'The Two Sociologies' *British Journal of Sociology.* Vol. 21, 1970.

Dayanand Shiksha Sansthan, U.P., Kanpur, *Rules and Regulations,* (year not known).

Denizen, N., *The Research Act.* London : Butterworth, 1970.

Desai, A.R., *Social Background of Indian Nationalism.* Bombay: Popular, 1948.

Desai, A.R., 'Social Change and Educational Policy' in (Gore, M.S. et al (eds.), 1967).

Desai, A.R., *State and Society in India : Essays in Dissent.* Bombay : Popular, 1975.

Desai, I.P., 'The New Elite' in (Unnithan, T.K.N. et al (eds.), 1965).

Desai, I.P., Kothari, I. and Gulati, I.S., 'Our Universities', *Seminar.* March 1960.

Desai, Neera, 'Role Expectation from Teachers and Available Inducement in Modernizing India' in (Ruhela S.P. (ed.) 1970).

Desai, S.M., 'Government and Private Agencies in the Administration of Higher Education', *The Education Quarterly,* Vol, XIX, No. 3, Oct. 1967.

Deshmukh, C.D., *In the Portals of Indian Universities.* New Delhi, U.G.C., 1957.

Dikshit, S.S., *Nationalism and Indian Education.* Delhi : Sterling, 1966.

Dreitzel, Hans Peter (ed.), *Recent Sociology,* No. 2. London : MacMillan, 1970.

D'Souza, V., 'Social Development, Education and Unemployment in India' in (Unnithan, T.K.N., et al (eds.) 1965).

D'Sousa, V., 'Education, Social Structure and Democracy in India' in (Ruhela, S.P. (ed.), 1969 (b).

Dube, S.C., *Contemporary India and Its Modernization.* Delhi: Vikas, 1974.

Durkheim, Emile, *Education and Society.* Glencoe : Illinois : Free Press, 1956.

Ehrlich, HansJ., 'Notes from a Radical Social Scientist: February 1970' in (Colfax, J. David and Roach, Jack L. (eds.) 1971).

Engels, Fredrick, 'Outlines of Critique of Political Economy' in (Marx, Karl 1974).

Floud, J. 'The Sociology of Education' in (Welford, A.T. (ed.), 1962).

Freidrichs, Robert W., *A Sociology of Sociology.* New York : Free Press, 1970.

Frey, Frederick, 'Comments : On Issues and Non-issues in the Study of Power', *American Political Science Review* 66. Dec. 1971.

Frisby, David, 'The Frankfurt School : Critical Theory and Positivism' in (Rex, John (ed.) 1974).

Gangadharan, K.K., *Sociology of Revivalism.* New Delhi : Kamlakar, 1970.

Garfinkel and Sack, 'On the Formal Structuring of Practical Actors' in (Mcknney, J. and Tiryakian, E. (eds.) 1970).

Garg, B.R., *Educational Crises in India.* Ambala : Associated, 1977.

Gaudino, R.L., *The Indian University.* Bombay : Popular, 1965.

Gautam, G.S., *Crisis in the Temples of Learning.* New Delhi : S. Chand & Co., 1972.

Gore, M.S., 'Crisis in University Education' in (Unnithan, T.K.N. et al (eds.), 1965).

Gore, M.S., et al (eds.) *Papers in Sociology of Education in India.* New Delhi : NCERT, 1967.

Gore, M.S., et al (eds.) *Field Studies in the Sociology of Education in India : All India Report.* New Delhi : NCERT, 1970.

Gould, H.A., 'Educational Structures and Political Processes in Faizabad District, Uttar Pradesh' in (Rudolph, Susanne H. and Rudolph, L.I. (eds.) 1972).

Guru Nanak Vidyak Society, Kanpur, *Memorandum of Association and Rules and Regulations*, 1965.

Guru Nanak Vidyak Society, Kanpur, *Annual Report* (1965 to 1974).

Gouldner, Alwin W., *The Coming Crisis of Western Sociology*. New York : Basic Books, 1970.

Gouldner, Alwin W., *For Sociology, Renewal and Critique in Sociology Today*. London : Allen Lane, 1973.

Government of India, Ministry of Education, *Report of the Education Commission (1964-66) : Education and Development*, New Delhi, 1966.

Gradd, E., 'The American Credo. . . of Higher Education', *Daedalus*. Vol. I. Fall 1974.

Halim Muslim Degree College, Kanpur, *Memorandum of Association*, 1965.

Hughes, E.C., *The Sociological Eye : Selected Papers*. Chicago : Aldine-Atherton, 1971.

Harvey, Mark, 'Sociological Theory : The Production of a Bourgeois Ideology' in (Pateman, Trevor (ed.). 1972).

Hogben, Lancelot, *Mathematics for the Millions*. London : George Allen and Unwin, 1973.

Horrowitz, Irwing L., (ed.) *Power Politics and People : The Collected Essays of C. Wright-Mills*. New York : Oxford University Press, 1967.

Horton, John, 'The Fetishism of Sociology' in (Colfax, J., David and Roach, Jack L. (eds.) 1971).

ICSSR, *A Survey of Research in Sociology and Social Anthropology*, Vol. II. Bombay : Popular, 1974.

Janowitz, N., (ed.), *W.I. Thomas : On Social Organization and Social Personality*. London : University of Chicago Press, 1967.

John, V.V., *Misadventures in Higher Education*. New Delhi : Young Asia, 1973.

Jenck, C. and Riesman, D., *The Academic Revolution*. Allahabad : A.H. Wheeler, 1972.

Kamat, A.R., *The Educational Situation and Other Essays on Education*. Delhi : People's Publishing House, 1973.

Kamat, A.R., *Education After Independence—A Social Analysis*. Bombay : Lala Lajpat Rai Institute, 1973-74.

Kanpur University, *Kanpur and Meerut Universities Act, 1965*. Lucknow, 1965.

Kanpur University, *Executive Council Minutes* (Annual Reports), (1967 to 1974).

Kanpur University Teachers Association. *Files*, 1965-74 (unpublished).

King, A.D., 'Factors Curbing Freedom, Initiative and Creativity of the Teachers in India', in (Ruhela S.P. (ed.) 1970).

Kondratov, A., *Sounds and Signs*. Moscow : Mir, 1969.

Kripal, P.N. 'Concepts of Education', *India International Quarterly*, Vol. 2, No. 1, 1975.

Kuppuswami, B., *Social Change in India*. Delhi : Vikas, 1972.

Lajpat Rai, Lala, *Arya Samaj*. London : Longman Green and Co., 1932.

Leach, Edmund, *Levy Strauss*. London : Fontana/Collins, 1970.

Lijderveld, Anton C., *The Abstract Society : A Cultural Analysis of Our Time*. Middlesex : Penguin, 1970.

Litchman, Richard, 'Social Reality and Consciousness' in (Colfax, J. David and Roach, Jack, L. (eds.) 1971).

Lomtev, T., 'Internal Contradiction as a Source of Historical Language Structure Development', in (*Engles and Linguistics*. Moscow : Nauka, 1972).

Madan, T.N. and Halbar, B.C., 'Caste and Community in the Private and Public Education of Mysore State', in (Rudolph Susanne H. and Rudolph L.I. (eds.), 1972).

Majumdar, D.N., *Social Contours of an Industrial City : Social Survey of Kanpur 1954-56*. Bombay : Asia, 1960.

Majumdar, R.C. et al, *An Advanced History of India*. London : MacMillan, 1953.

Malik, S.C. (ed.), *Management and Organization of Indian Universities*. Simla : IIAS, 1971.

Malik, Y.K. and Marquette, J.F., 'Democracy and Alienation in North India', *The Journal of Politics*. Florida, Vol. 37, No. 1, Feb. 1975.

Marx, Karl, *Capital : A Critique of Political Economy*, Vol. III. Moscow : Progress, 1971.

Marx, Karl, *Economic and Philosophical Manuscripts of 1844*. Moscow : Progress, 1974.

Marx, Karl and Engels, F., *Selected Works*, Vol. II. Moscow : Foreign Language, 1962.

Mathais, T.A. (ed.), *Education and Social Concern*. Delhi : Jesuit Education Association, 1968.

Mathur, R.S., *Higher Education*. Kanpur : D.A.V. College, 1973-74.

Mcknney, J. and Tiryakian, E. (eds.), *Theoretical Sociology*. New York : Appleton-Century-Crofts, 1970.

Millet, John B., *The Academic Community—An essay in Organization*. New York : MacGraw-Hill, 1962.

Misra, A.N., *Education Finance in India*. Bombay : Asia, 1962.

Misra, B.B., *The Indian Middle Classes*. London : Oxford University Press, 1961.

Mueler, Claus, 'Notes on the Repression of Communication Behaviour' in (Drietzel, Hans Peter (ed.). 1970).

Mukherji, D.P. *Diverisitios : Essays in Economics, Sociology and Other Social Problems*. New Delhi : People's Publishing House, 1958.

Mukherjee, H. and Mukherjee, Uma, *The Origins of the National Education Movement (1905-1910)*. Calcutta : Jadhavpur University, 1957.

Mukherjee, Ramkrishna, 'The Sociology and the Social Reality' *Sociological Bulletin*, Vol. 23, No. 2, Sept. 1974.

Myrdal, G., *Asian Drama : An Inquiry into the Poverty of Nations*. New York : The Twentieth Century Fund, 1968.

Myrdal, G., *The Challenge of World Poverty*. London : Penguin, 1971.

Nadel, Mark V., 'The Hidden Dimensions of Public Policy : Private Government and the Policy-Making Process, *The Journal of Politics*. Florida, Vol. 37, No. 1, Feb. 1975.

Naik, J.P., *Equality, Quality and Quantity : The Elusive Triangle in Indian Education*. Bombay : Allied, 1977.

National Archives of India, *Selections from Educational Records*, Delhi, 1965.

National Tribune, Kanpur, Vol. 10, June 18, 1966.

Nav Chetna Abhiyan, Kanpur, *Memo to U.P. Chief Minister*. 1974.

Nurullah, S. and Naik, J.P., *A History of Education in India*

During British Period. Bombay : MacMillan, 1951.

Nehru, Jawaharlal, *An Autobiography*. London : Broadley Head, 1955.

Nehru, Jawaharlal, *The Discovery of India*. Calcutta : Signet Press, 1956.

Padmanabhan, C.B., 'The Economics of Education : A Brief Survey', *Indian Educational Review*. 2(2), 1967.

Page, C.H. (ed.), *Sociology and Contemporary Education*. New York : Random House, 1963.

Pande Commission, *Report on D.B.S. College*, (unpublished), 1975.

Pateman, Trever (ed.), *Counter Courses, A Handbook of Course Criticism*. Middlesex : Penguin, 1972.

Petrosyan, M., *Humanism : Its Philosophical and Sociological Aspects*. Moscow : Progress, 1972.

Petrov, I and Prikulis, Y., 'Marxist Versus the Frankfurt School', *Social Sciences*. Vol. 4, No. 4(14), Moscow : Academy of Sciences, 1973.

Raghaviah, V. and Shrinivasan, K.V., 'University Governance in India—A Case for Lay Governing Bodies', *University Administration*, Vol. IV, No. 182, 1977.

Rex, John, *Discovering Sociology—Studies in Sociological Theory and Method*. London : Routledge & Kegan Paul, 1973.

Rex, John (ed.), *Approaches to Sociology—An Introduction to Major Trends in British Sociology*. London : Routledge & Kegan Paul, 1974.

Robertson, Roland, 'Major Axes of Sociological Analysis' in (Rex, John (ed.) 1974).

Roche, Maurice, *Phenomenology, Language, and the Social Sciences*. London : Routledge & Kegan Paul, 1973.

Rudolph, Sussanne H. and Rudolph, L.I. (eds.), *Education and Politics in India : Studies in Organization, Society and Policy*. Delhi : Oxford University Press, 1972.

Ruhela, S.P. (ed.), *Contributions to Sociology of Education in India. Vol. I*. New Delhi : Jain Bros. 1969(a).

Ruhela, S.P. (ed.), *Social Determinants of Educability in India*. New Delhi : Jain Bros., 1969(b).

Ruhela, S.P. (ed.), *Sociology of the Teaching Profession in India*. New Delhi : NCERT, 1970.

Sampurnanand, *Memoirs and Reflections*. New York, 1964.

Sanatan Dharam College, Cawnpore, *Prospectus*, 1921.

Sapir, Edward, 'Language—excerpts from his selected writings in Language, Culture and Personality' in (Thompson, Kenneth and Tunstall, Jeremy (eds.) 1973).

Schroyer, Trent, 'Towards a Critical Theory of Advanced Industrial Society' in (Dreitzel, Hans Peter (ed.). 1970).

Schroyer, Trent, 'A Reconceptualization of Critical Theory' in (Colfax, J. David and Roach, Jack L. (eds.) 1971).

Schutz, Alfred, 'Concepts and Theory Formation in the Social Sciences' in (Thompson, Kenneth and Tunstall, Jeremy (eds.), 1973).

Sen, Amritya, 'The Crisis in Indian Education' in (Malik, S.C. (ed.), 1971).

Sethi, J.D., *India in Crisis*. Delhi : Vikas, 1975.

Shah, A.S., 'Role of Private Colleges' in (Parle Tilak Vidyalaya (ed.) 1971).

Sharma, G.S., (ed.), *Secularism and its Implications for Law and Life in India*. Delhi : The Indian Law Institute, 1966.

Sharma, G.S., *Eudcation and Cultural Rights of Minorities*. New Delhi : ICSSR, 1973.

Shils, E., 'The Academic Profession in India' in (Singh, Amrik and Altbach, Philip G. (eds.) 1974).

Shukla, S. 'Control and Decision-Making in the Educational System' in (Gore, M.S. et al (eds.) 1967).

Shukla, Suresh C. 'Notes on the Educational Situations', *Mainstream*, February 6, 1971.

Shukla, S., 'The College as a Social System', *New Frontiers in Education*, June, 1974.

Singh, Amrik, 'The Fallacy of Mo(e)re Funds' in (Parle Tilak Vidyalaya (ed.). 1971(a).

Singh, A.K., 'Academic Politics and Student Unrest' in (Altbach, P.G. (ed.) 1968).

Singh, Amrik, 'Higher Education in the Seventies' *Quest*, Sept.-Oct. 1971(b).

Singh, Amrik and Altbach, Philip G. (eds.), *The Higher Learning in India*. Delhi : Vikas, 1974(a).

Singh, Amrik, 'Examination : The Strategy of Change' in (Singh, Amrik and Altbach, Philip G. (eds.), 1974 (b).

Singh, R.P., *The Indian Teacher*. Delhi : National, 1969.

Singh, Y., 'The Process of Socialization and Education' in

(Gore, M.S. et al (eds.) 1967).

Singh, Y., *Modernization of Indian Tradition*. Delhi : Thomson Press, 1973.

Srinivas, M.N., 'Education and Social Change' in (Mathais, T.A. (ed.) (1968).

Srinivas, M.N., 'Village Studies, Participant Observation and Social Science Research in India', *Economic and Political Weekly*, Vol. X, Nos. 33-35, Special 1975.

Statement of the Conference of Educators for Secularism, Socialism and Democracy. New Delhi, 19-21, Sept., 1975. *Secular Democracy*. Sept. 11, 1975.

Sorokin, P., *Reconstruction of Humanity*. Bombay : Bhartiya Vidya Bhavan, 1958.

Thompson, Kenneth and Tunstall, Jeremy (eds.) *Sociological Perspectives*. London : Penguin Education, 1973.

U.P. Government, Lucknow, *The Uttar Pradesh State Universities Act 1973*.

University Grants Commission, Delhi, *Report of the Committee on Colleges*, 1969.

Unnithan, T.K.N. et al (eds.), *Towards a Sociology of Culture in India*. Delhi : Prentice-Hall, 1965.

Upadhyaya, G.P., *The Origin, Scope and Mission of Arya Samaj*. Allahabad : Arya Samaj Chowk, 1937.

Vikramajit Singh Sanatan Dharma College, Kanpur, *Rules and Regulations* (year not known).

Vikramajit Singh Sanatan Dharma College, Kanpur, *Swarna Jayanti Smarika*, 1971.

Welford, A.T. (eds.) *et al Society*. London : Routledge and Kegan Paul, 1962.

White, Mary Alice and Duker, *Education, A Conceptual and Empirical Approach*. New York : Holt Rinchert and Winston, 1973.

Whyte, William Foot, *Street Corner Society : The Social Structure of an Italian Slum*. Chicago : University of Chicago Press, 1943.

Worsley, Peter, *Introducing Sociology*. Middlesex : Penguin, 1970.

Worsley, Peter, 'The Reification of Marxism : Rejoinder to Lazar'; *Sociology*, Vol. 9, No. 3, Sept. 1975.

Wrong, Dennis S., 'The Oversocialized Conception of Man in

Modern Society', *American Sociological Review*, Vol. 26, 1961.

Zeitlin, M., *Ideology and the Development of Sociological Theory*. New Delhi : Prentice-Hall, 1969.

Index